MAKING PANDEMONIUM

MAKING
PANDEMONIUM

NADEEM MASOOD

Matador
9 Priory Business Park
Kibworth Beauchamp
Leicestershire LE8 0RX, UK
Tel: (+44) 116 279 2299
Fax: (+44) 116 279 2277
Email: books@troubador.co.uk
Web: www.troubador.co.uk/matador

ISBN 978 1783062 492

British Library Cataloguing in Publication Data.
A catalogue record for this book is available from the British Library.

Typeset in Aldine401 BT Roman by Troubador Publishing Ltd
Printed and bound in the UK by TJ International, Padstow, Cornwall

Matador is an imprint of Troubador Publishing Ltd

MIX
Paper from
responsible sources
FSC www.fsc.org   FSC® C013056

For my children,
and for the WMW

Contents

Acknowledgements

It has taken me several months to create this book using the notes I made whilst I was rehearsing for the Opening Ceremony. Some of my notes were by no means exhaustive so I was relying on my memory when I began. At times my memory failed me, so I would like to thank the following for filling in some of the gaps and also imparting information that had passed me by: Danny Bigsmile, Adam Dalton, James Evans, Andrew Forey, Steve Fox, Bill Freeman, Nancy Harrison, Diane Mitchell, Dave Nattriss, Andy Newman, Tim Purcell, Anja Singer, Rob Smith, Suzanne Turvey, and Sally White. I'd like to thank James Evans, Andrew Forey, Daniel Musikant, Vin Patel, Saw Thurein Tun, and Brian Voakes for the use of their photos. Thank you to Steve Fox, Sean McManus, Jack Nunn, Nimisha Patel, and Paul Weaver for additional support along the way. I'd like to offer a very special word of thanks to Nancy Harrison for reading my manuscript and giving me lots of invaluable advice and encouragement, and to each and every member of Fife for making our county what it still is today. To Diane Mitchell, Katie Pearson, and the entire team of dance captains and Mass Movement Coordinators: thank you for your tireless energy, enthusiasm, encouragement and patience. I am eternally grateful to Steve Boyd, Toby Sedgwick, and Danny Boyle for all of the things they did for all of us. Finally, a truly heartfelt thank you to my amazing wife, for everything.

Introduction

Wednesday 6 July 2005

I can still remember the day it all began. I didn't realise then, but looking back now it is clear that it all began on this day. I was working as a Production Controller at Cedar Communications, employed on a 6-month contract. On this day a very important announcement was going to be made, and although I was interested in the result, indeed wanted the result to be in favour of the city in which I was born and bred, I hadn't actually followed the progress of London's Olympic bid. I think I was only aware of the forthcoming announcement because of the talk around the office. Now that I knew this, I was eager to hear the result.

At the time, Cedar Communications was based on Sackville Street in Piccadilly. The building name was Pegasus House. This was just down the road from Trafalgar Square, where large crowds had gathered, all waiting for what would ultimately be one word to be spoken by the President of the International Olympic Committee, Jacques Rogge. Moscow, Madrid, New York (okay, that's two), Paris, or London. Just one name was going to change one of these cities forever.

Everybody at Cedar wanted London to win. People were excited. They were looking forward to watching the announcement on the screen that had been set up in the boardroom, just over in the opposite corner from my seat by the window, where I was busy working on just another day in the office.

As the moment drew close, those of us who were interested had our own little gathering in the boardroom. We sat down, stood about, chatted, and waited, watching the live footage of the crowd that was but a stone's throw away from where we were. The atmosphere in the room grew a little tense as the announcement was mere seconds away. Eyes were glued to the screen, ears were anticipating that very first syllable, letter even, which would reveal all in half a second. Half a second the difference between absolute joy and sheer disappointment. A painful pause. The wait was over. All Mr. Rogge had to do was say the word. Complete silence ruled in that boardroom and in the square. He was taking his time.

"London."

The room and the square simultaneously erupted. Dame Kelly Holmes gave us all one of the most enduring images of the day. Wow. We had won. Applause, cheers, hands punching the air, and shouts of affirmation filled the room. This was amazing. Even I could appreciate just how incredible this was. The Olympic Games were going to come to London.

After just a couple of minutes the moment dissolved as our excitement waned, and we all returned to our desks. For now it was over. We had won and that was all we would know for now. I didn't religiously follow the Olympics. Nevertheless I was very pleased that the Games were coming to my home city. I am a Londoner. I did feel an enormous sense of pride. It was indeed amazing, and I expressed my feelings to Kay who was sat opposite me. We spoke about the effect this was going to have on London and how the city would be transformed. Yet it was seven years away, time to forget about it and get back to work. Seven years was a long time, beyond the current decade in fact. At that moment Tesco and Nikon Pro magazines needed our attention, so Kay and I returned to our work. When I finished for the day I went home.

That same evening, as I reflected once more on London's success, I had no idea, indeed could never have begun to imagine, what I would be doing in 7 years and 21 days from then.

This is my account of an incredible journey that began on Sunday 6 November 2011, as a result of what had happened on Wednesday 6 July 2005. But first, I must explain exactly how I came to find myself in a certain place at a certain time on that particular Sunday morning.

Thursday 7 July 2005

(   ).

On this day and everyday henceforth.

WAVE ONE

APPLICATIONS

1

Applying For The Role

July 2010

After London won the bid the London Organising Committee of the Olympic and Paralympic Games (LOCOG) had announced that it would be employing volunteers from local communities to help during the Games. I can remember thinking immediately that I would love to take part, although I wasn't sure if I would be eligible. Still, I registered on the LOCOG mailing list for updates.

During the first half of 2006 I had read that it would be good to do some volunteering to possibly stand a better chance of being allowed to help at the Olympic Games. I went on to volunteer at the London Triathlon that year. I had participated in this event during the previous two years, completing five triathlons in total. In June 2006, however, I had been diagnosed with Type 1 diabetes after several months of unknowingly enduring the symptoms. This had put my training at a standstill and I had lapsed as a result. I was in no condition to do a triathlon that year, so I had decided to volunteer, thereby at least having some involvement in the event, and I could also build up some work towards my portfolio for the Olympics. It turned out that this would in fact be my only volunteering experience that year, and over the next four. But it mattered not.

In July 2010 I learned that LOCOG was looking to recruit 70,000 Games Makers, as they called them, and anybody was allowed to apply. Previous volunteering experience was not mentioned, so any ill thoughts I had about not having done anything over the last four years were put to rest. I had a chance still, so I was going to apply. By now I had decided that this was something I just had to do. I wanted to be involved. Advertisements on the Underground only strengthened my resolve. They made no secret that this was going to be a lifetime opportunity, something to tell your grandchildren, something to be proud of. I didn't need any encouragement. I was going to do this. Applications were to begin soon. I made sure I was still on the mailing list, registering again just to be certain.

October 2010 – March 2011

On 5 October 2010 I completed my registration to apply to be a Games Maker, and by the end of the following day my application was complete. I was now in the system, and I could only wait to see if I would get an interview. It was going to be a long process. They needed 70,000 Games Makers, but they received 250,000 applications from people hoping to be part of the Olympics. LOCOG made no secret of the fact that it was not going to be a wait of a few weeks, or even a few months.

On 28 October 2010, applications for potential Games Makers closed. If you'd missed the deadline, it was too late. An email was sent to all applicants, asking us to ensure we had filled in the Skills & Experience in Step 2 of the form, as they would "look at this when deciding which role you might be suitable for". They also wanted us to complete the Diversity and Inclusion in Step 1, although this was optional. Any changes needed to be made by Friday 12 November. All successful applicants would then be invited to a selection event from January 2011. These events were to take place between February 2011 and January 2012, so some of us would not even receive an invite until later in 2011. I was right. This could take a long time. It was time to forget and wait.

On 10 March 2011, I received an email telling me that I hadn't been forgotten. Of the 250,000 applicants, around 3,500 people had been interviewed and over the next year or so, another 300 potential Games Makers would be interviewed every day. They would still be interviewing applicants in March 2012! At least I hadn't been told no. I was still in with a chance. I kept waiting, and soon enough I let my application and its progress drift into the background. Life continued.

Friday 19 August 2011

It was on this day that my Ceremony journey began, although I didn't yet know it. I still hadn't heard from LOCOG about my Games Maker application, but the following email landed in my inbox:

WAVE ONE: APPLICATIONS

Be a part of Danny Boyle's cast for the Olympic Ceremonies.

Artistic Directors Danny Boyle and Kim Gavin are searching for 10,000 volunteers to fill a wide range of performance roles in the Olympic Opening and Closing Ceremonies. To be part of an amazing show in front of a packed stadium audience and more than one billion people watching on TV around the world, all you need to be is enthusiastic, positive, have huge amounts of energy and a willingness to give up your time to rehearse in East London from March next year. Volunteer performers must be aged 18 years or over on 1 March 2012.

It was as simple as that. I wasn't sure why I had received the email. I suppose it must have been because I was on the London 2012 mailing list. I thought about it for a few minutes. Danny Boyle's cast. Now that would be something special. But what could I have offered? I had no performance skills. They weren't going to hire just anybody, not for something like this. But in the email it said they wanted just four things: enthusiasm, a positive attitude, energy, and time to give. I definitely had three of those, but wasn't sure about time to give. I already needed to give ten days, if successful in my application to be a Games Maker. Add to that training days. That much I knew already from the application process. I wasn't sure if I would have enough annual leave left to also cover any volunteering for the Ceremony.

In the end I clicked on the link and was given the full details. I learned that no experience was necessary. If successful, I would need to rehearse for up to five hours, maybe three times a week from May. That one fact put an end to any thoughts I had on taking part. With one baby and another toddler there was no way I would be able to manage that. It wasn't fair on my wife, Misbah. As much as we both loved them, I knew just how much of a handful they were! It would have been nice, but I could do nothing. I had family responsibilities.

Another thing I noticed was that they also wanted people who were trained in acting, acrobatics, and other such skills. I forwarded the email to my brother, who was training to be an actor. A day or two later I asked if he'd received the email. He had done, but didn't think it would be appropriate for him, and he couldn't give the time anyway as he would be off on his travels again the following year. I thought it was an opportunity wasted, but as in my case, he had priorities.

Further down the information panel it mentioned that if they received more than 15,000 applications, the selection would be determined by ballot. Surely this would indeed be the case. It would then just be down to pure chance. I left it at that, although I did take note of the closing date for applications: 31 August 2011.

Monday 22 August 2011

After a couple of days of careful consideration, I decided that I may as well fill in the form and apply. What harm could it do? It did say they didn't necessarily want any experience or specific skills – not for everybody at least. So why not? That was Misbah's view on it. I did ask her if she wanted to apply too, not actually considering who would look after the kids so often, if we were both successful, but she wasn't even interested in trying. At that point, I still didn't think I would be able to manage the commitment, but I felt that if I didn't apply, I could live to regret it. Besides, it wasn't certain that I would receive an audition. I was jumping the gun here, so instead of creating scenarios from nothing, I submitted my application. They only wanted very basic personal details, nothing more. In reply, I received this:

Application Confirmation: Ceremonies Volunteer Performer

Your application has been received and you will be hearing from us again in September following the 31 August application closing date.

If we are lucky enough to receive over 15,000 applications a random computerised draw will create the final short list for auditions.

If you are successful we will invite you to complete a full application form to receive an audition slot. We will also include more information about the audition process and details on what it means to be a Ceremonies Volunteer Performer.

If your application is not successful we will notify you by email as soon as possible after the 31 August 2011 application closing date.

London 2012 Ceremonies

Once again, I waited. The application deadline passed and we were into September. They did say that even if you were not successful, you would hear back from them. Still nothing. It was out of my hands now. Lots of people simply wouldn't get an audition.

2

Luck Strikes Twice

Thursday 15 September 2011

After more than three weeks of waiting to hear back, I received an invitation to audition.

Congratulations, your application to audition has been successful. You are invited to audition for a chance to become a Ceremonies Volunteer Performer in the London 2012 Olympic Games Opening or Closing Ceremonies. Please read the following points:

- You must complete the form and audition date choice in one application. You cannot save the information and go back.
- You will be able to choose one audition date from nine dates offered between 1 and 13 November 2011.
- There will be 200 people in each audition. You will not have to prepare anything.
- If successful, you will be invited to a role-specific audition in the last two weeks of November or the first week of December.
- Once you have chosen your date, please keep it free as you will not be able to change it once confirmed.
- In order to be cast you must agree to attend all rehearsals in East London.
- The deadline for application submissions is Sunday 2 October at 11.59pm.

Once we receive your application we will contact you after 2 October 2011. Please ensure you keep your requested date free. Good luck and we look forward to meeting you!

I was now rather excited, and felt very lucky too, although 15,000 was a lot of people, so I always had a good chance of being chosen at random, although I had no idea how many people had applied. It didn't really matter to me. I was going to audition for the Olympic Opening Ceremony! If nothing came of it, at least I will have had the experience.

I filled in my application as quickly as possible – there was no point in tarrying until the deadline. I managed to find a weekend audition, on a Sunday, which was convenient, although it was an early start at 9am. At least I was on the right side of London, in New Cross, with auditions being held in east London. They were, however, about a month and a half away, so more waiting ensued. I was now used to this. These things didn't happen quickly.

Wednesday 21 September 2011

Games Maker offers begin! So read the subject of the email I received from LOCOG that day. I hadn't even heard about my application, yet some people were being offered positions. I took comfort in the fact that I hadn't received a rejection. The email contained this crucial piece of information:

> Some potential Games Makers have not even had their interviews yet (and interviews continue until March 2012). If that's you, we haven't forgotten you and you are still under consideration for a Games Maker role!
> By the end of this year you will either have been offered a role, offered an interview or have been told that your application was unsuccessful (if you have not been told you are unsuccessful by 31 December, this means you are still in the running for a role).

At least I now had some kind of timescale. The end of the year was drawing closer, so hopefully I would have heard either way by then. It had been such a long wait so far – almost a year since I applied. All I wanted was an interview so I could show them why I was a perfect choice for a Games Maker. I was certain I could impress them. I would be extremely disappointed if I wasn't successful. Hopes were still alive though.

Saturday 8 October 2011

The deadline of 2 October for successful applicants to fill in their forms for an audition had passed some days ago. I now received confirmation of my time slot:

Thank you for registering for a chance to become a Ceremonies Volunteer Performer. We confirm your audition time as follows:

Date: Sun 06 November 2011
Time: 09:00

It is essential that you arrive punctually as we cannot accommodate late arrivals in alternative sessions due to the number of applicants.

Location: 3 Mills Studios, Three Mill Lane, Bromley-By-Bow, London, E3 3DU

IMPORTANT: This document contains a bar code that is exclusive to you and will enable us to quickly retrieve information and process your registration. Please bring this with you on the day. You will need to present your passport, full UK drivers licence or UK birth certificate.

Upon arrival at 3 Mills you will be checked in and then our Costumes Team will take your measurements in order to tailor an appropriate costume should you be cast in a role.

You will have your picture taken for accreditation purposes.

No filming or photography of any kind is permitted on site.

In the audition you will be put through a variety of activities to assess your attributes and it is important that you wear comfortable clothing and footwear that will not restrict your movement.

The total time that you will be on-site from check-in to check-out will be 3 hours and 15 minutes. You need to stay for the entire period.

If successful, you will be invited to a role-specific recall audition. There will be no choice of dates for this as each recall is dedicated to a specific role. We will let you know within 48hrs after your first audition when this date is. If you are unable to make the second audition, unfortunately you will not be able to continue with the process.

Whatever the outcome, we want to ensure that you have the most enjoyable experience possible and that you are able to demonstrate that you possess all of the necessary qualities to secure a role in the greatest show on Earth!

I had a look at the map to get an idea of where I needed to go, even though the audition was about a month away. At the time we were hoping to move to Croydon as soon as possible, so it could be from there that I would have to travel to the audition. That would mean a very early start, on a Sunday. I wasn't exactly looking forward to that, but I was certainly keen to see what would happen, what we would have to do. I was sure it would be quite an experience.

Saturday 29 October 2011

As the date for my audition approached, I was busy with packing and organising a house move. In a few days we were going to leave New Cross and move to something bigger and in a much more convenient location in Croydon. As could be expected, the audition was not at the forefront of my mind. But just so I didn't forget, the Ceremonies people sent me a reminder email.

The only new information offered was that there would be a sign on the way to the audition so we could find our way. It was made up of a red circle, a blue triangle, and a green square, all outlined in black and set in a white rectangle.

I looked up the route on the Transport for London website from East Croydon station. There was no way I was going to be late for this, so I aimed to arrive at Bromley-by-Bow by 08.30am at the latest. That meant I would have to catch a train at around 07.30am, which in turn meant getting up at 06.30 in the morning, on a Sunday, which I wasn't quite used to. I am not a natural early riser.

Friday 4 November 2011

Finally I heard from LOCOG about my Games Maker application. I had been successful! I was very relieved. I would have been more than a little upset if I hadn't even made it to the first stage. All I had wanted was a chance and now I had it.

> Congratulations, you are one step closer to becoming a London 2012 Games Maker! We have reviewed your application and would like to invite you to a selection event at 10 Upper Bank Street, London, E14 5NP.
> The selection event will take around 90 minutes and will include a 30-minute interview. We are currently considering you for a role as a Spectator Entry Team Member.
> If successful, you'll be performing a vital role, ensuring that spectators have a fantastic experience. You'll be working at one of our prestigious Games venues in a high-profile and busy position. Your responsibilities could include welcoming thousands of excited spectators to the venue and ensuring smooth entrance.
> You must take part in an interview in order to be considered for a Games Maker role.

Admittedly the role didn't sound particularly exciting, maybe just checking tickets, saying hello to spectators, that sort of thing. However, I really was just glad to have been offered something. All of the roles would play a part towards making the Games a success. Tens of thousands of people didn't even get offered an interview. I was fortunate, lucky, and very pleased indeed. Now that I had a foot in the door I was confident enough to believe that they wouldn't be able to refuse me. I was the right person for this. I logged into my account the same day, chose a selection event, and received a confirmation:

> Spectator Entry Team Member
> Date: 15 Nov, 2011
> Time: 16:00
> Duration: 01:30
> Location: LOCOG HQ – 10 UBS

I needed to leave work early, but I could arrange that quite easily. My manager already knew that I may need time off for Olympic volunteering the following year.

After all the waiting and wondering, things were beginning to happen. I had a chance to become a Games Maker at the Olympics and in two days I was going to audition to perform at the Olympic Ceremony. I was glad to be involved.

WAVE TWO

AUDITIONS

3

Audition 1

Sunday 6 November 2011
9am – 1pm
3 Mills Studios

I am lying in bed now on that Sunday morning in November. Very early on that Sunday. It's still dark when my alarm wakes me up. It's cold outside. I wonder if I really want to travel across London at this hour. My bed is warm and I can barely open my eyes. I continue to snooze, knowing that I really must get up soon. If I fall asleep now I won't make it.

Sitting up in bed, rubbing the sleep from my eyes, I feel apprehensive, wondering if it's worth the effort. Doubt enters my thoughts. I visualize my entire journey in a few seconds. What awaits me at the other end? An audition, I know, but it's still unknown territory. I have a deep apprehension of the unknown, though I always deal with it in the same way: take it in stages, break it up, and concentrate on one thing at a time. Forget about what's coming next.

Stage one: get ready and get as far as the front door. Stage two: to the station and on the train. Now just sit and wait until I have to get off. Stage three: make the necessary connections and arrive at my destination. Stage four: walk to the audition venue using the map that I have printed out and viewed countless times. I can picture the route in my mind, but I still look at the map. In this way, I arrive, but not without a few travel hiccups. On that Sunday morning in November there are line closures, station closures, engineering works, and delays. I'm glad I left early. The District Line is rather busy. I wonder if all of these people are on their way to the audition.

I eventually reach Bromley-by-Bow and alight. Back to stage four. Lots of people leave the train here and I consider the same thing I did 20 minutes ago. These people are probably going to the audition.

Through the ticket barrier and I see the sign with the coloured symbols. Out of the station, down some steps, through the subway,

17

back up some steps, passing another sign along the way, and now a large crowd is walking towards the Tesco that was mentioned in the email. A few people in front of me get talking about the audition. I don't hear much of the conversation but one of the girls is a dancer. She knows exactly why she is here and what she is hoping to do in the Ceremony. I observe a couple of numbers embroidered on the back of her grey tracksuit bottoms. It doesn't mean anything really, but I remember those numbers, imprint their image in my memory. I have no idea why.

As we walk past Tesco and along the road that leads away from the dual carriageway and towards the relative seclusion of 3 Mills Studios, over a small bridge, a queue becomes visible. There are plenty of people behind us and though we are a little late, they are surely not going to turn us all away. I can relax now. Just join the queue.

Up ahead they are checking people in, looking at our invitation emails and identification. Marshals are lined along the path, bidding us good morning and hello, asking us to have our invitations and ID ready for inspection. When it's my turn I show my passport and print out, and receive a wristband in return. Stage five is arrival at the audition, which I have just done. I've made it.

Onwards I go, following the crowd on a makeshift path made of interlocking tiles. Signs ask us to keep to it at all times. We take a right, walk about ten metres between a couple of buildings and come to a yard of sorts with trailers and Portakabins used for toilets. The Gents is off the path on the left. I take the opportunity now, not wanting to let even the call of nature get in the way of whatever it is that I'll be doing once inside.

Lots of people are still arriving as I rejoin the path and the crowd, veering towards the right and into another queue. I can see the entrance to the studio out of which a line of hopefuls is extending. I move forward slowly as more lengthy checks are being conducted, or so I assume. Behind me the queue is growing with every second that passes.

Once I reach the entrance area I can see some tables set up where people are sat with computers. Directly in front of me is a TV screen playing Olympic moments from the past, giving us a taste of what we could be a part of if we successfully get through today. The queue snakes to the left and right, between some barriers, although it's now very short and moving quite quickly. We are being called forward according to our initial, and then we get properly registered on the system.

Once that's done, we are sent to a series of booths where

somebody takes our photo and some measurements, for the costume we may be wearing. Costume. The thought of having one of those gives me a very small inkling of just how cool it will be if I am chosen. Yet there are so many people here, and this isn't even everybody. So many of us will be disappointed. Anyway, no negative thoughts. I just have to go with it and see.

The formalities seemingly over, we are directed to the studio area. There is one on the left and one on the right. I am told to enter the left hand one by a marshal in a yellow bib who also wishes me good luck. The studio is an enormous space, very high ceiling. There are a few platforms dotted about, and along the left wall at this end there are some clothes rails for us to hang our coats and jackets, and place our bags. I make sure I have my energy tablets in my pocket, and then proceed to the seating area made up of white plastic folding chairs, arranged in rows in two blocks with a wide aisle in between. The left block is full so I am directed to the next available seat towards the front of the right one. I have by now pinned the number I received from the registration team to my top using the safety pins they provided. It's a bit like a race number with Ceremonies written on it. My very first memento. Come what may, I will at least be able to show that I took part in an audition for the Olympic Ceremony. That's still something.

Once seated, we are kept entertained by some slightly overzealous individuals who are clearly going to be taking us through the audition. They are wearing pale pink bibs and they thank us for making the effort to turn up so early on a Sunday, especially with all the closures on the Underground. Indeed some of them are amazed at the high turnout. As the rows of chairs fill up conversations begin amongst the people on either side. We are all wondering what we will have to do, and whether or not we have a chance of getting through. All of us take comfort in the fact that nothing needs to be prepared and no experience is necessary. Looking around there is a very diverse range of people: male, female, old, young, short, tall, slim, slender, plump, athletic, muscular, and everything in between. There is no specific profile here; everybody is welcome.

After some time we are asked to introduce ourselves to the people either side and in front of us, then turn around and say hello to the people behind too. Some take to this better than others, the extroverts being distinguished from the less comfortable amongst us.

Once it is established that more or less everybody is here, we are asked to gather around a guy called Steve, who is standing on one of the platforms so we can all see him. From his accent I can tell he is American. This guy is far too enthusiastic so early on a Sunday morning, but if we are going to impress then his attitude is definitely the way forward today.

Over the next few minutes we learn that he has worked on the last few Olympic ceremonies. He is somewhat of a veteran it seems. What a job! And he knows every Olympic host city since before the war, or maybe even beyond that. Choosing a starting point he goes through all of the host cities of the summer Olympics, and asks us if we can remember anything about each Games. Naturally it's the older people amongst us who offer us their memories and thoughts initially, with the younger ones eventually contributing. For each city he picks one or two people to say something. He does this by calling out the number on their chest, which is unique in each case. Some can remember an aspect of the competition, some the Ceremony, others recall the socio-political climate at the time.

When it comes to Los Angeles 1984, I raise my hand but am not picked. I was going to say that it was the first time I was aware of a place called Los Angeles. I was nine years old. I don't remember much else, except maybe hearing the names Daley Thompson and Carl Lewis for the first time. We move on to Seoul 1988. I believe this was the era when people like Seb Coe and Steve Ovett were rivals.

In this fashion we move through the years, and my memories, although I am older, become more and more vague. I have never been a big follower of the Olympic Games, but the more we do this, the more aware I am becoming of just what I am involved in here. Steve possibly expresses it best by saying that when our friends are watching us on TV performing in the Olympic Stadium they are going to think "wow", and then they are going to want to be us. But we are going to be the ones there, in this once-in-a-lifetime situation. He reminds us that London will be the only city to have hosted the Olympics three times. Will it happen again in our lifetime? It's very unlikely. This is our best chance to be a part of it.

Soon the audition will begin we are told. I do hope so as we have been here quite a while and not much has happened. I'm not exactly aching to go, however. Until now I haven't had to do much, making it very difficult to mess up and secure my ticket to nowhere fast. But begin we must.

Steve tells us that first and foremost we are here to enjoy the experience. We mustn't worry about how we think we look, so when we are stood there getting the steps wrong, completely out of time, and thinking, "Man, I wish I'd just bought tickets!", we need to just carry on because we have no idea what they are looking for and they may just see something, at some point, that makes them think we can be good for this or for something else. That's slightly comforting, in an odd sort of way. Of course, I still want to do well and have an easy pass into the next stage of the process. I shall see.

We get told that we need to be aware at all times of the geography of the studio. Each side is marked North, East, West and South. We are asked to point to each side, as Steve calls them out. He then draws our attention to the floor layout. There are lots of coloured lines and markings drawn on, all in a certain pattern. He helps us to familiarise ourselves with them all. A lot of what we will do today is centred on coordination and awareness of space and direction. So we are asked to move to this point or that line, or group ourselves according to a number range, or by the initial of our surname, or maybe by month of birth. Speed is the key here.

We are each given a home base which is a single point in the room where we need to stand, facing a certain direction which will be called out. We have to memorise that point, using the lines and other markings, and the people around us, to help us remember where we need to stand. We will be asked to return to our home base at several points during the proceedings, as quickly as possible.

We do a lot of introductions, just walking around and meeting whoever you cross paths with. At one point we are asked to stand in a certain formation and then hold hands with the two people either side of us. We are then told to take two steps forward, still holding hands. What we have done without realising it is form the Olympic rings. All of the audition assistants can see this as they are standing on the platforms off the floor. This is one of the key moments of the audition for me, brief and relatively insignificant though it is, lasting just a few seconds. By holding hands we are all one, there is a sense of unity, and we moved together to form the rings. This is one of the reasons why I am here. I want to be a part of this sense of unity that the Olympics embodies, where we all work and move in unison to create something wonderful and awe-inspiring that the world will see, whatever that ends up being. I really want to be a part of it.

Steve hands us over to his assistants who are going to lead us through the main part of the audition. What we have been doing so far is just warming up, getting familiar with the area we are in, and bonding with each other.

There now follows a series of exercises involving dance, mime, movement and the like. Each of the assistants, of which there are four, takes us through a different exercise. The first of these is to form a very long line, and walk around the room, or in actual fact have a boogie around the room to music played on the PA, keeping the formation. "No inhibitions," we are told. It takes me some mental strength to agree to this. This is not the time or the place to feel shy or self-conscious. Everybody is doing it, so I just do so too, thinking about what could happen if I don't look enthused or able to move. I won't get called back, a high price to pay for being shy. Inhibitions out of the window then.

So off I go with everybody else, doing my best to dance whilst moving in a line. I don't find it easy, although clearly I am not the only one. After a while it is simply difficult to maintain any sort of rhythm, but no matter as we are soon moving on to something different.

For the mime exercise we are arranged in sets of rows, maybe four or five across and ten deep, I think. We are going to go through a daily routine, all done by mime. We are shown a move, which we have to repeat, for example switching the alarm clock off by raising our right hand and bringing it down sharply; pulling our coat on; taking a sip of coffee and feeling a "ting", waking us up; brushing our teeth, two strokes up and down, and three to the right, emitting the sound of the brush with each stroke. As we learn each move, another is added. In this way we build up to several actions and a long sequence is established.

It isn't as difficult to remember the combination as I first imagined. Plus most of us have somebody in front to take prompts from, although the front row moves to the back after a couple of rounds, so everybody is at the front at some point. This also makes it possible for everyone to be observed properly. There are plenty of officials looking at us with clipboards, making notes. We have numbers so they know who we are.

The girl in front of me is the one with the numbers on the back of her tracksuit bottoms, the same girl I walked behind on the way here. She is rather good, I must admit. She will surely get through. I take some of my cues from her and observe how she is performing, really emphasising the moves, with nice sharp actions. I learn from her and do the same. When it is my turn to be at the front I make sure I put plenty of emphasis on my movements, giving a really strong "ting" with an exaggerated facial expression when sipping the coffee, just like they showed us.

The next section is about dance choreography. Once again we are shown moves which we have to repeat, before moving on to another. Soon a whole routine is established. I can do the moves but on this one I am having trouble remembering the sequence. It's going a bit quick and I keep getting in a muddle and messing it up. This is not good. We are asked to bring a bit of individuality to the moves, so everybody isn't doing exactly the same thing, although the core moves are still there. We are given the example of doing our shopping. I have no idea what that is supposed to mean. I am not good at this. I think this is where I am going to fall apart. We go through it again and again, and I'm trying desperately to do the moves properly and in the correct order but I just cannot get it perfect.

One of the moves is to just look up to the ceiling, pick a spot, focus on it, and freeze on a move of our choosing. I can't even get that right. I come up with the most basic moves, where all I've done is put my hand in the air or something equally pathetic. This isn't going to get me through. I try again and again to do something interesting, and work that individuality into the routine, but I'm finding it hard enough to just remember the sequence. I try my best but it just isn't good enough. Despite all of this, it is still a lot of fun. They have looped a refrain from Beyoncé's 'Love On Top' and it is to this that we are performing our moves. It's very uplifting and by now there is a lot of enthusiasm in the room. The music is energising us and the choreographers are certainly enjoying it.

To end we are split into two large groups, where half of us stand on the side so the other half has more room to move. So now there are people right next to me watching me screw it up! When it is my turn to stand on the side, I can see people who are clearly better than I am, more comfortable with dance moves and more likely to make it through. I feel disheartened, but also remind myself that it's not just about dance. Maybe they have seen something else that I was good at, even if I flunked the dance portion. I do hope so because I will now be very upset if I don't get through. I have really enjoyed the experience and I want more of it. But there is nothing more I can do now.

Steve thanks us for auditioning, wishes us the best of luck, and says that we will hear back within 48 hours whether or not we have been successful. It's not quite 1pm, but that's fine. I get my things together and make my way out, back the way we came, and past the Tesco, where I buy some pastries for breakfast, and then towards the station. At least it's not a long wait to find out how we've done. Fingers crossed.

Wednesday 9 November 2011

Yesterday had been frustrating. They had said we would hear either way within 48 hours. All day I had waited and waited but no sign of an email. I continually interrupted my work to quickly check, refreshing my screen and feeling a pang of hope when the page went blank during those few seconds when it was reloading, only to feel deflated when there was clearly no email from the Ceremonies. All day I'd repeated this routine. In the end I had to just log off and go home, reminding myself that they did say they would inform us whether successful or not. As long as I hadn't received a rejection, there had still been a chance.

Today, on the other hand, was even worse. Still nothing. The day was ticking away and I still hadn't learnt about my audition. I was checking my email constantly. Mid-afternoon and I was beginning to accept the fact that they would not be emailing me because I wasn't chosen. It didn't matter what they had said. What mattered was they were in fact only contacting the successful ones. After all, they must have had thousands of people to email. Why waste time telling people they weren't good enough. They were not interested. Applicants would make the assumption for themselves in their own time.

I continued with my work, but all I could think about was the audition. Was I really that bad? Surely I'd done something right or at least worth considering. I couldn't have been amongst the worst people there. My mind was a myriad of thoughts, reflection, reminiscence, and refusal. There was no way I wasn't good enough. No, they said they would contact everyone. I needed to stop assuming. And wait. No, I couldn't wait any longer. This was driving me crazy. I had to know. I went online and searched for a number I could call. I looked through all of the audition emails but couldn't find one. Of course, they didn't want thousands of hopefuls hounding them. So I went to the London 2012 website. I needed to find a number and just speak to somebody, anybody. I eventually found some contact information and called. It didn't take me long to get through to somebody. That was surprisingly easy. I was quickly told that if I hadn't had an email, it meant I hadn't been picked. The lady was quite clear on this. Only successful applicants had been contacted. Well, that was that then.

Reluctantly and slowly, I put the phone down. What use was there in talking to her any longer? She could do nothing for me. There were no doubts now. I hadn't made it. I couldn't believe I hadn't made it. How could I have not been chosen? Let's be honest now: I was not expecting this. I kept telling myself that I may not get chosen, that it was very competitive and not everyone would be good enough. Just the way it is. Some people could perform, some people couldn't. But still, I did not honestly believe in my heart that I would not get through. This was now difficult. Failure. I had never handled this well. Ever since failing my first driving test, when I was 17, I had had a real problem with failure. Not that I had over-achieved in everything I'd done, but outright failure wasn't usually an option for me.

I started to think about all the happy faces that had been told yesterday that they had made it through the first audition. So many overjoyed people. Hundreds of them. Thousands. So many places there were, and I couldn't fill a single one of them. I was jealous. And I was mortified.

I thought as far forward as the night of the Ceremony. All those people on the TV and I could have been one of them. I was lucky enough to be granted an audition, and I screwed up such a golden opportunity. It was going to take a long time to quell this disappointment. What did those people have that I didn't... now this was becoming wrong. I had to stop and just accept that I hadn't been good enough. I'd messed it up. Yet the stubborn side of me refused to just accept this. I still believed I had done enough to get through to the next stage. I wasn't that bad. This must have surely been wrong. But the lady on the phone was unequivocal in her response to my question. Myriad.

One thing I was sure of was that I needed to do something about this. I was never, ever going to get this opportunity again, so I had to try just once to convince them that I could do this. I had nothing whatsoever to lose now. She did give me an email address for the Casting team. So at a few minutes before 4pm I wrote an email that I hoped would go some way towards me getting another chance. I knew this was pointless, and even silly, but I had to do it. I had to be able to say that I at least tried and didn't just sit down and accept defeat. By now I was no longer content with simply being able to say that I had auditioned for the Olympic Opening Ceremony, with a number to prove it. I had to be part of it. I needed to write an email and plead. I didn't care what anybody, or my inner self, thought. This was the gist:

> I attended the audition on Sunday 6 November at 9am and I am yet to hear whether or not I have been chosen to attend the next stage. I have spoken to somebody in the 2012 office and it seems like only successful applicants have been contacted. If this is the case, I feel very surprised as I felt I had done enough to at least warrant a recall.
>
> Is there any chance at all of some kind of feedback? I did make a few mistakes (surely lots of people did) but I am very confident that with practice I could perform very well at the Ceremony. I used to do martial arts, a lot of which is essentially choreography and coordination, so I am sure there must be something I could offer you.

Considering there were no second chances in this kind of thing, my email was a long shot, and in truth, more than a little pathetic. But emotion had taken over reason. It was the only way forward now. I'd been reduced to this.

I sent the email a few minutes before 4pm. Within about twenty minutes I received a reply. I couldn't believe they had responded so quickly, or even at all. I didn't delay opening it, even if it was just a quick and courteous confirmation of what I already 'knew':

> Thanks for your email. There has been a slight delay in the emails being sent out due to the volume and high standard of our auditionees. Please accept our apologies regarding this. The 2012 office did give you the incorrect information as in fact everybody will receive a result – I am sorry for the confusion.
>
> I can confirm that you have been invited to a recall audition on Wednesday 16th November, 5.30pm – 9.30pm.
>
> This will take place at 3 Mills Studios once again. You have been recalled to session 104B.
>
> You should receive a full email confirmation of this recall audition by the end of the week.

To say I was relieved and overjoyed was way off the mark. It is hard to say how pleased I was after reading that email. In a single second my mood completely changed and all of the negative thoughts, self-doubt and disappointment were replaced with relief and joy, I suppose. I couldn't believe it. Yet it was written there in front of me, so believe I did, and so glad I was.

I sent Misbah a text to tell her the news. She was pleased. I would be returning for another audition in a week's time. I reminded myself that this was not a second chance. Nobody had taken pity on me. I had made it through because they'd considered me to be good enough. Whatever thoughts I had had earlier on could now be cast from my mind. I was almost there. Just one more audition. In the evening I received an official confirmation of my recall.

Monday 14 November 2011

The second audition was getting close now – just two days. Just like the first one, I received a reminder email.

Slightly more imminent, however, was my Games Maker selection event. The following day, in fact. I was quite nervous about this as I did not want to somehow let the pressure affect my interview. I took some time to prepare for it, something I had only ever done on one other occasion. I tried to think about the sorts of questions they would ask me. They would no doubt be customer service oriented, so I thought of situations where I'd offered great service, where I'd received bad service, and what should have been done instead, what I considered excellent customer service to be, and so on. I had all of these responses prepared.

I thought about why I wanted to be a Games Maker, what it meant to me, how I wanted to represent London and welcome the world to my city, help people and ensure they would have a great experience. I was proud that the Games were coming here and I wanted to be part of the team that delivered them. I was confident that they would see in me the sort of the person they were looking for. I was almost certain. Tomorrow would be my one and only chance to convince them.

4

Games Maker Interview

Tuesday 15 November 2011

I spent the day at work, as usual, and in the afternoon I left, allowing plenty of time to arrive at the LOCOG HQ in Canary Wharf. It took me some time to find the address as the streets are oddly arranged over there. I used to work nearby, about a decade ago, and the area has changed immensely. Most of the buildings were not here all that time ago. Number 10 Upper Bank Street is a large office block with a vast reception lobby.

As soon as I entered the premises I could see a large reception desk several metres in front of me, flanked on both sides with a wide corridor leading to a world quite unknown to me. To the left some leather sofas were placed for visitors, and amidst it all was a pedestal with a lady behind it. A temporary sign showed me that this was where I needed to report in.

The lady had a list of people who were here for the same reason as I was, and she ticked me off. Since I was early she asked if I wished to be seen sooner than scheduled, to which I gladly agreed.

After a short wait a man came and asked us to follow him down the corridor on the left and to the lifts. We went to the 19th floor and into an area where we were welcomed and given a Games Maker selection event wristband. We could choose from three colours: blue, pink and white. Blue it was. We also received a brochure telling us about the process and what would happen over the next two hours.

Firstly we had to have our identification checked and registered, and a photo taken. We were then escorted to a small exhibition area where we were free to look around until called. This was quite interesting and included facts about the Olympics past, the venues and locations for 2012, and various other facts, figures and images. One display was a dedication from Seb Coe to the volunteers who had thus far made a commitment already to the Games by agreeing to various criteria to potentially become Games Makers, such as not expecting free tickets for our efforts, giving at least ten days of our time, and attending three training events. People who were thus committed were the people they needed, although of the 100,000 interviews taking place, there were only 70,000 roles, so today's interview was not necessarily going to lead to a concrete offer.

Having had plenty of time to look at the displays and read the information, we were asked to make our way behind a curtain into the theatre, which was really just a few rows of seats and a TV screen at the front. The video we were shown was a message from Seb Coe, wishing us the best of luck, and a more detailed offering from Eddie Izzard giving us advice on how to conduct ourselves and the sorts of things we should say, making sure that we disclosed as much relevant information as possible, all done in his usual humorous manner.

Once the video had ended we were shown to individual booths where we met our interviewers. I had a familiar face: the lady who signed me in downstairs. She explained that she was going to ask me a series of questions and I had to keep my responses as concise as possible. She could at times interrupt me in order to move on, if I had answered to her satisfaction already and no further information was needed. This did make me wonder if I was going to get a chance to disclose all relevant information about me, as Eddie had advised not too long ago.

The questions she asked were similar to what I had imagined the night before. I answered as best I could, but slowly I was losing my confidence as she questioned some of my responses. "Wasn't that just part of your job, rather than going the extra mile?" I couldn't think of another example of this on the spot so I continued to try to demonstrate why it was indeed over and above the call of duty. I didn't think she was convinced, but we moved on.

She asked me about past volunteering, so I told her about my day at the London Triathlon, showing competitors where to go and giving advice, from my own personal experience, about the race. I also included a bit of queue control that I had to do at a Lord of the Rings convention.

Throughout the interview she made notes on a clipboard. I could see that it was coming to an end after about 25 minutes, so I quickly asked if I could tell her about my linguistic skills. I can speak French, Italian, German, Urdu and Punjabi to varying levels. If I hadn't imparted that information I would have been very disappointed since all through my application process I had considered that to be a major factor in me being selected.

As the interview ended I wasn't completely satisfied with how it had gone, and hadn't expected some of the questions to be so specific, which had led to some unconvincing answers. A few of us compared notes and I wasn't the only one who had been a little surprised. But I did give some good responses so maybe I would be fine.

On one of the walls past the interview booths was a large message board where we could write a couple of lines, anything we wanted. There were all sorts of comments on there. I wrote something about feeling extremely proud to be involved.

There was also a London 2012 gift shop where we could buy souvenirs, but I chose not to take a look. A couple of minutes later, we were thanked for attending and then taken to the exit. The man asked if we would like any more wristbands, maybe another colour to the one we had received already. Some people gratefully accepted but I declined. I later reflected that I should have taken the opportunity to get another souvenir. It said 'selection event' on the band, so I would never be given one of these again. A missed opportunity.

On the way home I thought again about how the interview had gone. I really wasn't sure if I had given enough for them to offer me a role. As with the audition, however, it was now too late and I could only hope. My second audition was tomorrow. In the space of just two days, my entire Olympic experience could end. I had to do well tomorrow, especially now that my Games Maker role was possibly hanging on a thread.

5

Audition 2

Wednesday 16 November 2011
5.30pm – 9.30pm
3 Mills Studios

I leave work a little early today and get on the underground. There are no delays, just an easy journey to Bromley-by-Bow. Once we make it into the 3 Mills site, registering in the same way as before, there is a bit of a queue again. Some people are talking about the event tickets they have secured in the ballot. I haven't tried. I'm not even interested, but I am definitely interested in attending the event we are auditioning for, and not as a spectator.

Once inside I register, collect my bib number, and get measured again for my costume in case I am chosen. I am in the left studio once more. I follow the same routine of hanging my coat up (this time the clothes rails are at the back, on the left as we walk in), and then take a seat where we are told to sit. This is done according to people's surname initial.

After some time our group is told to join a line that has formed and is moving along at a medium pace. There are still people arriving so they need to move people towards the front end of the studio to make room at the back. One of the guys from the first audition, the one who led the portion where we had to dance and walk in a long line, is at the front of the queue. As each person approaches, he tells them to step forward and asks a random question, just something with a short answer. I am asked where I'm from. I reply London. Very simple. Other people have slightly more interesting questions, or ones that are maybe difficult to answer on the spot, but each one is different to the last. To do that for a few hundred people, every few seconds, is not as easy as it may seem. He does very well. I'm not sure if this is part of the audition, whether we are being tested with our responses, or if it is just a bit of fun to maybe help us relax, if we indeed need any help, but it is interesting to watch him think of so many random questions. It is something to do as we sit in some more seats and chat amongst ourselves, waiting for the audition to begin.

Eventually Steve, the very chirpy guy from the first audition, gets our attention and congratulates us, telling us that it is indeed a big deal to make it through since not everybody did. He introduces us to somebody called Toby Sedgwick, who was the Movement Director on War Horse. "I did say you were going to be in good hands," Steve offers as we applaud Toby. Well, War Horse is impressive, and it is surreal to be auditioning for somebody who is obviously held in such high regard, but it isn't quite Danny Boyle. I suppose it is asking a bit much to expect him to be here. It's only an audition. Whether or not we will see him later, if we get through this stage, remains to be seen, but I doubt it.

Steve goes on to explain that all of us are here because we can act. I can't speak for anybody else, but I know that I definitely cannot act. I have trouble changing my facial expression. Yet they thought I could act. Clearly I performed better in the miming sections than in the dancing. That I already know and here is confirmation. To say we can all act is a bit kind of them, in my case at least. I am actually a bit concerned about this, since I am now going to be expected to do some acting in front of a stadium full of spectators. I can't quite fathom how I have managed to get myself into that situation. However, I am jumping the gun here. I still have an audition to get through, which is just about to get under way. Back to the present, and back to the studio.

We are split into groups of about thirty to forty people, each with an instructor who is going to take us through the audition. Ours is called Paul, a nice guy. We don't have to worry about the lines and markings on the floor this time. That was all covered in the first audition. We only have to remember our home zone, the point at which we are standing. If we are asked to return there, we have to do so as quickly as possible, like last time.

Over the next couple of hours or so we are taken through various exercises and activities. The first one that my group does is to imagine we are holding a pole, the type that you spin around in your hands. We are shown various moves with it, holding it in different positions, and we just have to copy him. I don't do this particularly well, so it isn't a great start.

We then have to do some hand movements, imagining that we are balancing a plate on one hand, and taking it through one complete revolution, making sure that it doesn't 'drop' or 'slide off'. All the while judges are watching us, making notes on their clipboards, looking for the number we have on our chest so they know who they are marking.

Soon the lines are broken and we are told to just walk within our area. Not quite so simple as there are up to forty people and we have to keep moving, so frequent turns and manoeuvres are necessary. We are told to stop, then go, stop, then go. Then stop, and when told to go, we have to turn in another direction first, then go. This sometimes means that you bump into somebody as soon as you turn, so part of the exercise is to see how well you avoid people. It is all about coordination, but soon it also becomes about thinking at the same time. We are given different actions to do, like jump up, or kneel down, before continuing to walk. A few are introduced. This is then made more complicated as the instructions and actions are mixed up, for example, if Paul calls out jump, we have to in fact kneel. So the stopping, starting, avoiding, turning, and instructions are all combined, and called more quickly. In this way, things become quite messy, with people bumping into each other, getting confused about which action is actually being called. Sometimes stop means go and vice versa. At one point we also have to introduce ourselves to anybody we are walking towards. All of this goes on for what seems like a while.

Another exercise we do is to form a column about three people wide. The people at the back have to run down the side and freeze at the front. As soon as you find yourself at the back of the column, you have to run down to the front, and so on. A variation of this is to run to the front, hold a pose for a second, and then run to the back. We do this several times as it doesn't work too well the first couple of times. Paul makes it look easy, but the speed of movement, coupled with the pose, is not quite so simple. I doubt that they are looking for people who are as good as the instructors, rather people who are well coordinated and who can follow instructions, as well as give convincing expressions. The truth, however, is that nobody really knows what they are looking for. Everybody just does the best they can.

Plenty of people agree that although these are fairly simple tasks, under the circumstances they are twice as hard. There is a lot at stake here, and the pressure to impress is heavy. There will be no second chances. We either do well now, or our Ceremony journey will end before it has even begun.

After a while we are granted a short break. I make sure I drink some water, which is provided free. It is easy to eventually work up a sweat as we move from one exercise to the next. I have a quick chat with somebody sat next to me about the audition and how we think it is going, before we are invited to form our lines again, standing in our home positions.

It's back to miming. We have to imagine we are holding a shovel, bringing it back with our right hand and then driving it into the ground as we step forward twice, digging it in on the second step. Finally we pull the shovel out of the ground. That's four moves, all done in quick succession. Once we have done this, we have to throw our right hand over our left, and in this way the shovel has become a pickaxe. We then swing the pickaxe back and over our shoulder, bring it down into the ground, and finish by standing upright with the pickaxe in our hands. Four more moves. Eight moves in total. It appears fairly simple but once again it is hard to remember the sequence. The speed at which we have to do it also contributes to us making a mess of it. It's about a move per second. We are given a few minutes to practise on our own.

Part of the difficulty is that we are moving forward in the first part of the sequence. It's easy to overstep and get too close to the person in front. After a few tries I decide that I am finding this difficult. I am beginning to feel the pressure. I have to do something well, otherwise I will be out. It seems like there are eyes trained on us at all times. Somebody is watching me screw this up. I have to get it together.

A few minutes later Paul is back and we continue to go through the routine. Repetition is often my saving grace, but today it's not helping me at all as I still keep getting mixed up. I think it must be the situation. Try as I might I cannot really master it, and then we move on to something different. We are asked to move to the back wall and stand in a group. Five people have to stand in a row at the front. Paul demonstrates a walk in which we have to swing our arms at the same time, from left to right. As I watch other people doing it, it's easy to see that they don't look as good as Paul. When my turn comes I certainly don't feel like my movements are perfectly in time and cleanly delivered.

After a couple of rounds, they start to play a track on the PA – just a series of clicks which we are to use for timing, so we need to sync our movements with the clicks. I soon notice that the way Paul is walking is a bit like marching, which I have done a lot of, as I was in the army cadets at school. You step off with your right foot and raise your left arm, then step on your left foot and raise your right arm. Marching is simply an exaggerated walk. This exercise is much the same, except that we are swinging our arms instead of raising them, and both arms at the same time.

When it comes round to my row again, I concentrate on what I am about to do. Right foot forward, left arm swings out with the right arm following. If I start correctly it should be easy to keep the rhythm. All the while the click track keeps playing. After a while it becomes almost hypnotic. Click, click, click, click... constantly! When I move off this time I immediately get into a nice rhythm. Through the corner of my eye I see one of the judges look straight at me and then makes a note on her clipboard. I am convinced she must have written something positive because my steps were on the click, I swung the correct arm, and I kept my rhythm for a few steps at least. I believe that this is the one thing I have done really well this evening, and could be what gets me through. It can't be so simple, and it is all just speculation, but it does give me some hope.

We are almost finished. We end with the shovel pickaxe routine. This time we do it in a much larger group, in rows, and Toby is watching us. He acknowledges that the room is full of talent and they have a lot of good people to choose from. He tells us how pleased he is, before we show him what we have learnt. Part of what I do is okay, the other part is a mess and completely out of sync. I would have liked to have done better of course, but it's too late now. The audition ends and Toby tells us how great we looked. Steve thanks us and says that we will hear back in 6-8 weeks. That is such a long wait. It will be some time in January.

I look around and see so many hopefuls, some of whom will be chosen. As people gather at the front of the studio where the coats are, getting ready to leave and then filing out, Underworld's 'Born Slippy.NUXX' is played on the PA. It makes me imagine what it will be like in rehearsals. It'll be much like this – having rehearsed all evening, people will be walking out, chatting, talking about what only we know.

I don't quite know what it is about the opening notes of that song but as I hear them now I get an overwhelming desire to be a part of this. I absolutely have to be chosen and continue this experience. I'm already in too deep now, and though it is completely out of my control, if I don't get selected I will feel despondent for a very long time.

As I walk out of the 3 Mills site and onwards to the station, all I have in my mind is hope. But it's time now for a very long wait and life continues. I calculate that 6-8 weeks means the middle of January, which in turn means that I will be in Karachi when they declare their decision. We have booked a family trip already, departing on Boxing Day, so my holiday may be marred with bitter disappointment. It could be a holiday of two halves. I try to dispel all negative thoughts as there is no sense in ruminating now. The wait begins.

6

A Waiting Game

Thursday 8 December 2011

Over the next few weeks life simply continued. I hadn't heard anything about my Games Maker interview and of course any news from the Ceremonies was still a long way off. But on the first day of the fourth week, I received an email from London 2012:

> Congratulations, you are one step closer to becoming a London 2012 Games Maker!
> We have reviewed your application and would like to invite you to take part in a 30-minute telephone interview for a role as a Spectator Entry Team Member.

I wasn't expecting this to be part of the process, but it did at least indicate that they believed I was suitable for a Games Maker role, otherwise why even ask me for another interview. It wasn't an offer but I was sure that a phone interview would only serve to help them clarify a few things that maybe didn't get covered fully in the first one. I was more or less there, surely. At least it wasn't a straight rejection.

I logged onto my account in the Games Maker zone and confirmed a date and time for my interview: Friday 27 January 2012, 5pm. It said the interview would last half an hour. That was a lot of time for a bit of clarification and revisiting ground already covered. They were definitely not making it easy, especially since, in my mind, I was clearly the sort of person they were looking for. I wished they would just give me the role. I was willing to give them more than two working weeks of my time for nothing, yet this was proving to be the hardest and most nerve-racking interview process I'd ever been through.

One discovery I made today was that Underworld had been announced as the music directors of the Opening Ceremony. This was now too much. Danny Boyle directing and Underworld doing the music.

To be involved in anything that Underworld was doing was such a tantalising prospect, way beyond anything I'd imagined. I own almost every single song this group has ever recorded, including rarities, and have seen them live on five occasions. Now I could be performing in a stadium at the Olympics, whilst they play their music. Would they also be at the rehearsals? Surely they would have to be. I tried not to think too much about it as a rejection would now leave me in a very unfit mental state for a long time. Underworld and Danny Boyle – please God!

Saturday 10 December 2011

Finally I received an email from the Ceremonies, but it wasn't quite what I was expecting. In my momentary excitement I'd forgotten that it hadn't even been a full four weeks yet.

> Thanks again for the time and energy in the auditions for the Opening and Closing Ceremonies of the London 2012 Olympic Games. It was a pleasure to have you there and we hope you enjoyed your time with us. In 6-8 weeks we will be emailing with the results of your auditions and we wish you the best of luck.
>
> In the meantime, we have re-opened the applications to audition for the Olympic Ceremonies. Having completed our first phase of auditions, we now need more men – particularly if they have rhythm!
>
> So if you have a friend, a brother, or a father who could be interested in joining the Olympic experience he can apply and find out more about the commitments involved no later than 9 January 2012.

I picked up on two things in this email. Maybe they didn't have enough male dancers of a certain style – why else would they ask for rhythm. Secondly, the email mentioned that in 6-8 weeks they would be contacting us. Did that mean 6-8 weeks from now? It had been almost four weeks, and still they were expecting me to wait the same length of time they had mentioned almost a month ago. I found this very frustrating indeed. It was probably a case of simply not changing the lead time according to how much time had already passed, but the ambiguity in the email irked me as the wait had already been so difficult.

7

Offers Made

Tuesday 13 December 2011

With my Games Maker phone interview still about a month and a half away, I was very surprised and somewhat confused to receive the following email on this day in December:

Congratulations!
Following your interview to be a London 2012 Games Maker, we are delighted to offer you a role as a Venue Entry Team Member at the Olympic Games!
We received almost 250,000 Games Maker applications, many of which were of an incredibly high standard. Selecting our volunteers is a very tough job, but we were really impressed with your interview – we know you've got the passion, enthusiasm and commitment needed to make the Games happen. We hope that you are proud to be chosen to take part in the greatest show on earth.
We have taken lots of care to match you with the right role, so please note that you will not be able to swap. If you would like to be a Games Maker, you must accept the role that you have been offered.
Thank you for your patience over the last few months – we know you've had a long wait and we really appreciate your dedication to volunteering at London 2012.

So now they didn't want to interview me on the phone. I wondered if this offer was a mistake. I soon decided that I did not care. I logged on and accepted my role with no hesitation whatsoever. Within seven minutes of receiving the above email, I found a confirmation in my inbox:

Thank you for confirming that you will take on the role of Venue Entry Team Member with the SECURITY team at MAIN PRESS CENTRE during the OLYMPIC GAMES.

That was enough for me. It was official: I was going to be a Games Maker at the Olympics. I had no idea why I had been chosen to be in the Security team since I had no experience in this field at all, but it sounded interesting, and being in the Main Press Centre, where all of the journalists and writers would be based, was very appealing. I had to contain my excitement as I was at work. I'm not akin to public displays of joy, but that is what I felt.

It had been a long journey, one that had seen me experience a mixture of emotions, but no less than 1 year, 2 months, and 7 days after I applied to be a Games Maker, I was granted the rare privilege of telling my children, and maybe their children, that I was a vital part of an Olympic Games. I had seen a similar statement on a poster on the Underground and I had decided then that this was an opportunity to be taken. I now had the chance in the palm of my hand and I was grateful. A sigh and a smile, relief and pleasure. Thank you.

Wednesday 14 December 2011

Now that I had accepted my offer, I received another email containing an official welcome to the Games Maker family, which I thought was nice. There was also a video message from Eddie Izzard, essentially saying well done and good luck on our Olympic journey. Another link took me to the Games Maker uniform. I was looking forward to receiving this and wearing it during my shifts. That was certainly going to make me feel a part of a family, or an exclusive group of people who had been chosen to represent London and be one of the faces of the Olympic Games. I felt very proud.

Part of this communication was about the training that would now follow:

> Things are really starting to hot up and it's not too long now until the Opening Ceremony of the Olympic Games. As part of the build-up, we'll start to send out invitations to training soon.
>
> Orientation comes first, from February – an inspiring half-day event that will welcome you to the London 2012 team. You'll be joined by thousands of other passionate Games Makers – and some famous faces too!

After this you'll attend more specific training on your team, role and venue. Please keep an eye on your email inbox and make sure you accept your invitations quickly.

Around this time we were busy preparing for our forthcoming trip to Karachi. Boxing Day was fast approaching and I was excited about going. Once over there news of the Ceremony would be close. I would return knowing whether or not I would be performing. I took comfort in the knowledge that I was at least going to be a Games Maker so my mind was more at ease, but there was still an element of apprehension at the outcome. I kept thinking back to the rhythmic walk I did in my second audition when the marker looked at me and wrote something on her clipboard. That was the one thing I kept playing back that kept my nerves at bay.

Tuesday 10 January 2012

For the past fortnight I had been checking my emails a few times everyday but not a single message was from the Ceremonies. Tomorrow was the end of eight weeks; I had been counting. They were not making this easy. I knew from experience that they would definitely get back to me but what was taking them so long? For two weeks I had waited and waited, thinking that even though they had said 6-8 weeks, I wouldn't have to wait the maximum time. Sadly I was wrong, and it was now looking like it would stretch beyond even eight weeks. At times I was refreshing my inbox every few minutes whilst doing other things, in the hope that an email would suddenly appear. It was all in vain.

On the other hand things were progressing on my Games Maker journey:

The London 2012 Games are getting closer, and it's time for you to sign up for your first training event – Orientation.

Orientation training will give you a fantastic insight into the London 2012 Olympic and Paralympic Games, the sports, venues and life as a Games Maker. You'll find out more about the Games and the next steps on your journey. You'll also meet lots of other Games Makers.

The session should leave you feeling inspired about the Games and the key part you'll play in making them happen.

> Training is compulsory for all Games Makers, and will be taking place in the city where you'll be based during the Games.

As always there were a range of sessions available. I chose Saturday 18 February at 8.30am. The venue would be Wembley Arena. Travelling from Croydon would be another painfully early start to the day. Early mornings aside, however, I was very much looking forward to the training.

Wednesday 11 – Sunday 15 January 2012

Eight weeks and beyond. I was now in new territory, and becoming increasingly frustrated at not knowing the result. I had a 9-month-old daughter who had travelled across five time zones and was by night driving both me and my wife just slightly mental (bless her) by refusing to adjust to her new routine even after more than a fortnight of being in Karachi. By day I was driving myself crazy when nothing showed up in my email. I kept telling myself today is the day I'll find out, but for five days I only found out just how patient I was required to be. I had more than enough to keep my mind off not knowing, but still, by now I was getting rather agitated and I just wanted to know if I was in or out. I logged on to my email continually, kept refreshing, waited a while then tried again, went away and came back, logged on, refreshed, over and over. My patience was really being tested, the fear of rejection also lingering. I'd waited so long. I just needed to know now.

Monday 16 January 2012

So it went until I received an email in my inbox where the subject header told me everything I needed to know, without even opening the message: "London 2012 Olympic Games Ceremonies – Cast Offer."

I looked at those last two words for far longer than two seconds. I looked at each of those two words individually. I looked at the shape of the letters. I just stared at them. I looked through them and around them. Without raising a finger I touched those two words on the screen before me. And finally I came to my senses. A smile formed on my lips. My mind said "Thank God for that". I laughed inwardly. I felt an immeasurable sense of relief. Through gritted teeth I forced an affirmation that was in reality no more than a whisper. Cast Offer.

From here I moved quickly and opened the email. There was no sense of dread at what I may or may not see. I had nothing to fear. I already knew the content. It was confirmed. I was in. All I had to do was read the details. I read with great pleasure.

Congratulations! You have been successful in your audition to become a Ceremonies Volunteer Performer.

We hope that you are able to accept this once-in-a-lifetime chance to be part of a global event that expresses and celebrates the passion and creativity of the United Kingdom in front of the entire world.

Below is a brief overview of the cast group that you have been selected for together with general information regarding rehearsals.

Cast Group	Olympic Opening Ceremony: Segment 44 Group B
Role Outline	Character/movement and utility role in spectacular sequence in Opening Ceremony
Rehearsal Site Facilities	• There will be rehearsals at three venues in East London including 3 Mills and the Stadium. • An overview of your rehearsal schedule is attached. • Security will be strictly maintained at all venues and only accredited performers will be allowed on site.
Travel	We will allocate Oyster cards to cover transport costs from Central London to the individual rehearsal venues. These will be valid from Zones 1 – 6. Unfortunately no other travel costs can be covered
Cast Coordinator	Your lead cast coordinator is Laura

Participation as a Ceremonies Volunteer Performer is a significant undertaking and you will need to commit to the period of time required for rehearsals and the Ceremonies themselves. Before accepting this offer please remember that from April 2012 there will be two to three rehearsal sessions per week, lasting up to four hours, either on weekday evenings or at weekends, and a number of all-day rehearsals in the three weeks leading up to each Ceremony. Please consider carefully whether you can fulfil the requirements of your schedule before completing your acceptance agreement.

In order to deliver the Ceremonies successfully it is extremely important that everyone attends all rehearsals. If you miss more than two rehearsals throughout the whole period you will automatically move to the reserve cast and we cannot guarantee you will perform.

This offer is conditional pending formal validation of the identification provided at registration and satisfactory background checks in accordance with the requirements stipulated by LOCOG and UKBA.

If you wish to accept this offer, please confirm by returning a signed copy of the Agreement to us. The deadline is 31 January 2012. If you have also been offered a role as a London 2012 Games Maker you will need to choose which role you prefer, as it isn't possible to accept both.

Once again – congratulations! We look forward to receiving your response and to welcome you as a London 2012 Ceremonies Volunteer Performer. Remember everything we do is confidential, including the information in this email. Be part of the secret!

So I had been chosen for the Opening Ceremony and it was to be a spectacular sequence. Those were the two things that registered before anything else. The Opening Ceremony of the Olympic Games. I was so excited. In my eyes this was the main one – the one that everybody would be looking forward to and anticipating, and I was going to be in it.

The words character/movement got me thinking. I could see some kind of mime sequence, or just a scene where I would be required to act. I wondered what costume I would be wearing and how long I would be performing for. A few minutes at least. For that short period of time I would be in the middle of an entire stadium full of people. It was pointless even trying to imagine how that would feel. I had no idea. I searched online for the Opening Ceremony at Beijing, which I had never watched. There was no time to start now. It was getting late in Karachi and the kids had to be put to bed. Nonetheless I could at least watch a few minutes of it, and show my wife the kind of event I was going to participate in. She had very little understanding of what the Olympics even were, having never been interested in sport at all.

Although Pakistan always sends athletes to the Olympics, and have also won gold medals, my wife knew nothing of it. She knew nothing about opening ceremonies. It was hard for me to explain what this meant, so it would be easier to just show her. She sat beside me as I played the footage I'd found. Literally a few seconds into it and she was summoned to help with the kids.

When she returned I explained to her that I was going to be performing in a stadium like the one on the screen. She enquired as to what I would be doing, so I replied that I had no idea. She wondered what was so exciting, but if I wanted to do it then I should just go ahead. All the joy and excitement was lost on her. It mattered not. She would realise in time.

One thing that we needed to discuss was the rehearsal schedule, although it was really just the bare bones of it for now:

DATE	TIME	VENUE DETAILS/NOTES
Wed 02 May	17:30 to 21:30	3 Mills Orientation + Rehearsal
Wed 09 May	17:30 to 21:30	3 Mills
Sun 20 May	10:00 to 15:00	1:1
Sun 27 May	10:00 to 15:00	1:1
Sat 02 June	10:00 to 15:00	1:1
Sat 09 June	14:00 to 19:00	1:1
Sun 10 June	14:00 to 19:00	1:1
Sat 16 June	14:00 to 19:00	1:1
Sun 17 June	14:00 to 19:00	1:1
Sat 23 June	TBA	Stadium Orientation + Rehearsal
Sun 24 June	TBA	Stadium

Fri 29 June	TBA	Stadium
Sat 30 June	TBA	Stadium
Sun 01 July	TBA	Stadium
Sat 07 July	TBA	Stadium
Tue 10 July	TBA	Stadium
Sat 14 July	TBA	Stadium COMPULSORY
Wed 18 July	TBA	Stadium COMPULSORY
Fri 20 July	TBA	Stadium COMPULSORY
Sat 21 July	TBA	Stadium Dress Rehearsal COMPULSORY
Mon 23 July	TBA	Stadium Dress Rehearsal COMPULSORY
Wed 25 July	TBA	Stadium Dress Rehearsal COMPULSORY
Fri 27 July	TBA	Stadium SHOW DAY

They hadn't lied when they'd mentioned that this was going to require a significant commitment. It was in fact going to take over most of my summer. And Misbah would have to look after the kids whilst I was off rehearsing. I did feel bad about this. I decided not to accept the offer just yet until I had had time to really consider if it was going to be possible. Besides I didn't have to accept until 31 January. I was due back in London before then, and it would also give me a chance to speak to my manager at work and discuss time off for rehearsals.

One line in the offer email was very significant for me. I had already been offered a role as a Games Maker and I had even accepted it. Now I was being told that I would have to choose between the two. This was a body blow indeed and was going to be a tough decision, one that I didn't want to make too hastily. I would wait until I had returned home. I'd waited so long for the chance to be a Games Maker and felt so proud when I was offered a role. I was looking forward to wearing the uniform. It was ten days' work. The Ceremony would be over in a few minutes, and I wouldn't get to experience the actual

Games. I hadn't bought tickets as I'd decided long ago that I wanted to volunteer instead. I felt almost devastated that I had to make this decision. It was unfair. Maybe it was because they wanted to give more people an opportunity to be part of the Olympics, so only one role per person, or maybe the reason was more practical. Maybe I was being greedy. Over the next week and a half, I mulled over these points and others like them.

8

Only One Allowed

Thursday 26 January 2012

Now back in London I'd decided that I wanted to be part of the Ceremony and I would very reluctantly have to cancel my Games Maker role. I was extremely disappointed but the thought of performing in a packed stadium, and also the experience of going through a long rehearsal process, outweighed what I'd decided would essentially be a volunteering role that I could possibly get a chance to do again. Maybe not at the Olympics, but still the type of volunteering experience that could be repeated, whereas the Ceremony opportunity would never come again. Ultimately it wasn't a difficult decision to make.

Having signed and scanned my Acceptance Agreement and Assignment of Rights, the two documents attached to the offer email, I emailed my Cast Coordinator, Laura, to accept the role. I'd already clicked the link they'd included in the email when I was in Karachi, just in case not doing so would cause a problem, but sending these two documents was final acceptance.

I asked if it would be possible to receive an acknowledgement email, and took the opportunity to ask about doing both roles – whether it was definitely not allowed. I didn't want to cancel the Games Maker offer until my performer role was confirmed. I asked why I wasn't permitted to accept both roles, as I was really looking forward to becoming a Games Maker too.

I never did receive a reply from Laura, not even an acknowledgement of receipt of my acceptance. I therefore didn't cancel my Games Maker role, which I could do by simply logging into my account and selecting the right option. Once confirmed there was probably no going back, so I was reluctant to do this just in case there was a problem with my Ceremony offer and then I would be left with nothing. So I left it alone.

Thursday 2 – Friday 3 February 2012

I was now beginning to wonder if I shouldn't just cancel my Games Maker offer. If they found out that I was signed up for both that and the Ceremony, they may cancel one themselves, or worse both. I received a reminder of my Orientation Training, booked for 18 February, and on the Friday I was told that I would soon receive an e-Ticket for the event. I still hadn't heard back from Laura, so I decided that I would definitely attend the training session. It would be an experience in itself and one that I wouldn't be able to do again. It was in Wembley Arena so would be worth a visit.

Friday 10 February 2012

I finally received my e-Ticket today. My chosen training session was just eight days away and I was looking forward to it, even though I probably wouldn't be able to use any of the training. I printed out the email, which contained a secure and personal barcode for scanning at the venue. I wouldn't be able to enter without it.

Saturday 11 February 2012

I received an email today which had the heading 'Eddie Izzard and the Games Makers':

> Way back in July 2010 we started the search for up to 70,000 people to be London 2012 volunteers. Comedian Eddie Izzard helped us lead that search and almost 250,000 people applied. After a careful selection process, training is under way.
> Eddie went along to the first training event at Wembley Arena last weekend, along with thousands of Games Makers who braved the weather to get there. He met some of those who will be giving up at least ten days this summer to help with every aspect of the Games.

There was a video attached which showed Eddie at Wembley Arena during the first Orientation event, and a few interviews with people who had been confirmed as Games Makers. They said how privileged they felt and they'd volunteered because it was a once-in-a-lifetime opportunity – the usual sentiments. In one snippet Jonathan Edwards was addressing the audience and said, "I've waited a long time to say this: Good morning, Games Makers."

As I watched this video I felt dejected that I would no longer be one of them. Being a Games Maker was such a big deal, and the chance that I had in my hand was being taken away. I'd not fully considered the numbers until now. Of almost 250,000 people, only 70,000 were being given the opportunity – less than a third of applicants. And I was one of those. I felt proud to have come so far, but at the same time disappointed that I couldn't complete the journey. There had to be a way around this.

In the video I saw people being given a special Games Maker handbook or guide as they walked into the venue. It was a binder with information inside. This was a souvenir indeed. I was at least going to get my hands on one of those. I would have something to show that I did get accepted.

9

Orientation Training

Saturday 18 February 2012
8.30am – 12.45pm
Wembley Arena

Travelling from Croydon to Wembley in time for an 8.30am start on a Saturday morning isn't the easiest of journeys. Just like the morning of my first audition for the Ceremony more than three months ago, I have a very early start. I wish it didn't have to be this way as I very reluctantly get up and get ready. But early it is, and in the same way as previously I go through the motions of travelling to the venue, although there are no nerves this time.

Walking from the station to the arena, which I have done many times before when attending concerts, I look at the people around me. Every adult age group, every ethnicity, seemingly every walk of life are each represented several times. The only common thread in the average concert crowd is the event that everybody is attending. Yet with this extremely diverse group of people, there is one other thing that unites everybody: a willingness to give up our time free of charge for a global event.

As I reach the venue I look for the North East Entrance, as instructed. There are plenty of marshals available to direct people. Turning a corner and then walking up some steps, a long queue becomes apparent, as expected. Long lines of people are snaking up and down beside the entrance and moving slowly. I make my way to the end and wait with everybody else. I can see this is going to take some time so I occupy myself with the book I've recently begun to write. I manage to slip an Olympic-related simile into the narrative. I will forever remember where I was when that line was written.

After a significant wait, I am approaching the front of the queue. We are asked to have our print outs and identification ready for inspection and scanning. Once checked, I am given one of the handbooks I saw on the online video. Mine to keep forever. Only

Games Makers receive one of these. I thank the friendly lady and make my way inside. I don't have long before the training begins, barely enough time to grab myself a coffee to help me stay alert at this early hour. There is a lady giving out Cadbury's chocolate bars, ostensibly an act of generosity, but clearly it isn't just about this. There are many corporate sponsors who are involved in the Games.

Block D2, Row 7 is where I need to go. I am sufficiently familiar with Wembley's seating plan to know that I have a floor seat towards the back of the arena. Going inside, I walk down the aisle to my seat in Row 7. There is a stage in the centre and a screen above it. On one side there are a couple of bright pink sofas, arranged like they would be in a studio chat show setting. To the right of these are two swivel chairs and a large desk. In terms of atmosphere it is indeed like being at a concert, just no music being played on the PA. People are still taking their places. Looking around there are large patches of empty seats, but this is slowly changing.

I sip my coffee and flick through the handbook I've received. It contains lots of useful information including some facts about the Olympics, a list of all of the Functional Areas for the volunteers, some training exercises, plus lots of things that we, as Games Makers, must familiarise ourselves with before we begin our shifts, including trying to memorise all of the pictograms that represent each of the sports at both the Olympics and Paralympics, and also the British Sign Language alphabet. This is something for the train journey home.

Eventually the lights go down and we are introduced to our host for the day, John Inverdale, who takes a seat on one of the sofas. He takes us through the format of the day and what will happen. A break is planned half way through the proceedings.

The very first thing we have to do is introduce ourselves to everybody around us. One of the aims of the day is to take the opportunity to meet fellow Games Makers, regardless of the role we've been appointed.

We watch introductory videos about the history of the Olympics, and what it means to be a Games Maker, including words from some famous Olympic athletes who state that the volunteers for them are the people who do indeed make the Games possible. We are told about all of the venues that will be used, both in and out of London, and shown what a typical day could be like, including the journey to our shift. We will be wearing our uniform before leaving home as there will be no changing facilities.

In amongst all of the video footage, some key personnel from London 2012 are invited on stage to discuss the Olympic bid and the logistics required to host the Games. The Paralympics are not left ignored when Tanni Grey-Thompson makes an appearance. A senior member of the police force talks to us about the security operation, and a representative of McDonald's, another of the principal corporate sponsors, speaks about customer service and the training programme they have devised.

Throughout the training there are breaks for simulated news bulletins by acting presenters on stage, to give us a taste of what Games time coverage will be like.

During the break, which lasts about half an hour, I decide to go to the information point and enquire about my role to see if I have to definitely decline my offer. Getting past a security guard to gain access to a set of stairs that take me down to a lobby area, I approach the information desk. I am careful not to give my name. I still carry with me a sense of paranoia that keeps telling me that somebody is just waiting to catch me out. This is slightly irrational but my malaise stems from an intense desire to continue both of my journeys.

Several times throughout the training so far I have felt an excruciating sense of disappointment that soon I could no longer be part of this incredible team. I have to find a solution. The lady I speak to tells me that I will have to contact the London 2012 office directly as the information team at the event are in no position to help me with my query. End of conversation. I make a mental note to call as early as possible in the coming week.

With that out of the way I return upstairs and have a look at the official merchandise stall which is selling all sorts of London 2012 memorabilia which I have no real interest in. Not far from here people are having their photos taken with the now ubiquitous official mascots, Wenlock and Mandeville. I've not yet decided if I like the mascots, just consider them a little odd. I move towards the small crowd. There is no queue, just a free for all, with people asking others to take photos for them. I take a couple of photos myself and wonder if I also want to take back with me a memory of my day here. I eventually decide that I may as well take the opportunity – why ever not – as I may later regret not having done so. I ask a fellow Games Maker to return the favour I've just done him, and so get a photo of Wenlock and Mandeville standing either side of me. By now it is almost time to return to our seats so after texting Misbah, who is still in Karachi with the kids, I re-enter the auditorium.

One of the key sections of today's training is now played back on the overhead screens: the mnemonic I DO ACT. This represents all the things that London 2012 wants every Games Maker to embody and apply to everything we will do during our shifts.

I – Inspirational
D – Distinctive
O – Open
A – Alert
C – Consistent
T – Team

Eddie Izzard presents examples of each of these by using role plays, where one scenario shows Games Makers failing to apply these qualities, and another where they successfully manage to do so. Predictably the former is exaggerated and comical, whilst Eddie, in between each example, is equally humorous.

The final portion of the day sees the Games Maker uniform being modelled on stage. Once again I feel very frustrated that I may not be able to get my hands on it now, but I banish these thoughts as I am sure there is no reason why I can't do both this and the Ceremony. That, at least, is what I believe.

A musical finale follows, and with that the first real stage of our Games Maker journey ends. It is time to leave. Before doing so I take a couple of photos of the crowd that has amassed outside Wembley Arena. Thousands of Games Makers, holding their training handbooks, are heading towards the station, or just milling around and chatting to their new colleagues. Some spend a couple of minutes to take in the scene before leaving and catching pre-booked trains to what is probably all parts of the country. It has been an inspirational day. I have a serious phone call to make on Monday.

10

Still In The Games

Monday 20 February 2012

Whilst at work, I went online in the afternoon to search for a phone number for the London 2012 volunteer office. Unlike a lot of consumer websites it was relatively easy to find. Once I had dialled and was connected it was equally painless getting through to a real person. I explained my predicament to the voice on the other side, without having given my name, and said that I didn't wish to relinquish my Games Maker role without first receiving absolute confirmation of my Ceremonies role acceptance, which hadn't thus far been acknowledged at all, a constant source of unease. I had wanted to call the Ceremonies office, but they were much less willing to take calls. Try as I might, I could not find a number anywhere.

I also asked why I couldn't perform both duties, to which the man replied that it was probably just a case of clashing schedules between Games Maker training and Ceremony rehearsals. If this was the sole reason, indeed no other was mentioned, I felt a sudden glimmer of hope that I could take both roles without any issues arising. Yet the Ceremonies offer email stated categorically that it would have to be one or the other. I held this thought until I had finished my phone conversation. The man advised me that the best plan of action would be to keep both positions until such a time when I would be forced to cancel one due to unavoidable clashes. I thanked him kindly.

By now I was beginning to understand that the Games Maker programme and the Ceremonies were two separate entities who were only aware of each other's activities, but did not work closely together. They both had different email domains, different contact details, and different offices. If I kept both activities close to my chest during training and rehearsals, and I intended to do exactly that, then there was no reason why I would be discovered. Ceremonies didn't have to know that I was also pursuing my role as a Games Maker.

There were only two more Games Maker training sessions

remaining: role-specific and venue-specific. I was allowed to miss up to two rehearsals. Therein lay the very simple solution to my problem. I had no actual intention of missing any of the rehearsals, as I wanted the complete experience and would avoid this eventuality if at all possible, but if there was no other option, then there was a way out. I was still confident that I would be able to attend every rehearsal as there were always several training sessions available for Games Makers, to ensure everybody could attend a session convenient to them. With these thoughts I was in higher spirits, and I looked back upon my Orientation Training from the opposing perspective.

Tuesday 21 February 2012

The following day I heard from London 2012 again:

> It was great to see you at Wembley Arena for Orientation training last Saturday – we hope you enjoyed it!
>
> Please take some time over the next few days to read through the workbook you were given at Wembley. You can access the training materials on the DVD at the back of the workbook.
>
> We know that the next few months are going to be a busy time as you prepare for your role at the Games – you'll have additional training to attend, you'll be collecting your uniform and accreditation, and you'll also find out your shift pattern.

I was hearing about my Games Maker role regularly now. There was still no news from Ceremonies, although according to the initial timetable I received with my offer email, rehearsals were due to begin at the beginning of May, so still over two months to go. I couldn't wait to get going but all I could do was continue waiting.

Wednesday 14 March 2012

Finally I heard back from the Ceremonies, although this was a general email, not from my Cast Coordinator. Whatever the case, it meant that I was still in and my acceptance had surely been received if I was still on the mailing list. I breathed a sigh of relief as I opened the email:

GROUP 44 – LONDON 2012 CEREMONIES – Cast Update

We wanted to give you a quick update before your first rehearsal.

Signed Performer Agreements: If you haven't sent in your signed performer agreement, we need it before the first rehearsal.

Accreditation Information: Now we have collected all the relevant information, this is being checked to secure your Ceremonies and Games Time accreditation. All queries need to be resolved in advance of your first rehearsal to facilitate access on site.

1:1 Rehearsal Space: In your offer letter rehearsal schedule we referenced our third rehearsal site which is the large outdoor space where we will replicate the scale of the Stadium and conduct full scale rehearsals. This is a fantastic resource and indispensable to delivering four world class Ceremonies. We now have this venue confirmed. It is in Dagenham, which is in Zone 5.

We are organising a shuttle bus to the rehearsal site and we anticipate some parking available. We are currently establishing what car-pooling opportunities there may be and will send further information when available.

Rehearsals at the 1:1 Rehearsal space will mainly be on evenings or at weekends until we require longer rehearsals.

Rehearsal Schedules: Although we try to minimise changes they are inevitable and we will communicate with you as soon as possible.

Confidentiality: Just a reminder: please do not speak to the media about your participation in the Ceremonies. If you get approached contact your Cast Coordinator.

With about a month and a half to go now before the first rehearsal, I was becoming rather excited at the prospect of discovering what we would be doing in the Ceremony. I'd received my cast offer all the way back in January. I was just over half way through the long wait to rehearsals. That first session couldn't come soon enough, but these things always take time.

Monday 19 March 2012

Just a few days later I heard about my Games Maker uniform and accreditation collection.

> The London 2012 Games are getting closer and it's almost time for you to collect your Olympic uniform and accreditation card.
> You've been invited to a Uniform Distribution and Accreditation Centre (UDAC) in the town or city where you'll be volunteering during the Games.
> You'll need to bring your **unique volunteer number: 2137550.**

I quickly logged on and chose a time that was convenient, although every slot offered meant that I would have to interrupt my working day for more than my lunch hour allowed. I was relieved to have a very understanding and flexible manager as I didn't want to use any annual leave for this. I needed to save my remaining leave for training, rehearsals, and my shifts, and already I didn't have my full allowance available, owing to the family holiday at the beginning of the year.

I received my confirmation shortly after selecting my slot:

UNIFORM AND ACCREDITATION COLLECTION
Class: Group E
Date: 29 May, 2012
Time: 12:00
Duration: 01:00
Location: UDAC – LONDON COLLECTION

I was now looking forward to collecting my uniform, although once again there would be a long wait. Despite my previous assurances that there would be no issue with me accepting both roles, I couldn't help feeling that something would go wrong and the system would expose me in due course. Paranoia was still rife.

Friday 23 March 2012

The emails and updates continued to come. Ever since my Orientation Training, this was the only activity taking place. The occasional communication aside, life had once again become normal. On this day I received a Games Maker update, which contained the following news:

Games Maker shifts

We've been really busy over the last few months arranging almost a million shifts for our volunteers! From April you will find out the exact dates and times when you'll be volunteering during Games time. Not everyone will get their shift pattern at the same time, but we'll email you when yours is available.

Please make sure you stick to your shift pattern. Your role is essential to the Games, so if you can't make a shift we'll need to find someone else to do it – that involves a lot of work behind the scenes.

Training

Games Makers need to attend Role and Venue training. These sessions will go into more detail about the tasks you'll be performing at the Games, as well as the venue(s) where you'll be volunteering. They're also a great chance to see the people and places you'll be part of this summer. You'll be sent invitations over the coming weeks and months so please accept them quickly.

Saturday 21 April 2012

Almost a month passed with no further updates and no news about rehearsals, although things would soon begin to move forward. My Orientation Training had taken place over two months ago. The next stage of my Games Maker journey would soon arrive:

Now it's time to sign up for Role-Specific Training.

At this session you will learn everything you'll need to carry out your role at the Games, from skills and knowledge to how you can best represent London 2012.

You will be trained with other volunteers, and you'll be able to try out the duties you'll be doing – whether that's using specific equipment or directing people. Most importantly, you'll find out who you'll be interacting with during the Games – from spectators to athletes – and how to be the best host possible.

What to bring to Role-Specific Training:

1. Your Games Maker workbook
2. Valid photo ID
3. Your reminder email – you'll receive this a few days before training. It contains your unique volunteer number.

As always I logged on as soon as possible and booked my session. I'd noticed that some slots got booked up very quickly, usually the evening and weekend ones, so it was always important to secure my place promptly. I managed to book the following training session:

ROLE-SPECIFIC TRAINING: Security – Venue Entry TM RST
Date: 11 May, 2012
Time: 18:00
Duration: 04:00
Location: Hackney Community College

This was a four hour session beginning at 6pm, so after work. It was going to be a long day, but it was something to look forward to.

11

Rehearsals Approach

Wednesday 25 April 2012

The first Ceremony rehearsal was now only one week away according to the initial schedule that we had received. Today I received confirmation of this when Ceremonies finally wrote to us:

44 GROUP B

We are looking forward to seeing you at your first rehearsal next week. Please bring this letter with you, as the bar code is exclusive to you and will enable us to scan you in quickly. Your rehearsal is on **Wednesday 2 May – 17.30 – 3 Mills Studios.** It is essential you arrive punctually – there is a huge amount to achieve!

Your first rehearsal will include:
1. Registration and distribution of key information.
2. Distribution of your Ceremonies accreditation and Oyster card.

Attached to this email are the conditions of use for both your Ceremonies accreditation and Oyster cards. You will be required to sign this before either of these items is issued. Accreditation and Oyster cards will only be issued on presentation of the I.D that you used for registration. No I.D – no entry to the rehearsal.

We can only admit those who have submitted their Performer Agreement form and have satisfied accreditation requirements.

There will be a creative cast orientation prior to your first rehearsal, to give you some more information about your role and segment. And then rehearsals begin! Have fun!

IMPORTANT INFORMATION

Rehearsal Schedule: Please check the updated rehearsal schedule attached.

Attendance: Remember if you miss more than two non-mandatory rehearsals you will go on a reserve list. We have a healthy reserve list of people who are waiting to get the chance to be part of the Ceremony, so do make every effort to keep your place.

Confidentiality: In signing your Performer Agreement you are agreeing to keep all details confidential. You can tell people that you are taking part in the Olympic Opening Ceremony, but you are not allowed to give any details about what you are doing. This includes all forms of print, broadcast media, forums, social media channels, and blogs.

Due to security, you may not indicate your location at any time using GeoLocation services. No cameras are allowed in rehearsals, including camera phones.

If you are approached by the media you should contact your Cast Coordinator. Please be aware any breaches in confidentiality will result in you not being able to take part in the Ceremony.

Branding: Rehearsals will be filmed by the Ceremonies team. We ask you to not wear anything too overtly branded.

You should wear appropriate clothing but do NOT need to prepare anything or bring any equipment with you.

Admission will only be for those who have the appropriate confirmation information. Non-cast will not be able to come on site.

Oyster Cards: At your first rehearsal, on receipt of your signed confirmation of terms and conditions you will receive a pre-paid Oyster card. This will have a certain number of trips to cover journeys to and from Central London to the rehearsal venues. When this runs out we will issue subsequent cards.

We look forward to seeing you very soon on this next exciting step of the journey!

I read this email more than once to make sure I understood everything, but also because I was now very excited about rehearsals finally beginning. It had been a long wait, but I was going to enjoy every minute of the experience. It would be incredible, and I was going to savour it.

Also sent with the email was an updated rehearsal schedule which was much more detailed than the previous one. It now looked like this:

DATE	TIME	VENUE DETAILS/NOTES
Wed 02 May	17:30 to 21:30	3 Mills Orientation + Rehearsal
Wed 09 May	17:30 to 21:30	3 Mills
Sun 20 May	10:00 to 15:00	1:1
Sun 27 May	10:00 to 15:00	1:1
Sat 02 June	10:00 to 15:00	1:1
Sun 03 June	10:00 to 15:00	1:1
Sat 09 June	15:00 to 20:00	1:1
Sun 10 June	15:00 to 20:00	1:1
Sat 16 June	15:00 to 20:00	1:1
Sun 17 June	15:00 to 20:00	1:1
Sat 23 June	09:00 to 17:30	Stadium Orientation + Rehearsal
Sun 24 June	09:00 to 13:00	Stadium
Fri 29 June	17:30 to 22:00	Stadium
Sat 30 June	09:00 to 17:30	Stadium
Sun 01 July	09:00 to 13:00	Stadium
Sat 07 July	13:00 to 22:00	Stadium
Sun 08 July	09:00 to 13:00	Stadium
Tue 10 July	17:30 to 22:00	Stadium
Sat 14 July	09:00 to 17:30	Stadium COMPULSORY
Wed 18 July	TBA	Stadium COMPULSORY
Fri 20 July	TBA	Stadium COMPULSORY
Sat 21 July	TBA	Stadium Dress Rehearsal COMPULSORY

Mon 23 July	TBA	Stadium Dress Rehearsal COMPULSORY
Wed 25 July	TBA	Stadium Dress Rehearsal COMPULSORY
Fri 27 July	TBA	Stadium SHOW DAY

There were going to be some long rehearsals – 1pm until 10pm. Nine hours! Two very significant additions to the schedule were rehearsals on Sunday 3 June and Sunday 8 July. This now meant that from Sunday 27 May I would not have a single free weekend until Sunday 15 July. Misbah was not going to be happy and I wasn't looking forward to breaking this news to her. The summer is our time for family days out but there would be none of this throughout June and half of July. And she would be left with the kids. I felt bad but I just couldn't say no to this opportunity. I would have a lot to make up for once it was over.

That evening I told her what we were both in for, and my prediction was not far off the reality. She was not happy and was even left a little stunned at the commitment I had signed up to. I don't think it had fully registered when I had received the cast offer in Karachi and I'd shown her the basic schedule.

We discussed exactly what I'd thought we would be discussing: her having to look after the kids the entire week with no breaks, and no weekends free for most of the summer to spend days out. I could understand this. Whenever I have the children for just a few hours, because of their age, it is relentless. I continued to feel a heavy sense of guilt, but equally I could not stop myself from being completely selfish. I asked her to think about how proud she would feel when she was watching me perform on TV, even if she wasn't able to see me. I think she relented a little, but maybe not quite enough. I was sure she would come round eventually. At least I hoped so.

Friday 27 April 2012

I received another Games Maker update today, this time from the Security team.

With only 91 days to go until the London 2012 Olympic and Paralympic Games, we know you're eager to find out about shifts during the Games.

All Games Makers who were chosen to volunteer in the Security team have now accepted their positions. This means we can move into the next stage of planning – coordinating shifts. As you can imagine, with 70,000 volunteers to allocate shifts to across the entire Games, this is a mammoth task!

Over the coming weeks we will plan your shifts according to individual venue requirements, competition schedules and, more importantly, access to public transport, so you don't need to worry about not getting to your shift on time.

We plan to complete this by the middle of May. This means you will receive the details of your shift pattern in the **last week of May.**

WAVE THREE

3 MILLS

12

Rehearsal 1

Wednesday 2 May 2012
5.30pm – 9.30pm
3 Mills Studios

Today begins as any other Wednesday. I go to work in the morning and carry out my tasks as I would do on a normal working day. Except that today I can't quite concentrate as much as usual, because this evening I have my first rehearsal for the Olympic Opening Ceremony. Thoughts of this are getting in the way of my work. It has been a long wait, almost four months, but all waiting eventually ends. Tonight I am going to discover what I will be doing in front of a stadium full of spectators. In front of a global audience. My sense of anticipation is immense and the end of play couldn't come soon enough. But this wait is also eventually over and a little earlier than usual I log off my computer, gather my things, and leave work.

On the way to 3 Mills I try to imagine what rehearsals will be like. An exercise in futility. All I know is that I will be involved in a spectacular sequence and that we will be acting or miming something. This could mean absolutely anything. Whatever it will be, I take comfort in the knowledge that there is no pressure to perform well tonight. They are going to teach us and ensure we get to the required standard. Auditions are over and they believe we have what it takes, which is why I am soon walking along the now familiar road past Tesco and over the bridge.

Once inside, it's the same process as the auditions, having already shown my passport and email print out with my unique bar code, which they scanned to authenticate me. Some people, me included, have forgotten to print out and sign the agreement that was attached to the last email they sent: the conditions of use of our accreditation and Oyster card. They do, however, have copies of this, which I duly sign and feel thankful that this isn't going to cause any problems. They seem to be very strict about their rules and procedures, so this lapse is welcome.

I receive my Oyster card, but my Ceremonies ID with lanyard isn't ready for me yet. I'm told I will receive it at the next rehearsal. I need to have my photo taken again so I walk to the booth I'm directed to, examining my Oyster card as I go. It's a special Ceremonies design, so it will be a nice souvenir when it's all over.

After I've had my photo taken, it's time to enter the studio. Before I do so I stop to have a coffee. There are people stood about chatting, some making drinks. Lots of plastic cups are arranged on a long table on the side. Some contain coffee, some coffee with powdered milk, and others powdered tea. I didn't realise there was such a thing as the latter. Sugar is provided separately. There are also pallets of bottled water. I take one of these and save it for later, and get to work making my white coffee, which conveniently involves adding hot water to the pre-filled cup. Hot is an understatement. It seems to be way past boiling point as I almost burn my upper lip within a second. It takes a while to finish it.

Eventually I walk into the same studio that we used for our auditions. Once again I hang up my jacket, put my bag down and then I'm told to join a queue to collect our bibs. Towards the far corner I can see what looks to be a model of the Stadium, which we will no doubt be shown later on. The line is quite long so it takes some time to reach the front, where they have a list of our names. I am handed Bib Number 461. It seems to be a random allocation. The bib is a mid-blue colour and has WMW written above the number. I think nothing of this as I put it on and take a seat where shown.

Rows of the same white chairs are arranged and we are told to take the next available seat moving front to back. No gaps are to be left. There are introductions with the people sitting either side and around me. I remember just one name: Jay. We all get talking and notice that there seems to be a high ratio of men against women, although the range of faces is really quite diverse, much like the crowd I was part of at my Orientation Training. At the front of the seating area there is a large TV screen, so it looks like we are going to be shown a video at some point.

A while later the same guy who I remember from auditions, Steve, addresses us. Firstly he congratulates us for making it. Not everybody did. He introduces us to some key people and then points out the model of the Stadium where, he tells us, Danny Boyle is doing a briefing in small groups. We will be called over by our bib numbers. I wonder if I heard that right. I look over to catch a glimpse, but can't see him. But if Steve says he is here, then he must be. I didn't think he would be around, surely having more important things to do, but he is present at the first one. How very nice of him. Maybe he's here tonight, just to see us and brief us, and then that will be it. I start to feel excited now and can't wait to be called.

A bit of waiting around and chatting follows, and then a range of numbers gets called, which includes 461. I make my way towards the model with around 50 others and find a place at the front on one side, and there right opposite me is Danny Boyle, about a metre and a half away. I have to confess I am a little star-struck, even though he is just a director. I say this, but it is in fact quite a big deal for me. I went to see his first film, 'Shallow Grave', in the cinema twice, all the way back in 1994. I can remember it well. I was in my second year at university in Salford. Two years later I watched 'Trainspotting', again whilst at university, and was blown away. We played the soundtrack to death in our student flat that summer, especially 'Born Slippy.NUXX' by Underworld. After watching 'A Life Less Ordinary' on satellite TV I lost track of his career somewhat, although I did watch '28 Days Later' and 'Slumdog Millionaire'. Now I am here, about to be briefed by him on something he is directing. It is a little surreal.

As people gather round I can't quite believe the sight before me. The model of the Stadium isn't so surprising, as I have seen images of it before, but what is incredible is the inside of it, the set I believe. It is a countryside landscape. There is a patchwork of fields with hedges, even a cottage or farmhouse. This surely can't be the set. There is barely time to take this all in when Danny begins.

The first thing I think is just how down-to-earth and friendly he seems to be. He starts by talking about the volunteers and how he considers them to represent what is most important about the Olympics, not the profiteering that is such a major aspect for the corporate sponsors and in some cases the athletes, who cash in on the advertising opportunities. He mentions some well known athletes as examples, not in a disparaging way, but just stresses that for him the volunteers like us embody the true Olympic spirit.

He then moves on to the Stadium, which he says is just down the road, pointing "that way", and how it is really quite small and compact. They have taken the standard venue design, gutted it and removed all but the most necessary aspects, leaving just the bare bones, to make it rather intimate. He says that the audience will be closer than we imagine and we will be able to see their faces. He confirms that this

71

before us is indeed our set, spoken so casually. There will be real turf, fences, and farm animals. I thought they were in the model just for effect, but there will be real sheep, cows, horses, ducks, geese and chickens. I continue to listen in disbelief. At one end of the set there is a hill which represents Glastonbury Tor. It looks rather high. At the bottom is a moshpit of spectators, with another one at the opposite end. Here there is also a large bell. He goes into some detail about this. It is the world's largest harmonically-tuned bell and will be rung for the first time at the beginning of the Ceremony. It was made in Whitechapel Foundry and is intended as a lasting memory of the Games.

Soon we make our way back to our seats. Some people hang back to speak to Danny but I keep walking. Besides I have no idea what I'm going to say to him. Maybe we will see more of him. I do hope so.

When everybody has been briefed attention once again turns to the front of the seating area where Steve addresses us, essentially to just hand us over to Danny. He asks us to raise our hands if anybody has worked with an Oscar-winning director. Very few, if any, hands are raised, but Steve's hand goes up. This is all very surreal, but also very special. We all applaud Danny as he takes over, and then he introduces us to some of the people who are present, including none other than Rick Smith from Underworld. I catch a glimpse as he stands up to show his face. He is at the far end of the seating. I immediately wonder if I will be able to meet him. I have to seek him out if I get a chance during the rehearsal.

Danny explains that we are about to see a video simulation of what we will be doing at the Ceremony. It's a segment that will last around 17 minutes. This is getting better and better. I would have been thankful for just five minutes, but 17 is amazing. We are going to be performing in front of the audience for that long. I find it difficult to suppress a smile. Once Danny has finished his introduction, the video begins. There is silence as the lights dim. I think most of us have been looking forward to seeing this for a long time.

Some classical music is playing and somebody is making a speech. It looks like this will be the beginning of the Ceremony. That in itself is an honour. I can see a very basic depiction of the countryside set that we have just been shown. Soon the music changes to a more electronic beat, the same few bars in a loop. Out of what looks like a tunnel underneath the set appears a large group of people arranged in straight lines behind each other. They are marching, it seems, and doing some kind of hand movements at the same time, all in time with each other. This is all computer simulated. We see some grass being pulled out of the ground by a few people standing in a row. Elsewhere more groups of people are entering the set, doing the same marching and hand movements. There are hundreds of them, appearing from all over. This looks incredible and with the help of the music, it already looks like something quite epic.

All of a sudden a chimney rises up out of the ground. A full size chimney. And then another one. And another one. I now notice that there are workers at the bottom of the chimneys, and some even standing on top of them as they rise out of the ground, which is still being pulled up in pieces. There are incredulous laughs coming from the audience at this point. I don't think anybody can quite believe what we are viewing.

Some of the footage is snippets of actual videos that I recognise as the auditions. I see the shovel and pickaxe sequence I had so much trouble performing. It looks like I am going to have to learn it properly. The rest of the video largely passes me by as I lose focus, probably because this is all so awesome. I do remember seeing more miming and four more chimneys rise up, making seven in all. All of the grass has been taken off. Out of somewhere the Olympic rings appear and we see them from up above. Soon it is all over.

"So that's what we are trying to achieve," says Danny as the lights go back up, a comment which is greeted with a bit of laughter. He informs us that it is going to be the biggest live set change ever attempted, in both scale and time. Well that is something to shout about, if we ever manage it. He goes on to tell us that his friends in the business are sceptical and think we won't be able to do it. I think about this for a few moments. That entire set that we marvelled at not too long ago has to be removed completely, as in all of the grass, the fences, and the hedges. The house too. This is crazy. I can't believe I am involved in something like this. I am very happy that I am. Steve kindly explains that this is the sequence everybody will be talking about the day after the Ceremony, and asking how the hell did they do that. Well I am wondering that now, although I suppose that's not for me to work out. I just have to do what they tell me.

Danny tells us that he can't stay for the rest of the rehearsal as he needs to rush off to a meeting so he excuses himself as he leaves. The rehearsal now begins. We've seen what we are doing. Clearly there is a lot to learn. Steve divides us up into small groups of around 20 to 30 people in bib number sequence. Each group is assigned to a dance captain. As this is going on I continue to think about our section. I want to be one of the workers on top of a chimney. Can we choose our role, I wonder. I know I'm just being silly as those people will likely be stuntmen. They're not going to put one of us all the way up there.

The group I'm in is assembled not too far from the entrance of the studio. Our dance captain introduces herself as Polly. She appears to be very friendly and enthused – just the sort of person we will need. After a very quick warm up and introductory pep talk we begin. We are going to learn some choreography which involves movement and miming. I think this might be the hand movements I saw on the video.

The first sequence we are going to learn is called Shut Boot/Sliding Doors. In eight movements we have to shut a boot, slide one door from left to right, then change from right to left, and finally we finish by pulling something towards us, a bit like opening a filing cabinet by pulling it out. Polly goes through it with us several times. It's easy enough but the difficulty lies in making it look real since it is all miming. We are told to picture a car boot in front of us, we have to 'see' it in order to convincingly make it look like we are wrapping our fingers around it and pulling it down. Our hands have to go just above head height, which is different according to your height, so there will be a bit of individuality in this, which is fine. We also have to concentrate on closing our fingers only once we have 'grabbed' the door handles with our hands. We repeat the sequence many times before moving on to another set. We are going to come back to each one anyway.

One very important aspect is where we are looking. We need to be staring straight ahead, focussing on one spot, and keeping our eyes set on that one point. No looking left or right. And we need to have a deadpan and determined look.

The second piece of choreography is called Levers/Pull. This one is a bit more complex. We have to grab hold of a lever in front of us with our right hand and pull it towards our right side. At the same time as pulling it back our left hand pushes another lever forward. This one is harder to pull back so we have to use our right hand to get a firmer grip and then pull it towards our body. We then grab another lever that is on our right side and pull it across to our left side. Finally we take hold of two handles in front of us, crossing our arms right over left, and uncross them with some emphasis. The visual aid we are given here is to imagine we are banging our knife and fork down on the table.

This is all done in eight movements again, and what's more it has to be done in eight beats, which roughly translates as eight seconds. Once again we are shown the sequence and go through it several times until we are more or less comfortable with it. As we learn the moves better Polly brings in the rhythmic element to it so we are all in time and doing more or less one move per second. Visualizing the levers and actually seeing what we are doing does help to get the moves right.

Before long we are on the third sequence which is called Chisel/Hammer. With our left hand we put a chisel down in front of us. With our right hand we hammer it. Then both hands come back and round to the left and right, ending up in the centre again. We then bring both hands to our right hip, keeping them both together. The next action is like mixing a bowl of cement, so it's a circular motion, but just one semi-circle. We finish by wiping our hands clean by clapping them together, and then slapping our thighs as if we are finishing our day's work. Eight moves, eight beats.

By now I am beginning to get into a bit of a muddle as I still have the previous sequence in my head so I am getting confused between the two. Which hand goes forward first? Of course it is different for each one. I am finding that if you get one move wrong the whole sequence falls apart. Keeping in sync and to time is also rather difficult at the moment. I suppose we are very early into the proceedings, so not to panic just yet. Polly is very patient and is more than willing to repeat the moves more than once, answer questions, and explain again what we are actually miming, to help us 'see' what we are doing. She explains to us that in order to convince the audience we have to fully believe in what we are doing. She is very clear on this point. The more vividly we can picture the boot, the handles, the levers, the chisel, the hammer, the more real our moves will look to the audience. For somebody who has had no experience in this sort of thing at all, it is easier said than done. I am going to have to practise all this, again and again, until I get it right.

Before I can think about when I'm going to get a chance to do this, we are on to our fourth sequence. This one is called Work Prep and thankfully it is much easier than the last two. Here, as the name suggests, we are getting ready for work. We give both legs a small shake, left then right, we roll up our sleeves in the same order, we wipe our brow with our right hand, stretch our necks in both directions, and finally roll our shoulders forward, as if we are putting our coats on.

We quickly move on. There is a lot to learn and they are not hanging around. Clearly they want to just teach us everything first and then concentrate on practising and perfecting. Polly has said more than once that it is fine to make mistakes. It is a relief that we are no longer being judged.

So it is on to Dials. The first two moves of this one are not so simple. We are operating some machinery and we have a control panel in front of us. To the left there is a pair of dials, one at head height and the other at chest height. With our right hand we grab and turn the top one clockwise, and then do the same with the lower one, but this time anti-clockwise. The grabbing and turning has to be one single movement, one beat. From here we twist to the right and grab a sheet with both hands, one hand on either side of the sheet, and twist back to the front, keeping the sheet level. With both hands we grab a press above our heads, then bring it down and back up in one beat. Finally we grip a lever on the right and bring it over to the left.

I think this one requires us to visualise everything more than the others because the two dials are in a straight vertical line and on the same plane so our hand positioning is important. When bringing the sheet over, we have to keep the same distance between both hands, since the sheet we are 'holding' is solid, not flexible. Also, it is heavy, so this needs to be conveyed to the audience. As with the others we try it several times and Polly answers queries. My head is beginning to spin. In less than two hours we have learnt 40 different moves. The short break that we are now allowed is most welcome.

I bought a sandwich before I came so I grab that out of my bag and head outside. There is very light rain, but it doesn't bother me as I need to cool down. Doing all those moves, again and again, has actually caused me to work up a bit of a sweat. I go inside once I've finished my sandwich and make a coffee. I notice somebody only filling the cup about two thirds with hot water and topping up with cold bottled water to make it more drinkable. That's good thinking. I adopt the same strategy, so I can finish my coffee quicker as the break is only about 20 minutes.

I go back inside the studio and see people chatting, walking around, and going through their personal belongings. Some people are practising the choreography. One girl from my group, Liz, seems to have it down already. I should probably do the same but I feel a little self-conscious. Instead I walk over to Polly, who is chatting to a few members of our group. I mention to her that I'm finding it a bit difficult and that it's rather daunting that we will have to perform this to perfection in front of so many people. She reassures me, however, that they are going to drill us until we know it inside out. After the break we continue with the choreography. We have now been taught all of the different sequences, so it's just a case of practising. We revisit all of them, with Polly once again going through them to remind us. She cues us in by counting eight beats. At times she talks us through the sequence whilst we are doing it, but she does so rhythmically, almost rapping it, and at times she goes into a sort of beat box to help us with the timing and synchronisation. She certainly has a way about her that is quite amusing. Sometimes we loop the choreography so we go straight into another set after finishing one.

With a few runs of each sequence completed, she brings in a new element to the moves where we are stamping our feet to the beat. The first move in the set of eight starts on the left foot and so on. It is quite hard to keep in time. We only do this for Shut Boot/Sliding Doors, Levers/Pull and Chisel/Hammer. Work Prep and Dials are done whilst stationary. Following on from this we now have to walk whilst doing the choreography as this is what we will need to do during the Ceremony. This is what we have been leading up to. We walk from one side of the studio to the other, which isn't far so we only fit in a couple of runs each time. Putting the two together isn't easy but it will just require practice. We also try doing combinations of more than one sequence, which adds yet another complication. There has been an awful lot to absorb but as Polly indicated we will have plenty of time to make this all second nature by the time we are in front of an audience. I'm not as convinced as her at this stage.

Our first rehearsal finishes with everybody divided into two large groups. Half of us have to stand on the sides whilst the other half is going to walk from one end of the studio to the other whilst performing a combination of all three moving sequences. I am in the group on the side. There are 125 people in each half. The music from the simulation is cued on the PA. As they begin and start to go into Shut Boot/Sliding Doors, seeing it en masse makes it look so much better and before the group is half way down the studio, applause is given. Everybody appreciates what has been achieved in such a short time. When they reach the end they are asked to turn about and prepare for one more run. In this way the people who were at the back the first time are now at the front. Again they receive applause. It looks superb.

Time to change over. For me personally it doesn't go perfectly but it still feels great being amidst this mass of people doing the same moves as one, not quite in unison, but we all have a common purpose. We have all been taught separately but we are all speaking the same language when we move together doing the same moves. The people watching are kind enough to return the applause, even cheers of appreciation. We turn for another run before being told that it's the end of the rehearsal.

I have a lot of practising to do before the next one which is a week away. An email is going to be sent during the week which will contain instructions for all of the choreography we have been taught, just in case we forget. We need to hand our bibs in, keeping them in order, so each group organises a person to collect them all and then hand them in. This proves to be more difficult than it should be but we get there in the end.

As I walk out of 3 Mills once more, I eventually get talking to somebody and we discuss the rehearsal, what we think of the task ahead of us, and the video we watched. There is a common sentiment of wonder and awe regarding the latter, and of how we will have to take things up a few gears to really pin down the choreography. Already the video is becoming vague and I hope we get to see it again. At the moment my mind is filled with forty mimes. As we reach the Tesco we introduce ourselves to each other and shake hands, before he makes his way to his car. I'm not sure how he managed to get away with parking without being fined. I say goodbye to Wasif and make for the station. Nobody knows what this mass of people has been up to for the last four hours. It's our secret and one we have agreed in writing to keep. I decide that I won't even tell my wife, although I am sure she will not appreciate this.

Thursday 3 May 2012

I was right about Misbah. She wanted to know what I would be doing, and I didn't tell her. She wasn't impressed. I think this may become an issue but I shall see.

True to their word, I received a short email today from Vanessa, the Volunteer Performer Cast Coordinator, telling us that we all did a great job in the first rehearsal. The following notes were included:

WAVE THREE: 3 MILLS

WORK PREP

1) Shake left leg
2) Shake right leg
3) Roll left sleeve
4) Roll right sleeve
5) Right hand wipe brow
6) Tilt head to left
7) Tilt head to right
8) Roll shoulders forward

LEVERS/PULL

1) RH forward LH back
2) LH forward, RH back
3) Both hands grab left forward lever
4) Pull lever towards body
5) Both hands grab lever on right side
6) Pull lever across to left side
7) Grab handles, right over left
8) Uncross arms holding fists in front

DIALS

1) Top dial RH
2) Bottom dial LH
3) Get metal sheet on right
4) Pull sheet round to centre
5) Hands up for press handle
6) Press down and release up
7) Grab lever on right
8) Pull lever across to left hip

SHUT BOOT/SLIDING DOORS

1) Hands up grab boot handle
2) Shut boot down
3) Grab door handles Left (RH top)
4) Slide door to right
5) Grab door handles Right (LH top)
6) Slide door to left
7) Grab both handles in front
8) Pull towards you bending elbows

CHISEL/HAMMER

1) LH holds chisel in front
2) RH hits chisel
3) Both hands down, circle to front
4) Both fists to right hip
5) Both hands mixing bowl
6) Round to left and back to centre
7) Clap/wipe hands in front up
8) Slap down both hands on thighs

79

SHOVEL/PICKAXE (not taught)

Standing LF forward – holding mimed shovel, LH in front of RH:

1) Weight back on RF, shovel pulled back on right side of body

2) + 3) Moving forward LF-RF-LF and push shovel head into ground

4) Pick up shovel head out of ground weight on LF

5) Change hand position RH in front of LH

6) + 7) Swing pickaxe in circle, past right of body, up in air and land in front

8) Pull pickaxe out of ground

Change hands, LH in front of RH on shovel handle, and repeat moves

So this at least gives a taste of what the next rehearsal may include: Shovel/Pickaxe. During the week I try to find some time to go over the routines but fail to do so. This is partly because I am just a little self-conscious about what I am doing. I fear I will look silly if Misbah sees me doing these seemingly random hand movements. I have to admit that in isolation it does, to me, look a bit ridiculous. I definitely wasn't born to perform. I have no conviction and I am overtly shy. Yet I have committed to perform in front of tens of thousands. They say there is safety in numbers. I will be invisible amongst everybody else so I should be okay.

13

Rehearsal 2

Wednesday 9 May 2012
5.30pm – 9.30pm
3 Mills Studios

The week has passed quickly and so once again I am on my way to 3 Mills, although this is going to be the very last time as the next rehearsal will be in 1:1. Tonight there are separate queues for those that already have their passes and those that do not. When I reach the front of my line my Ceremonies ID is waiting for me. It does look rather nice. It's official and exclusive, although the photo of me is by no means the best I've ever seen. The lanyard has a special Ceremonies design, rather than being plain, so this is another souvenir.

After a coffee I queue up inside to collect my bib, which takes a while. I get talking to the person in front and the subject of volunteering comes up so I quietly tell her that I am also going to be a Games Maker, or at least I hope so. She says she knows a few people in the same position as me. One of them was unfortunately too honest and told the Games Maker team that they won't be able to volunteer now due to being part of the Ceremony – a decision her friend sorely regrets, as other people she knows have kept their positions safe and are going to see how things progress. She advises me to do the same. It is a source of some comfort that I am not the only person in this predicament.

Once I have collected my bib I try to mingle as rehearsals are not going to start just yet since plenty of people are yet to arrive, even though the stated time has passed. I have never been good at this and I always feel self-conscious and lacking in confidence when surrounded by strangers. In the far corner of the room, beyond where the Stadium model was last week, is a hospital bed. I momentarily wonder what it is for – maybe part of the Ceremony.

Eventually I recognise somebody so I say hello and we exchange the usual pleasantries before introducing ourselves. His name is Chris, a plumber by trade, and he has travelled from Brighton. That is quite a commitment, both time-wise and financially. There must be others like him who wanted to be part of the Games even though they live outside of the host city. He tells me that his girlfriend also auditioned but was unfortunately not chosen after the second round. That must be hard for her. It makes me appreciate even more the very fortunate position I am in.

Rehearsals begin and it is more of the same. We recap what we learned last time. This does mean that Polly has to show us the full routines again, although some people clearly know it. I am a bit rusty myself. I really need to practise more in my spare time. We spend some time going through all five sequences. This time Polly introduces some more elements. One thing we have to do is to stagger the starts. So the first row begins, and the second row waits until the row in front has completed the first four moves. They begin the routine on the fifth beat. The same for the other rows. In this way the last row is finishing their moves after the rows in front have stopped.

Another variation is what they call falling in. One person is nominated to stand in front of the group and begin the choreography. The people in the first row then start their routine, but in their own time and on the same move as the head person. They may begin on the third move, and then they carry on as normal, looping the sequence. Each person in each row only begins once the person in front of them has begun. They could wait a couple of beats until they know where in the routine the person is, if it isn't obvious. We do this until Polly tells us to stop.

We continue like so for a while, alternating between the five routines, doing different combinations, staggering and falling in, performing stationary, moving on the beat and also whilst walking. We also do the fall in whilst walking, which isn't easy. I absolutely must practise during the week otherwise I will find it increasingly difficult.

During the break I go for a coffee and get chatting to a few people, Daniel and David amongst them. A few of us exchange looks of acknowledgement but no conversation as yet. Once we are all lined up again we do some warm-up exercises and then continue. We are going to go through Shovel/Pickaxe to complete all of the choreography we will learn. It is exactly the same as the routine we did during the audition. Unlike all of the other sequences this one must be done whilst moving forward.

Throughout the rehearsal today groups of men have been called off to get fitted with their costumes. Soon it is our group's turn, so we leave all the women to continue choreography and are led out of the studio, a few steps to the left and into the adjacent rehearsal space where there is a different group going through a dance routine. They are all wearing roller skates and are paired up in couples. The music playing is a jazzy big band-style number. This is the first time I get a sense of just how diverse the show may be. There will likely be dancers, performance artists, actors, acrobatics, pyrotechnics, and more, all employed in one enormous spectacular. We are going to be just a very small element.

At the back of the studio is a doorway which we are led through and into a costume area where we queue and wait to be called. We register and get told to move to a smaller room behind this one where there are costume fitters with a row of crates in the middle. Each crate is labelled with a number to match our bibs. Once called forward we have to try on our costumes. Some people from another group are already dressed in their outfits. They look like they could be miners or factory workers from the nineteenth century maybe. Thinking about the video we saw, this makes sense as that was an industrial scene that developed and I do now recall some of the animated characters we saw.

I look through my crate and I have a baggy pair of dark grey corduroy trousers, a cream coloured buttonless shirt with no collar, and a pair of braces. I'm not sure if I am pleased with this. Some people have waistcoats, or jackets, or both. Others have belts instead of braces. There are lots of different outfits, in different colours, but mainly in shades of grey, black and brown with lighter coloured shirts. Everybody has to take what they are given; there is no swapping or negotiating.

They had previously taken our measurements so everything should fit but we still need to try everything on. The fitters are on hand to help if required. I need some assistance with my braces, which need adjusting. My trousers are very loose but once the braces are properly fastened they stay up fine. I ask one of the costume team if this is our final costume, and it is indeed what we will be wearing on show night. A lot of planning has gone into this and for them it is the culmination of it all, pending any adjustments.

Once fitted and back into our own clothes we go back into the first part of the room where they are allocating footwear. There are boxes upon boxes of brand new Doc Martens, not all exactly the same design. Some of them are slip-on, some of them are with laces. Again, we take what we are given. I receive a pair of black laced boots and try on a size nine. I take a size ten just in case. I'm not sure how much time I will spend in these but comfort will be the main priority. Once we are happy one of the team notes our size and style of boot, and then we make our own way back to the rehearsal, past the roller skating dancers who are not doing any dancing, but taking instructions about positioning and posture.

It's not long now before the end of the rehearsal. We manage to fit in some more choreography practice, which gives rise to questions about walking whilst doing the routines. As ever Polly is more than happy to help. Despite this I'm a bit confused about whether we all need to be moving in time with each other, as if we are marching in ranks, or if there is an element of individuality in the size of our steps and our pacing. The conclusion I draw is that they are not quite sure themselves yet and they are merely testing the water at this stage.

As with the first rehearsal we finish by splitting into two large groups, one performing and one watching. I am again watching first. I take a place on the side and look over to where Steve and the rest of the team are standing, and right there, wearing a green jumper, is Danny Boyle. I wonder if he has been here all along, watching us all. Does this mean we will see him at every rehearsal? I suppose this has been his life and soul for a long time now. This is his current project so of course he needs to be here seeing it all unfold and making decisions.

This time the group is instructed to fall into the combination of Shut Boot/Sliding Doors, Levers/Pull and Chisel/Hammer when given the cue. So we will see a staggered start. As before it looks amazing en masse and we applaud the group. They turn and go through it again, and then it's our turn. Changeover. I take a position in the middle of the group and fall in as best I can once the person in front of me has begun. On the way back Danny Boyle is right in there with us, managing to find a place in between a column of people, and he is filming us with his camcorder. At one point he is right next to me and I am completely conscious of him as I try my best not to mess this up. I actually don't do too badly, and if I am on his video hopefully he won't think I look terrible. I'm sure he isn't expecting perfection just yet. He does seem to be very aware of how much is being asked of us in a short space of time.

That brings us to the end of the second rehearsal. We do a bib collection like last time, but before we leave we are asked to gather round one of the staff to be briefed about the next rehearsal as it will be at a different venue. We will be in Dagenham in an outdoor area so we must be prepared and appropriately dressed for inclement weather.

It is the end of May but the sunshine doesn't look like it will appear any time soon. Full details about directions and what to do once we reach Dagenham will be emailed to us.

We are also told about a car pooling scheme they would like to introduce for anybody who wishes to drive to rehearsals. There is a board where people can write their name and number down under different locations around London. If there are enough people to fill a car they will be given a parking space. Because they are trying to keep the Games as sustainable as possible only cars with at least three people will be allowed into the secure site.

One final thing before we head home: we need to collect a pair of coveralls to wear at each subsequent rehearsal, to help us protect our clothes from dirt and the elements, and keep us warm. It is our responsibility to bring them with us. Queues quickly form according to size. I collect and try on a Medium, but as these are to be worn over our clothes I exchange it for a Large instead, which is much more comfortable. The man issuing my coverall asks me for my bib number so he can write it on the label. I hesitate at first but am pretty sure it is 461. He tells me that it's very important to remember our bib numbers. During the first rehearsal Danny did say to us that we will be known by our bib numbers. They will become our identity. He apologised to us on behalf of everyone but it's simply not possible to learn so many names and it is easier to call out bib numbers. This is the last time I will have any doubt about my number. I am 461. In this place, that is me.

Thursday 10 May 2012

The following day I received an email from Vanessa, which was actually emailed the night before. It contained information about Dagenham, as promised, but also something a bit different:

Dear Cast Member
     It's really exciting, rehearsals are great – you all look fantastic. We've seen pictures of the fittings and you will all look stunning.
     To complete the picture it is really important that Hair & Make-Up can complete the look. So we can do that – it is important that we start from a good base and would ask you a HUGE favour to not cut your hair, colour it excessively or indulge in weird and wonderful hair designs (unless Costume ask you

to!). We know this is a big ask but seeing as the Ceremony is only 11 weeks away and the look is so important, with the cameras getting close, we do ask this of you. For the men you are requested to grow stubble for the show; don't worry if you can't grow stubble as we can fake it too.

I didn't have a problem with this but I wouldn't start to grow my hair for another month at least otherwise I would be able to tie it in a ponytail. As for my stubble, if I left it for 11 weeks I would have a full beard, so this was all something for later.

The information about the new venue included the following details:

Congratulations! You have done brilliantly in your first rehearsals at 3 Mills and now we continue our journey to create these amazing shows. We have managed to secure a large rehearsal space where we can put the shows together. This is so important for us to be able to deliver the actual show to our TV and live audience.

You MUST have with you your ceremonies ID. You will need this to enter the rehearsal venue, and also to get onto our shuttle bus from Dagenham East.

Our site at Dagenham is OUTDOORS. Please dress appropriately. We recommend lots of layers and appropriate shoes with closed toes. It is a tarmac surface so shoes with support would be good.

Bottled water, tea and coffee will be provided at rehearsals. The site is close to local shops and a McDonald's. We always encourage you to be well fuelled for a rehearsal, so please eat before you come!

Thank you all for maintaining confidentiality; it really does make the Ceremony special. We are aware some journalists have been approaching cast on their route to 3 Mills and we really appreciate you all smiling and walking on.

There will be a bus shuttle service between Dagenham East station and the 1:1 venue. This will run regularly before and after rehearsals. The shuttle is free but you will need your ID.

We look forward to seeing you very soon on this next exciting step of the journey!

14

Role-Specific Training

Friday 11 May 2012
6.00pm – 10.00pm
Hackney Community College

With Wednesday's rehearsal still fresh in my thoughts, I spend the day at work as usual and at the end of play I have to travel to Hackney Community College. I haven't received a reminder this time but I know the address from the confirmation email I received so I have looked it up on the map before leaving.

This is my second Games Maker training session and today I will find out exactly what I will be doing for ten days. I finally managed to read through my Games Maker handbook that I received in my Orientation Training all the way back in February. I should have read it a lot sooner but at least this way the information is fresh. One thing I learned diligently is the British Sign Language. It's actually not that difficult after you've been through the alphabet a few times. I do remember learning it when I was in primary school so some of the letters were familiar.

From Old Street the college is about ten minutes away on foot, on Falkirk Street. I am conscious of the late finish so I look for a place to buy some food. There isn't much choice in the vicinity, but eventually I find a restaurant that does take away. I've been to nicer parts of London. Having lived in New Cross I am quite used to deprived areas and this also strikes me as one of those localities that seem to have been neglected by every government since before I was born, although I always considered this entire area trendy and artistically developed. I think I'm just in one of the less attractive parts.

One of the legacies of the Olympics is the hope that they will inspire a generation. The venue for my training today is a bit out of the way and not in the most affluent or developed area. However, being all-inclusive is one of the major aspects of the Games, and London 2012 is trying to embrace that wholly and entirely. I shut away my preconceptions as I wait for my halloumi salad wrap, which I have been doing now for longer than I would have liked. It is fast approaching 6pm, and although the venue is just around the corner, I do not wish to be even a minute late.

Outside the college there is a large branded sign welcoming Games Makers. This isn't just confirmation for us that we have found the right place, but also an advert to the local community. As I walk inside I see a small group of people congregated at the far end. I step over to the reception desk on my right and explain that I do not have an email print out to show them, which is no problem at all. I join the group and we are ushered through the building and into another, following a bright pink line that's been painted on the ground. This will also be our way of remembering the way out when we have finished.

We are shown to a room which is already full of people so there are not many seats remaining. Before long the training begins. First on the agenda is a general overview of what the evening will bring and then we are asked to spell our names in British Sign Language. It's a good thing that I learned this last night, although it is okay if we don't yet know it. The girl next to me is going to be volunteering in Earl's Court. This makes me feel glad that I am in the Main Press Centre and the Olympic Park. The girl on the other side of me, who has just arrived, has been assigned to the same venues as I have. I notice her name is Lucy according to the sticker she has. Maybe she will be one of my team members during the Games. She may have had a bad day as she isn't overly friendly and just a little uptight! She can't have been so in her interview otherwise she would not have been here now.

Once everybody has broken the ice with their group members, we move on to a section in the handbook about equality and diversity. There are a series of multiple choice questions, which we may already have done in our own time. We are now going to answer them individually using a hand-held electronic device which we use to key in our answers. Each question focusses on a minority group, or an aspect of racial prejudice or equal opportunities. Most of the responses are obvious, but the purpose of the exercise is clear. This takes up about a third of the training time, and then we move on to our actual roles. We are handed over to one of the heads of the Security operation.

Each of us has been given a set of notes, which we can add to our handbooks in the relevant section, and a small envelope containing some key fact cards, which we can keep on our person during our shifts to refer to. We are taken through the main duties we will be performing, which will be to help out in the Pedestrian Screening Area (PSA). This is like an airport security area that most of us are familiar with. Some of us will be Queue Assistants, whose job will be to welcome spectators and prepare them for inspection by asking them to have their tickets ready, and to take coats off and put metal objects into their bags. There will also be Queue Pacers who will direct people to the next available lane, where there will be tray loaders, and ensuring that the queue is moving as quickly as possible. The tray loaders will do just that and pass them into the scanners. That is as much as we will do. Everything else, particularly the checking of bags that have been singled out, will be checked by the professional security personnel from G4S. They will also perform full body checks.

Quite a lot of time is spent explaining how the scanners work, what the various lights mean, where to send people with pushchairs or those who are in a wheelchair, what is and isn't allowed through security, filling in Incident Report Slips if even the smallest incident occurs, and what to do if we need assistance. In between all of this there is a break where they bring us some dinner: a vegetable curry and rice for me. I don't need the wrap I've bought so I save that for later.

All the while I am thinking that this is not at all what I was expecting to be doing at the Games. Before today I thought that there may be something more interesting about the role, especially since I was going to be at the MPC, but it is now clear that I am going to be spending my entire shifts in the security area, doing what seems to be a rather mundane activity. I can speak five foreign languages. I have worked as a holiday rep in Italy, so surely I could have been put to better use. I think the only reason I've been given this role is because I've done some crowd control at a convention. Yet I am in two minds about this. Part of me thinks it will nonetheless be an experience, just maybe not the one I was expecting. And I have enjoyed tonight's training a little. I shouldn't be so negative, instead be thankful that I am here. Not so long ago I was bitterly disappointed that I may not be allowed to make it this far.

Soon the training is over, a little earlier than scheduled, and we are all making our way outside and following the pink line. We have a lot of information to read and digest before our shifts. I decide to remain positive. I am going to be part of the Security operation at the Olympic Games. How many people I know can lay claim to that?

15

One Free Day

Tuesday 15 May 2012

The next rehearsal was still five days away. The 11-day break in between the second and third rehearsals was the longest one in the schedule. Saturday was going to be the final day of complete rest. From Sunday the weekly onslaught would begin and it wasn't going to end until the Ceremony was over at the end of July.

In the meantime, there were a few developments with my Games Maker role:

> We hope you're looking forward to your Games Maker role in the Security team at London 2012.
>
> We want to let you know that, as well as the Media and Press Centre, we'll be assigning you to some Games Maker shifts at the **Olympic Park Common Domain.** This is the name for the shared space between our different competition venues in the Park, where we'll be hosting up to 170,000 spectators on any given day.
>
> The actual role you'll be performing has not changed, and you do not need to do anything as a result of this email.

I was relieved that I would still have some shifts at the Press Centre as I was looking forward to seeing that. It was likely that not everybody would be allowed in. The additional venue was treated as a new role so I had to log on and accept it. I received confirmation the following day.

Thursday 17 May 2012

It was not long now until I had to collect my Games Maker uniform and accreditation, and as such I received a reminder email from the

Uniform Distribution and Accreditation Centre (UDAC), with the details confirmed again.

I also received an email asking me to book the final training session for my role:

> Now that the London 2012 Games are just around the corner, it's time for you to sign up to Venue-Specific Training!
> This will take place at: IBC/MPC Olympic VST and will be really exciting! It will be your first opportunity to get to know your venue and meet everyone else who'll be based there.
> During this session you'll find out about the activities taking place at your venue during the Games and you'll be given key information like emergency procedures and transport points.

I logged on and booked a slot, making sure that it didn't clash with any of my rehearsals. There was only one of three slots that was possible so I took the first available. I received my confirmation shortly afterwards:

VENUE-SPECIFIC TRAINING: IBC/MPC Olympic VST
Date: 20 Jun 2012
Time: 18:00
Duration: 04:00
Location: IBC/MPC TRAINING

I was very pleased with this outcome as this was my third training session of three, meaning that I would have no clashes between my Games Maker training and rehearsals. There was still my Common Domain venue training to go but I was now confident that it would work out fine. No clashes meant there was no issue with performing both roles as far as I was concerned.

WAVE FOUR

DAGENHAM

16

Rehearsal 3

Sunday 20 May 2012
10.00am – 3.00pm
1:1

Today is the first of four morning rehearsals at the new venue, which is further out than 3 Mills but on the same branch of the District Line. All rehearsals will now be held at weekends only, until the final fortnight when we will be rehearsing during the week too. The day is cloudy and windy, but it is not raining. The first outdoor rehearsal in the rain wouldn't exactly be a morale booster.

Upon arrival at Dagenham East station I follow the directions we have been given and reach the Sanofi car park where there are marshals directing us to some bendy buses. So this is what has happened to them, or at least some of them. They have recently been taken out of service permanently, so LOCOG clearly jumped at the opportunity to shuttle us as efficiently as possible since a lot of people can fit on each one. Nobody asks to see either an email or my Ceremonies ID, which I have in my pocket, so not as high security as I thought. I just board the bus, take a seat and wait until it is full, which doesn't take long since there is a fairly constant flow of people.

As we leave the car park another empty bus is arriving to take more volunteers to the venue. The journey lasts about 5-10 minutes. On the way we pass the McDonald's that has been mentioned in the emails. It is nowhere near the venue, at least not within quick walking distance. Anybody who was hoping to nip out during a break to grab a burger will be disappointed.

When we arrive the bus is given clearance by Security and we drive in. It does seem rather secure so it is a privilege to be allowed in. A banner attached to a railing advertises to the local community, in no uncertain terms, that this site is being used for the Olympic Ceremony rehearsals. We do a circuit of the car park before being set down, when everybody gets off, following the instructions given by the marshals.

Over the fence I can see the top of what looks like a very large marquee with bright yellow and dark blue stripes. I thought we were going to be rehearsing outside.

We walk along a pavement for about 50 metres and then we are all checked. Each and every ID is examined. We enter the registration area, which is more or less the same as the one at 3 Mills. Our passes are scanned and this records our attendance on the system. Once we have registered we move into the bib collection area, which is divided into groups. Mine is 44B, a few steps to the left. Once I've been given bib number 461 by the lady behind the table I walk in the direction where I think I'm supposed to be going. We are now in the open again and the main marquee is about 20 metres ahead. There are more marshals along the way, welcoming us, and pointing out the toilets and refreshments area. Everything is either in a Portakabin or a tent, completely makeshift and converted for our rehearsals. A coffee is definitely required at this hour so I head there first. I walk past a burger van, which already has a queue of people. In the drinks tent we have the same powdered tea and coffee plus hot chocolate too. There is also a cold drinks machine and the now familiar crates of bottled water.

Walking through the entrance to the blue and yellow marquee, coffee in hand and bag over my shoulder, I can now see that this is not a rehearsal area at all – silly of me to think so. There are rows and rows of the white seats we had at 3 Mills, arranged in two large blocks, a wide aisle in between. To the left of these are the clothes rails, more than usual. The place is teeming with performers, officials and stewards, far more than there were during the first two rehearsals. I try to find a place I will remember. The mass of bags is going to grow, since lots of people are yet to arrive, so mine will probably just get buried, or so I think. I pick a memorable spot where a large flap of canvas juts in and hang up my coat. I will probably adopt the same system throughout our time at Dagenham. Getting into my coveralls easily requires just an ounce of method which I soon get used to, and then I go to take a seat amongst the many who are already seated and conversing.

Above our heads and at the front of the seating area is an information screen. I watch images of the rehearsal space which shows the location of the toilets, first aid and smoking areas, and exits. Other screens ask us to stay well hydrated and refrain from taking photos, which is strictly forbidden. A red and black electronic device appears with instructions on how it works – probably something for later as I have been given no such device as yet. The information is looped so after some time I decide to take a look around.

Before long I am back with another coffee as there isn't a great deal to see. It is way past 10am and nothing has happened so far, although the seats are gradually filling up. An announcement is being made for people to go to a desk at the front and collect some gloves, but only when your bib number is called so I find another seat and wait.

Eventually a lady walks through the centre aisle and hands out pairs of gloves to whoever hasn't got any. She writes my number on them and hands them over. We must bring them to every rehearsal. They are bright yellow workman style gloves, and once on are quite comfortable. I have to confess that they do give me a sense of wanting to do some work. Before I have time to think more about this Steve is talking on a microphone in his inimitable way which is by now becoming very likeable. He has a way of enthusing us whilst being overtly enthused himself. Very infectious it is. And so the rehearsal begins with a fairly lengthy introduction to Dagenham.

Steve explains that there are two fields of play (FOP), one on each side of the marquee and a plan is shown on the screens. Each one is a full scale representation of the Stadium – just the arena of course – so we will get a sense of the space we are going to be performing in on the actual night. Around the FOP there are six voms, short for vomitorium, which dates back to ancient Rome when they built amphitheatres aplenty. The voms are both the entrances to and exits from the FOP. He explains where each one is located on the plan.

Soon we are all making our way onto the FOP and we are shown the lines and markers that they have mapped out, a bit like in the auditions, but on a much larger scale. One set is numbers and another is letters. We are asked to get into rows and columns in bib number order. There are now one thousand of us – four groups of 250, 44A – 44D. This is how it will now be. No more splitting us up. Where we are standing is our home position. I look around for any markers as we are not necessarily on a line or a spot. To the left is Jay who I met in 3 Mills and to the right is Brian who I have just this second met. We are at the very front of our lines so that in itself makes it easier to remember our positions. To the left of Jay is the letter F, duly noted.

The first thing we are required to do is some choreography practice. I have been going through these a little at home, in the shower of all places, away from any enquiring eyes, although maybe not as often as I should have done. I notice Danny Boyle and Toby are here. They will be watching and I am at the front. About 30 metres directly ahead is a tower, essentially a large mass of scaffolding, from which they can see us all from above. On raised platforms just ahead of us, all along, are the dance captains. Polly is just to the right. It's nice to see her. They give us a quick reminder of the routines, which we do a couple of times each, moving on the beat but not walking. Shovel/Pickaxe is difficult for some as the platforms are in the way. For me they go quite well and I am no longer concerned about being at the front. Seeing us performing the choreography all together, from the viewing platform, must have been an impressive sight, even if it wasn't all perfect.

As soon as we have been through each sequence we are split into groups. Today is not about choreography – it's time to move on. We are going to be shown different aspects of the set we will be working in: fences, turf, hedges, Astroturf and crops. Each section will involve a different activity, which will not only give us a chance to get a feel for our props, but will also give them an opportunity to see how best to deal with each one, and how to approach the removal of it. There will also be a different element with Toby. We are going to rotate around each section, which means moving around the FOP, which is rather large. It's hard to perceive the full scale of it because it is full of people so you can't see the perimeter, but it is big. The breaks will also be rotated so one group is asked to leave the FOP straightaway for about 20 minutes, whilst the rest of us move to our first sections.

I am on hedges which are on the far side to where I am. They aren't really hedges, just long black troughs with handles on the sides. We are told that the actual hedges are still growing and they will eventually be planted into these troughs. We soon find that the troughs are on wheels and the idea is that we will use the handles to lift them on one side and wheel them off. So we all try that, following each other. This is quite simple so far.

Next I go to the fences. Another group goes on their break and the current one returns. The fences have three beams going across, connected to the ends. They are very irregular, made with different shapes of wood, the only common element being the length of each beam. They are not treated so have lots of opportunities for splinters, which is one of the reasons why we have gloves. The activity involves lifting the fences, which are placed together in a pack, and taking them to the other end of the FOP. There are two people per fence and some are heavier than others so we need to be careful when lifting them. Again, this is very easy but we are also being timed to see how long it takes. I am paired up with somebody called Sarah and we go through the exercise, which doesn't take very long. After another round it's time to rotate again.

This time I am on my break so I return to the marquee and check my sugar level which is fine. Twenty minutes is not long so one coffee later I am back on the FOP standing on a large turfed area, not real but fake, cut up into smaller bits which resemble a dartboard. That is exactly what this is, as Nathan soon confirms. Diane is also present who I remember from 3 Mills, another one of the dance captains. Nathan quickly begins to assemble people onto the dartboard. Most segments of turf need three people, but some need more and some need less. Not everybody is needed for the exercise so about half of the group stands around the edge.

All of the pieces are numbered, which will help us put them all back together after we have moved them. The idea is to drag one piece onto the one to the right and then drag both pieces off. This will momentarily give a pin wheel effect. We are not just moving turf, we are also trying to make it look attractive, although everything we are doing at the moment is just experimentation. Each piece has a handle underneath each corner. The narrow end has one person and the wide end two. Once we have dragged one piece onto another, the solo person walks over the turf and joins the other two. All three then drag both pieces off the FOP. The turf is surprisingly heavy and takes some strength to drag it quickly. In this way the outer ring comes off, then the inner ring, and then the centre – the bull's-eye – which is the easiest to drag. At the end there is a bit of time for those who didn't get to drag any turf to step forward and take a look at the pieces, get a feel for them, and see where the handles are, but unfortunately the exercise is not repeated for them. They will have plenty of time to have a go in subsequent rehearsals.

Once again we move round. Real turf is next, although for now they are using canvas sheets with poles slotted into the edges to weigh them down. Even with those we have to be very careful since it is windy and the sheets are not quite heavy enough to withstand it. Each sheet is cut into a square and they are all laid down in a grid. Of all the exercises we do today, this is the one that I follow the least. The first part is easy: each piece is moved one square across to create a chessboard effect. After that I just do the best I can but I haven't really understood the instructions. It is very confusing and in all honesty a bit of a mess. We are timed again and apparently we haven't done too badly but I have no idea how we managed to reach the end. We are asked for our opinions and input on how we think the process could be improved. I don't say a word but Jay seems to have followed this far better than I have as he makes some suggestions which are taken on board.

Toby now calls us over. He is near the viewing tower and we are assembled into a long column, about three abreast. He wants us to create a Roman candle effect whereby we all walk forward as a group and then the back row breaks off on either side, running down to the front. We keep it going in this way. I don't remember anything like this from the computer simulation. Maybe we are going to do this as a visual effect at some point. We soon establish that it will only work well if it's done quickly so we concentrate on that until it's time to move on.

The final section is crops which are represented by large pieces of foam, not at all heavy, so not ideal to work with in the wind. I imagine the crops will be inserted into the foam, but for now we are just working with the bases. The pieces are all laid out and we need to pick them all up and recreate the same set up elsewhere. We manage it eventually but in the wind it's a little difficult since pieces keep getting blown about.

That brings us to the end of the rehearsal. It's been a long day so far but there is plenty left of the afternoon and evening. We are told to go back to our home positions so I walk towards the front of the crowd of people and look for Jay, Brian and F, which doesn't take me long. We need to do a bib collection so being at the front of my line I collect and hand them to the Casting team.

After bib collection we are free to go. With so many people it takes some time to get back into the marquee, find my things, change out of my coveralls, and make my way out. There is a queue for the buses which will take us back to Dagenham East. It's already 3.30pm and I haven't even left the site. It will be at least 5pm before I get home. The journey home was a bit of an oversight.

It's been a fun day and one where I feel like we are getting into the core of what we are going to do. Nothing has been clearly defined yet but the foundations are being laid. They have covered choreography, and now props. We are moving along nicely.

Tuesday 22 May 2012

I received another email from Vanessa this morning, after our rehearsal on Sunday:

> Good job everyone on our first weekend in Dagenham! Here are a few updates from last weekend.
> Bibs may change next week so please be patient with us. Bib changes do happen when you are allocated and cast into groups.
> We have given coveralls and gloves to everyone. It is your responsibility to bring them to each rehearsal. We cannot issue more if you forget.
> We really appreciate your eagerness to arrive early for rehearsals, but there is no need to do so and will lead to confusion as rehearsals become larger. Please come at the time stated.
> Just so you are very clear, your group number is 44, and you are in a group named 44 A, B, C, or D. 'A' bibs are numbered 1-250, 'B' are 251-500, 'C' are 501-750, 'D' are 750-999. Your group is named Industrial Revolution or Working Men and Women, so when we make announcements in the holding area it is imperative to pay attention when your group name is mentioned.
> We shall see you back in Dagenham on Sunday 27 May.

So now I knew what the WMW on our bibs meant: Working Men and Women. I was already looking forward to the next rehearsal.

17

Games Maker Shifts

Tuesday 22 May 2012

Today I also received news of my Games Maker shifts, although it was only for my shifts at the Main Press Centre (MPC), not the Olympic Park Common Domain:

> Your shifts with the Security team at the Main Press Centre are now available to view in the Games Maker zone! We need you to check them and let us know you have accepted them.
>
> Thank you for your patience over the past few months – with almost a million shifts to arrange across the Games, it's taken time to plan and coordinate. We can only agree to changes in exceptional circumstances.

It was with some excitement that I logged on to my account to see which shifts I'd been given. This was followed by an equal measure of disappointment when I learned that I only had three shifts in the MPC. I'd been looking forward to working there and now less than half of my shifts would be at that venue. I would have to make the most of it. My shifts were:

> Thursday 26 July: 1pm – 10pm
> Friday 3 August: 1pm – 10pm
> Saturday 11 August: 6am – 2pm

Of much greater concern than my lack of shifts at the MPC was the fact that I had one very early start at 6.00am. I had no idea I would be required to start at such an hour and I wasn't even sure how I would travel across London at that time. On a more positive note all of my shifts so far were on non-rehearsal days so no clashes. Lots of Games Makers had shifts before the Ceremony. My first one was the day before, but we had no rehearsal planned. I still had seven more shifts to be allocated, however, so there was a chance that I could be asked to work on show day. Judging by the comments about shift changes, this could prove to be problematic so I couldn't relax just yet, although I didn't have to wait very long to find out.

Wednesday 23 May 2012

I now received my remaining shifts – same email, different venue: the Common Domain (CDM). I quickly logged on and was happy to see that I wasn't expected to work on Friday 27 July. This was the final hurdle and now I knew that I would have absolutely no problem being both a Ceremony performer and a Games Maker. I was very pleased indeed. My final shift pattern:

Thursday 26 July: 1pm – 10pm – MPC
Saturday 28 July: 6.30am – 2pm – CDM
Tuesday 31 July: 1pm – 8pm – CDM
Friday 3 August: 1pm – 10pm – MPC
Saturday 4 August: 6.30am – 2pm – CDM
Sunday 5 August: 6.30am – 2pm – CDM
Monday 6 August: 1pm – 8pm – CDM
Tuesday 7 August: 1pm – 8pm – CDM
Saturday 11 August: 6am – 2pm – MPC
Sunday 12 August: 1pm – 8pm – CDM

This was a mixed bag. On the plus side I only had five weekday shifts, so less time to take off work, thus saving holidays, which I could use to spend time with Misbah and the kids. Conversely I would have five more weekend days away from them, leaving her to do all the hard work, yet again. Even the weekday shifts were going to take up most of the day and night, if travel time was included. For some reason I'd thought that I would be working a standard nine to five – so completely wrong I was. She wasn't going to be happy, but would as ever accept it, albeit begrudgingly.

The four early shifts were worrying too, not only because of the time I would have to get up, but also because there would probably be no trains at those times. Unless Transport for London were going to operate much earlier trains. I logged on to the website and it wasn't looking good. I think my greatest concern was that I had an early shift the day after the Ceremony. So I was going to perform in the Opening

Ceremony, finish very late no doubt, then I would have to get across London, get dressed into my uniform and probably travel all the way back with no sleep before a seven and a half hour shift. This did not seem possible, and absolutely did not appear favourably in my plans for the night after the Ceremony. I had to do something. I made a mental note to email the Security Volunteers team to try to change my shifts, but before I could do that I had another rehearsal to go to.

18

Rehearsal 4

Sunday 27 May 2012
10.00am – 3.00pm
1:1

Today is the first day of a long run of weekend rehearsals. If this is to be seen as a form of work then I will be doing full weeks for the next month and a half. I arrive more or less on time and quickly walk through registration. It seems that most people arrive a little late. When I've collected my bib I look at the letters on the front again, except this time they are more meaningful. We are workers in the Industrial Revolution. I remember learning about it in History at school with Mr. Cheyne, although whatever he taught me has been pushed back to unreachable depths. I momentarily wonder what Mr. Boyle will now teach me about this period in history.

On the front of my bib today is a laminated card, held in place with staples. It has the abbreviated name of our segment printed on it: WMW. There is also a large F on the left of the card. On the right there is a list of Waves, going from One to Seven. One is Structures, a few are Terrain, and one is curiously called Hail Mary. Is there a religious element to this that I don't quite remember? A couple of Waves just have 'Coming Soon' printed next to them. I'm sure all will be explained in the rehearsal, which I am now looking forward to even more as more details are going to be revealed. I also notice that the FOP has turf and fences on it. The set is in place. Things are moving forward.

The sun is beating down today so it is nice to be in the shade of the marquee where it is much cooler than elsewhere. On the way in I see a large metal sculpture of a bicycle with a figure sat upon it, just in a very basic form. I have no idea what that is for. Once inside I go through the same routine, and make sure I have a coffee before the rehearsal begins. Despite the warnings, I don't wear my coveralls as it's just too warm. Others are doing the same. There is a desk set up where we need to go and collect ear plugs to be used with the monitors that we haven't yet been given. These are for us to keep and we need to bring them to all rehearsals.

There are so many people in the seating area that I rarely see somebody from my group or whom I have spoken with, so I usually sit alone. I spend most of my time looking around, seeing people conversing, noticing other people who are sitting solo, and staring at the endless loop of information on the screen above. It's been quite a long wait so far and it doesn't look like it will end any time soon. There seems to be little value in arriving on time, although I suppose some people have to arrive early to ease the passage of those who arrive late.

Eventually I see somebody from my group at 3 Mills walking down the aisle. I haven't met her yet. We both recognise and acknowledge each other so she takes a seat next to me at the end of the aisle. We introduce ourselves but I don't quite catch her name so I ask again. She repeats Elia, I am sure, but getting a glimpse of her ID card around her neck, upon which her name is prominently printed, I can see something that sounds completely different. I am left confused but I don't say anything.

She tells me that she was in the Closing Ceremony of the Athens Olympics in 2004, Greece being her home country. She lives in London now so has incredibly been granted the very rare opportunity to be in another Olympic Ceremony. She didn't have a large role at Athens but it was an amazing experience and it made her very proud. I'm sure I will be sharing these sentiments come July. She goes on to mention that they were allowed to watch the Opening Ceremony dress rehearsal, and in return those performers watched the Closing. I haven't thought much about the dress rehearsal until now, or even what it actually means. Of course, performing in front of an audience of 80,000 people isn't going to be sprung upon us as most of the performers are anything but. Indeed the mere thought of it gives me stage fright, a full two months before the event. We have three dress rehearsals planned so they are going to get us well prepared for show night. There is no other option. All of the volunteers at Athens were given a DVD of the show afterwards which was nice. I hope London will be just as generous. It will be great to walk away with a souvenir to show to my children.

After quite some time Steve welcomes us back to Dagenham. He is as chirpy as ever and is very fluent on his microphone, a seasoned Olympic instructor. Today we are going to be introduced to our set, or as much of it as is possible in this rehearsal space. A plan of the FOP appears on the screen and he tells us that we are going to be divided into counties. For the next few minutes he states bib number ranges beginning at one and continuing numerically, and gives each resultant group their county name. I have been assigned to the county of Fife, which is why my laminate has F printed on it. There are over 100 people in Fife and Elia is also in my group. Each county is a different size and the number of people allocated to each one is a reflection of this. Essex is the largest so has the most people. One or two counties only have 20 or so volunteers. Fife is at the larger end of the scale.

Eventually we see another plan of the FOP but with all of the counties now showing, and with their boundaries indicated. Our county is going to be our area, our responsibility, the space we will be working in. This is the section of the FOP that we will be clearing or moving. I suppose it was never going to be a case of piling us all on and everyone be free to walk anywhere, as required. They are containing us and each county will concentrate on their own patch. This is the first major development of the day. The full list of counties is: Ayrshire, Berkshire, Cornwall, Devon, Essex, Fife, Gloucestershire, Hampshire, Isle of Wight, Jersey, Kent, Lancashire. A – L.

All of them have their own difficulties to deal with. Fife, for example, will have sheep going through. There are animals in other counties too. My mind goes back to the model we saw in 3 Mills. There will be a herd of real sheep in the area we are attempting to clear, although the sheep will be in Essex at the start. This does mean that there may be more than just turf to move as the animals will do what they naturally need to do, so to speak. This is now getting very interesting and amusing. I am not the only person wondering what I have gotten into here.

Steve now explains what the rest of the information on the cards means. This is essentially how our segment will play out. First we have to remove the structures, so the fences, the hedges, the crops, etc. This is Wave One. The terrain is next, meaning all of the turf. This is in three waves as there is so much of it and will take a lot longer. Once we have completed this, we have Wave Five, or Hail Mary. This means removing everything else that remains on the FOP. If you see it, get it off, and with haste. Waves Six and Seven are marked as 'Coming Soon'.

The FOP has now been tiled so it is much smoother than last week, and not as dusty. We are going to be concentrating on structures during this rehearsal. Steve calls out each county and tells us which exit from the marquee is best, depending on the location of the county on the FOP. This also reduces congestion. Slowly we trickle out and find our respective counties. We are asked to just wander around our patch and familiarise ourselves with our structures, the general layout and our boundaries.

County Fife has a long line of turf about three metres wide with two lines of fences, creating a sort of channel that leads onto the main area, which spreads to the right. It is shaped a bit like the letter P. The fences continue all the way up the left edge and we have hedges snaking through the middle. The curve of the 'P' is made up of a dartboard in the centre and other bits of turf surrounding it. All of the pieces are numbered F01, F02, F03, and so on all the way up to around F160, so we have that many fences, hedges and pieces of turf to remove. The fences at the very top of our section are labelled E followed by a number, so these are for County Essex and therefore not our responsibility.

We spend quite a lot of time in our counties, just looking around. It's important we know the layout. We are asked to introduce ourselves to anybody who we don't know. These are the people who we are going to be spending most of our time with from now on. We are also introduced to Katie who is going to be our Mass Movement Coordinator, essentially the person who is in charge of us. Each county has a member of the Mass Team allocated to them. They all wear pink bibs; Katie's has a large K on the back in black sequins. She organises us into lines to the side of the long row of fences, which are now on our right. We are put into bib order and in pairs. Whoever is standing next to us is our buddy. If we are asked to get into our buddy lines, this is the formation we need to adopt. I am paired with Josh. Chris, who I met at 3 Mills, is a couple of rows behind me.

Soon we are asked to walk into our county via the ramp, which is the long line of turf. This will eventually be an actual ramp although it is flat here. We then walk round our area and back out again. They just want to see how it works, the best route to take, and how easily we can form our lines again. The route we took meant some people had to walk over a hedge so it wasn't quite perfect. It was only the first time. We do this a few times, including a couple of runs when we move the hedges, walking in a pre-determined line. There are long waits in between.

It is a very nice day today so in between tasks we take advantage and sit down on the turf, lie down and relax. There is no sense in standing as it takes what seems like an age to organise anything.

On one side of the site is a residential area. It is a little way off, but not so far away that somebody looking out of the top floor windows wouldn't be able to see us. What a sight we must look. These are the rehearsals of the Olympic Opening Ceremony and there are hundreds of us essentially just sunbathing. Any of us who are not partaking are doing little else. Somebody may be mocking us right now.

Around this time there are auditions happening for soldiers. I'm not sure how they have chosen people but they have to go and meet somebody elsewhere and take part in a short audition. I don't know what they are required to do, but it does sound interesting and the lucky few who are chosen will at least have a proper part to play. I can't remember seeing soldiers in the simulation though.

We now move on to fences. Once again in our buddy lines, Katie works out how many people will be needed according to how many fences there are. Those people then walk into the county and pair off starting from the very top fence and working down to the bottom of the ramp. We then spend a lot of time standing by our fences. They are held together by a strip of Velcro fastened to the right post which is tied to the post next to it. We are only going to be required to unfasten the Velcro strip, lift our fence and walk with it to the outside of our county and place it down, forming a pack of them, like they were arranged during the previous rehearsal.

It seems so simple yet it takes a long time to organise and coordinate 12 counties, as we all need to do it at the same time. Steve is talking to all of the Mass Team remotely. They are waiting for instructions and cues, which they convey to us. It may seem easy but even this must be a challenge in communication. In our case, having to coordinate over a hundred people, some of whom are getting frustrated and bored, can't be easy either. Yet we do finally move our fences, alternating sides as we move along the rows, to give a staggered effect. Once we have set our fence down we walk back and form our buddy lines. That is as far as we are taking it for the moment. We are told it looked good. I'm sure they are just being kind. We put the fences back, ensuring they are in the correct order and the right way round, label facing out, there is another long wait, and then we go through removing them again. And so we continue, with a break slotted in.

Towards the end of today's rehearsal we are asked to go to a different part of the FOP where there is some haka practice, meaning our choreography. Different counties have been alternating throughout the rehearsal. There is no turf here and through the thin soles of my plimsolls I can feel the heat. My feet are almost burning. I may have to wear some different shoes to future rehearsals as it is only going to get warmer now.

We get into rows and go through the routines, walking whilst we do them. Some of the dance captains are scattered amongst us. After a few combinations up and down, we are allowed to go. One guy asks me to show him some of the choreography as he missed one of the first two rehearsals so is a little unsure about Chisel/Hammer.

Next week is Jubilee Weekend. It is also the first weekend where we have rehearsals on both days. We are told they will be critical so we are urged to come if we can. They repeatedly express their appreciation for the time we are giving. They know it's a big ask, and are more than likely expecting plenty of people to be absent. I know Josh will be in Croatia next weekend so he will miss both rehearsals. A few other people in our group will definitely only come to one of them, so we may be a little thin on the ground.

19

Uniform Collection

Tuesday 29 May 2012

Today I have to go and collect my Games Maker uniform from the Uniform Distribution and Accreditation Centre (UDAC). My time slot is 12pm and it should last around an hour. My boss has kindly allowed me to go during work so I leave around 11.30 and head to Star Lane on the DLR. It takes longer than I anticipated but I don't have to arrive exactly on time. The UDAC is a short walk from the station and on the way I see several people walking towards me carrying large black bags. There is no mistaking where they have just come from.

On the side of the building there is a large purple sign with "Welcome to the UDAC" written on it. The steward outside directs me to the main entrance where my trip through the centre will begin. It all has a very makeshift look about it. The standard queue barriers are mapped out, but as there are not many people here I walk all the way up and down, up and down, until I am near the front, where I wait to be called forward to a long row of tables almost spanning the width of the room. There are work stations and Games Makers manning them. The lady I go to takes my details and registers me on the system. They are all wearing their uniforms. Maybe this is the only role they will perform for the Olympic Games, their duties ending before the competition even begins.

Once I've been verified I am given a sheet of paper that shows everything that I will receive today, and am told to follow the red line on the floor. There are also green and orange lines. The red one takes me round and behind the row of tables. I notice there is a lot of branding: London 2012 logos, colours and labelling. Eventually I come to some more desks where I will collect my accreditation. This is a very large laminated card, A5 size. Not something you can keep in your pocket. I think they want to be able to easily tell who is accredited and who is not by forcing you to wear this around your neck at all times. The lanyard that comes with it is fully branded. The card has my photo, my name, and some codes to show where I will be given access to. I only have MPC and CDM on mine so I will not be allowed into any of the competition venues, no exceptions made. This also means that Games Makers who are working at other venues in London will not be allowed into the Olympic Park, which is somewhat harsh I feel.

I move on to the 'shoe store' where they are fitting people for their trainers. I am greeted by a very pleasant man who asks me my shoe size and then tells me to take a seat. Soon he returns with a pair of trainers for me to try. They are surprisingly comfortable, although between us we think it is best to get a size up as I will be on my feet for several hours at a time, not to mention all the walking I'll be doing. He marks my sheet with my size and shows me which way to go to get myself measured for my uniform.

I meet a lady, as pleasant as the man in the shoe store. We follow the same routine, except this time I am being fitted for my Games Maker trousers, jacket and t-shirt. I consider the fact that it is going to be hot, or at least I hope it is, so take a size up of everything, for comfort, and to give a nice loose fit. All of the uniform is very comfortable. They have at least put some thought into its manufacture. After trying on a couple of sizes the lady marks my sheet with a Large next to each uniform item and sends me to the next stop which I find is for my Games Maker bag. This contains a water bottle, a branded umbrella which has 'Just In Case' printed on the sleeve, a pocket guide with a branded pen, a baseball cap, a set of postcards, and a Games Maker Swatch watch. This last item I was not aware of and I don't welcome it if it's part of our attire. Ever since my gran gave me a watch when I was 17 or 18, I have vowed never to wear any other. Not a single watch, other than hers, has ever been worn on my wrists ever since, and this one will be no exception. It is also here that I receive the large black bag that I saw earlier. It is branded with an Adidas logo.

The next stop is to collect my actual uniform, now that my sizes have been confirmed. Throughout my journey through the UDAC everything has been very smooth and quick-moving. It is all very well organised and efficiently run. I come to a bank of tables about 20 metres wide, behind which are more Games Makers. About ten metres behind them are stacks and stacks of boxes on shelves, stretching as wide as the tables. There are hundreds of them. A man greets me and asks for my sheet which he uses to find my uniform in the sizes indicated. He gradually fills my bag, making it all fit in like a jigsaw,

probably having done this many times before. When everything is in I
have a bag of the following items:

1 Jacket
2 T-Shirts
2 Pairs of Trousers
1 Pair of Trainers
2 Pairs of Socks
1 Baseball Cap
1 Shoulder Bag
1 Pocket Guide
1 Pen
1 Umbrella
1 Water Bottle
1 Swatch Watch
1 Set of Postcards

I get to keep all of these items once my shifts are over. Quite a set of
souvenirs, I must say. I think the only items that do not have Olympic
branding are the socks, which are by Adidas.

There are just two stages left before I can leave. Firstly, I have to
go to the checkouts. Although everything is free it must all be
scanned and then signed for. There is a bit of a queue and it is not
moving quickly. Very slowly in fact, speed of service clearly not a
priority, despite there being one person scanning and another re-
packing on some tills. I am aware that I've been away from work
longer than expected and I become agitated when I see one operator
talking his 'customer' through every item. I have no idea what he
could possibly be telling her about a pair of socks, or indeed any of
the other items, that she doesn't already know. When I finally reach
my till I am thankful that I have two people, making my exit all the
more quicker. The operator confirms that the watch is only a gift and
not part of the uniform, only to be worn if I so wish. She hands me
a receipt detailing each item I've been given, all of them costing me
exactly £0.00. I sign a declaration to confirm that I have indeed
received all of the items listed, and then it's off to the final stage:
Oyster card collection.

I leave the main building and get directed to a small hut. A man
behind a counter asks to see my accreditation, which he checks and
then issues me with an Oyster card, having registered it to me

specifically. He tells me that it will start to work on the day of my first shift. It says Olympic Volunteer on it. I have another souvenir Oyster card. As I leave the site, walking past another souvenir shop, I feel pleased with what I am carrying in my hand – essentially my passport to the Olympic Games, and a uniform that only a select number of people will ever be allowed to have.

20

A Special Message

Friday 1 June 2012

A few days after my uniform collection I received an invite to my final Games Maker training session. I'd forgotten about this when my shifts had been confirmed, so once again I would have to see if a clash with rehearsals could be avoided. The email was exactly the same as the previous one, just concerned with a different venue.

As always I logged on quickly and looked at the options. There were only four sessions this time: Sunday 8 – Wednesday 11 July. I had a rehearsal on both the Sunday morning and Tuesday evening. I could have opted for the Sunday afternoon but thought it best to keep the two activities completely separate, so I settled for the Wednesday. I had narrowly escaped a clash but escape I did and now there was no chance of any clashes at any point. All of my Games Maker training sessions and shifts had been confirmed.

The next rehearsal was tomorrow – the first of two over the Jubilee weekend.

Later that day I received a rather unexpected but very welcome email in my inbox:

44 B – A Message from Danny Boyle

Thank you for your attendance so far. You're doing an amazing job and I hope you're enjoying it. The ambitions of the show can only be achieved through your energy and continued commitment to the rehearsals.

This coming weekend is a huge one for the Opening Ceremony Rehearsals at Dagenham. I know the Queen has organised lots of alternative distractions. Don't be tempted! Come to Dagenham instead! She will approve when you walk into the Stadium on 27 July.

And even more importantly – you, your friends, your family and the world will be dazzled by your collective star power!

Look out for each other and thank you!
Danny Boyle

PS: As a thank you for attending this Jubilee weekend we will have a special thank you gift for you (sorry, only available on Sunday)

It had been sent via Vanessa but it seemed authentic enough, so it was a pleasant surprise. I had always intended to go to both rehearsals so if I was going to receive a gift for my efforts, no matter how trivial or small, then so much the better. It did seem to reveal some fears they may have had about our willingness to come to rehearsals during such an important weekend for some. People would have made plans and rehearsals would not be given priority. I felt quite the opposite. When I signed up for this I made a commitment and I intended to honour this by attending all rehearsals, unless it was absolutely unavoidable. For me, wanting to just do something else on a rehearsal day was not a good enough reason.

21

Rehearsal 5

Saturday 2 June 2012
10.00am – 3.00pm
1:1

It is now June though it is not warm today, instead wet and cloudy. I pack my cycling jacket, which is waterproof, and head off for another early session. Today there will be less people, by all accounts, so I'm not sure how much we will be able to achieve. There is a long wait at the beginning whilst everybody arrives and preparations are completed. Members of the Casting team are handing out ponchos so I take one, but I don't think I will use it. They are very cumbersome things and I have my jacket on underneath my coveralls, although admittedly that will serve more to keep me warm rather than dry, if it should rain.

Most of my time at the beginning is usually spent drinking coffee, loitering and watching the same messages appear on the screen overhead. Today, however, there is another TV screen set up at the front of the left aisle, where there are cyclists seated. It is clear from the gear they are wearing that they are BMX riders. Some of them have DOVE written on their bibs. There is a crowd forming on their side so I go and see what's happening. I soon discover that there is going to be a video played of their segment, or some of it at least. Their leader, who introduces the clip, informs them that they will be on for the final five minutes of the show.

The video plays and we are treated to footage of BMX riders performing all manner of clever tricks and moves on their bikes. I recognise the music as The Chemical Brothers' 'Star Guitar', a track which always lifts my mood. As I watch and listen to the flowing melody of the song, I feel a real sense of how fantastic this experience has been so far, regardless of the intermittent boredom and frustration, and just how amazing it is going to be as we approach show night. We are involved in something very special indeed and this is the underlying feeling I get from hearing this song. I am sure that it will forever conjure up images of rehearsals in Dagenham, of being inside this blue and yellow marquee.

I can now see riders who are flying around the Stadium. We have moved on to a computer simulation, rather than real footage, and they are all wearing large white wings on their backs to represent doves, I presume. At the end one rider flies over the middle of the Stadium. So this is how the Ceremony will end. These guys only have five minutes, but what a thrill, flying around the arena on their bikes.

After more waiting, more than I would have liked, the rehearsal begins. I am beginning to wonder if there is any point in arriving on time. Vanessa makes a few announcements first and then it is over to Nathan, not Steve, who tells us that we are going to concentrate on flow today, so more of what we were doing last week, where they are looking at how everybody moves around the FOP and trying to make the traffic as smooth as possible. We get called out one or two counties at a time and then it's off to Fife, our area.

We all gather around Katie and she gives us a briefing, going through what we will be doing today and mentioning any other details that may be relevant, before asking us to form our buddy lines. She also asks if there are any people who would prefer not to do any lifting, for whatever reason. It is physical work after all, and not to everybody's liking. A few people volunteer themselves, so they are asked to stand in a group away from the buddy lines. They will be given other tasks. As Josh isn't here today I am paired up with Gaudi, who I met in the shuttle bus earlier on. He is from the Philippines but lives in London. The diversity and dedication that is so apparent here is not lost on me. Elia, who I met last week, must have felt so proud to be performing in her country's Olympic Ceremony. So many people here are not even from London, or even the UK, yet they are giving up so much of their time to represent my city.

Eventually we walk through our county with our buddies whilst the Mass Team watches. We go back to our buddy lines and wait again. There is a lot of this in between runs. Sometimes we strike fences, sometimes we do some turf. Whichever we do, it never seems to go completely smoothly. I wonder how the other counties are finding it. At times we concentrate on one section of turf and then stop for a regroup. Those people who are not required for that piece can only stand and wait. It is becoming very frustrating, but this is what we have to do. We don't really have the big picture so we just do what they ask. This section of turf needs to be moved in this way, this area in another way, this one comes first, then that one. In this fashion we continue, but it is very slow-paced. And it isn't exactly warm. During break time we get some respite, with a chance to warm ourselves with a hot drink or two, before going back out.

The turf on our fence line is split vertically into three very long pieces. Having moved the fences and hedges off before the break, we are going to practise this for now. The idea here is to strike the middle one first. Two people take hold of the inner end, one on each side, and run towards the outside of the line, thereby creating a rolling tongue effect. Some more of us are positioned at the top of our county, where there is a row of triangular pieces, all interlocking, next to some much larger irregular bits. There is one person on each corner of each piece. Yet more of us are positioned on the dartboard. We go through short bursts of striking in different ways, working out cues, and who is going to strike first in each area. We wait whilst the Mass Team confers. We try it all again, varying it a little.

After a while we put all of the turf, hedges and fences back and prepare for a full strike, where we are going to move everything. So now, instead of stopping after a certain point, we just keep going until everything is off, so we need to be mindful of what needs to be moved next. We all know which fence or hedge to go to, as we went through this earlier and each one was allocated to a pair. Some people are then allocated to a certain piece of turf, but most of us will need to just strike whatever piece we come to. This is something we are going to have to get used to as there is a different number of people present each week. Sometimes those given specific items to move will not be here so somebody else will need to fill in, moving everybody else out of sync. Some people will maybe not even make it as far as show night, so flexibility is essential. Because of this, it is impossible to allocate each and every piece to a particular group of individuals. There still may be many changes to come.

We form our buddy lines and wait for the strike to begin. We wait a very long time for what appears to be nothing, but some things are happening behind the scenes, one of which is getting the music ready to be played over the speakers as we strike. The looped drum beat from the simulation kicks in as we are given the cue to begin. Striking the structures is relatively smooth. The fences are now put onto dollies that they have placed in front of our county. Three fences are to be placed on each side. We rehearsed this earlier. As soon as we place our fence we have to walk around the back of the dolly and back into our buddy lines, ready to walk onto the FOP again to strike something else. The chain continues in this way.

By the time I make it back onto the fence line, with all fences removed, the turf has also gone, so I walk to the top section to find something to move. This is where it gets a little disorganised as it isn't immediately clear who should be on which piece of turf. As some people are dragging turf off, other people who are walking back get in their way, so they have to stop in their tracks, causing others to stop too. There are too many people in a small area and this is not quite flowing. In short it is a mess. Confusion is written across many faces, but we continue, somehow clearing the first area whilst others are already trying to clear the dartboard. Their path is hampered, however, so they change course, walking over somebody else's turf, which in turn causes those people to wait.

Once we reach the bottom of the fence line with our turf, there is a queue forming to deposit the pieces, as some people are dragging quicker than others. Once deposited we have to make our way back again to our buddy lines, this time not necessarily with our buddies, it just depends on who you end up next to because everybody is walking at a different pace and therefore could have moved a different piece to you. However, trying to walk back isn't as easy as there are people constantly walking off with turf behind them and the available space is slowly reduced due to the ever-increasing pile of turf that is forming beside us. The inevitable mêlée is becoming harder to get through, almost like trying to walk straight through a field of runners.

Nevertheless we continue and somehow we clear the FOP, all counties doing their bit and transforming the green blanket into the dark grey of the tiled ground. We are congratulated and praised. But that was embarrassing. Any coordination and flow that we established earlier was dismantled very quickly as we were reduced to a rabble. This is not going to be easy and I have no idea how we are going to manage to pull this off. It is early days though.

Walking back to the shuttle buses after the rehearsal has ended, I see Danny Boyle walking in the opposite direction. He thanks and greets us as he walks past. It was a nice way to end today's session. I wonder if we are going to get a chance to actually talk to him personally at any point. I do hope so as there is plenty I would want to say, mainly about his films and influences.

With a three o'clock finish it's usually around 5pm when I get home, enough time to help with the kids, put them to bed, and share what's left of the evening with Misbah. She has stopped asking me about rehearsals as I've already made it clear that I don't want to say anything. I am beginning to think this is the wrong call. Who is she going to tell? I'm not quite sure how to explain to her what we are doing anyway. The choreography has been left behind, so I don't know where that will fit in, and to tell her that all we are going to do is a set change will only frustrate her more. Still, I'm going back tomorrow for another session. Who knows what it will bring.

22

Rehearsal 6

Sunday 3 June 2012
10.00am – 3.00pm
1:1

Today it is raining. And it is still much colder than it should be at this time of year. Reluctantly I pull myself out of bed and make my way to rehearsals at the usual early hour, on a Sunday. Considering it is Jubilee Weekend, the transport system is running well and I have no problem with my journey. When registering we are asked to take an In Ear Monitor (IEM), like the ones I have been looking at before every rehearsal on the overhead screen, so it looks like we will be using them today. We are also asked to hand in our Oyster cards, even though there is still credit left on them, and exchange them for new ones. As always, I get changed and walk to the refreshment tent to grab a coffee, except this time there are large puddles to walk around and jump over. The rain isn't heavy but it doesn't look like we have seen the last of it just yet. I have my poncho in my pocket just in case.

Back in the main tent we have company today. There are rows and rows of dancers all the way down one half of it, where the BMX riders were sitting yesterday. They are busy rehearsing. There must be a couple of hundred of them, and more are arriving. I take a seat and watch them as I drink my coffee. I can now see why I wasn't chosen to be a dancer: they are really good, with quick, sharp movements, and well coordinated. Just learning their routine would probably take me an age. As I watch them I notice that some are clearly better than others.

Through the rows of predominantly female volunteers I also see something familiar. A pair of numbers that I am sure I've seen before. They are on the back of some tracksuit bottoms. I am sure, in fact certain, that their wearer is the same girl who was in front of me at my first audition several months ago now. She was blonde, as is the girl I am now looking at. It is definitely her. I remember those numbers. I knew she would make it as a dancer. It seems odd to see her here, after all this time, both of us having made it but in two very different roles. I almost make up my mind to go and thank her when I get a chance as I distinctly remember taking my lead from her during the miming segment of the audition, and that is what made me look good, but I soon decide that approaching her with that will seem just a little strange. Instead I go to use the facilities, opting to try the ones on the other side of the marquee as I overheard somebody saying they are less busy than the main ones.

On the way over I notice that there is a Prayer 'Room'. I should make use of that as it would save me having to catch up with my prayers when I get home, but it's not really convenient. Still, it's nice that they have thought of it. As I enter the toilets, just before walking into a cubicle, somebody walks out of the next one. I do a double take, and it is clearly Danny Boyle washing his hands. I automatically close my door but I'm thinking that I should take the opportunity since it has presented itself. I could still walk out and chat to him, but in the toilet? Within a second he leaves. It would have been a little awkward anyway. At least he has turned up, after urging us to make this a priority, despite the Jubilee celebrations.

When I return to the tent I once again sit and wait for something to happen whilst watching the dancers, who are quite entertaining, even though they are going through the same routine over and over. After some time, frustrated at the lack of activity, I decide to walk down the aisle to get a different point of view. I see Jay at the back of the dancers, a few paces removed, going through their routine with them, although he is only doing steps. He actually looks quite good. The judges clearly didn't deem him good enough though. I wonder which he would have preferred now.

Looking at the time I see that I have been here almost an hour and a half and we have done nothing at all. Surely something is going to happen soon. I look around and over near the front rows of seats, on the dancers' side, is Danny Boyle, chatting to a couple of volunteers. One of them is having his photo taken with him. After the toilet incident I can't now miss this opportunity. Without hesitating I make my way over and patiently wait, at the same time taking my phone out of my pocket and setting the camera. They have stated very clearly that all photography is prohibited, but if the Artistic Director himself is okay with it, then that is fine with me. I have no qualms at all when I ask him politely if I could possibly have a photo. He immediately agrees very kindly and puts his arm around me as I ask the person opposite to take a photo for me.

"You'll probably want to update these when we get to the Stadium," he says, possibly meaning that it's not the best backdrop for a photo.

"Well, I may not get another chance," I reply, smiling, mindful of the fact that a large proportion of the 1,000 volunteers in my segment alone must surely want to have a picture with Danny Boyle. The photo is taken. I thank him kindly and then return the favour just offered me by taking a photo for Daniel, who has also seen what has been happening. I look at my photo and luckily I am happy enough with it. My bib number is clearly visible, which is a nice touch, and in the background some of the dancers, who have by now dispersed and are on a break, can be seen. I have a backdrop that can never, ever be repeated exactly. I am pleased to have secured a photo so early in the proceedings. A few other people have now arrived to have a chat or photo taken. The voice of Nathan is on the microphone. Finally, after such a long wait, we are getting ready to begin. Before I go to take a seat, I get Danny's attention and tell him: "I just wanted to say that I'm really, really pleased to be working for you…"

"Ah, cool."

"…and I hope to be able to talk to you at length at some point."

"We will do," he replies, in a very amicable and sincere tone. Nathan once again asks us to take our seats.

"Well, I'd best get to my seat as we're about to start." He has been very accommodating and down-to-earth. It is clear to see how much he appreciates us being here, and he is more than willing to give us his time, if we ask it of him. We are all essentially here to make his vision a reality, and he needs us to be able to do that. I am conscious of this as I sit down, and I am indeed proud to be working for him, to be a small part of his production, and I want to perform well for him, as does everyone. He has asked a lot from us, and is still expecting a lot more yet.

After a quick update from Vanessa, we begin with a video of our full strike yesterday. Of course they are filming pretty much everything we do so it's good to be able to see how it looked. The video was filmed from the tower, which is also where the Royal Box will be on the night, so this is the Queen's view of our segment. She will be able to see Fife quite clearly. As the footage on the screen unfolds it is hard to discern what is actually happening from that angle. It seems rather far off, which is just the effect of the camera I suppose. Eventually it is clear that the turf is slowly disappearing. Some of the dancers who are on their break are also watching. I wonder what they must think. It looks just like how it felt last week: a disorganised mess. I can now see the queues forming at the bottom of our ramp. More Tarmac is visible now, but it happens in short bursts rather than a constant flow, which is the intention. There seems to be a lot of stopping and starting as we decide what comes next. There is no way to tell how the counties on the other side of the FOP are getting on.

The music continues. The longer it does the more embarrassing this is becoming. I wouldn't feel this way if we didn't have an audience but they surely can't be impressed with this, even as Nathan is singing our praises as the strike ends and the FOP is clear of all structures and terrain. It took us around 13 minutes. Our segment will be 17 in total, so at the moment we have four minutes for two as yet undisclosed waves. I'm glad we still have a lot of rehearsals remaining.

We are now asked to switch on our IEMs and choose the channel that Nathan nominates. He assures us that they are constantly learning from our strikes and once again they are going to be looking at flow, although they are concentrating on the inner counties today. The rest of us are going to do some choreography practice. Half the rehearsal time has already passed. It doesn't look like we are going to spend much time doing strikes today. The inner counties move to the FOP and the outer ones are asked to move into a large shelter, a bit like a hangar with no ends that has been built away from the marquee and our FOP. Maybe this is where the dancers usually rehearse when it is raining and there is no room in the marquee. We don't get that luxury as we can't rehearse without our set, but this is a welcome escape from the rain.

We all move inside and form long rows spanning the width of the space which is about 30 metres. I try to find space where there isn't a puddle as my shoes are not waterproof. Some people have come prepared and are wearing wellington boots. They are kindly asked to occupy the puddles if possible so others can stand in a dry area. Once we are all in position all eyes are on the dance captain at the front. We are still on our IEMs so there is no issue with not being able to hear clearly. We go through each of our routines, but we are now fine tuning each of the moves, so she breaks it all down again and goes through them one by one, explaining exactly how each arm, each hand, each fist needs to be positioned. Elbow raised, left fist next to hip, right hand over left, hands waist high, right hand goes up first on the clap. We are concentrating on the smaller aspects, now that we know the moves well. When pulling a lever we can't have a tight fist as there is supposed to be a handle in there, so this needs to come across. This is also why it's important that we can 'see' the lever we are pulling.

As we go through each routine, the dance captains invite those people who are not so familiar with the choreography to move to the right side of the shelter where some of them are leading a crash course. This may be because some people were absent during one of the 3 Mills rehearsals, or they were not there at all, meaning some people have dropped out and people on the reserve list have been given the opportunity to join us.

Soon we move on to the combination, so Shut Boot/Sliding Doors, Levers/Pull, and Chisel/Hammer, concentrating on making them look as good as we can, bearing in mind what we have just been taught. We do them synchronised, and then falling in row after row. She gives us different instructions to see if we are listening, which isn't always the case with everybody, it turns out, as some people continue when they should have stopped. Sometimes she asks us to do just half the routine, or stop at a random point, or we do a different combination. She is certainly keeping it interesting, but this is also serving to make us learn and know each sequence inside out.

The best thing we do is the individual routines, and then the main combination, in double time. This is not only challenging but also a lot of fun, watching everybody move twice as quickly and trying to keep it together. If we can do it at this pace, then doing it at the normal pace will be even easier. We do this several times, and then the session ends. I enjoyed that a lot and it was very useful, not to mention encouraging. I go to the front as we walk out to go on a break, and tell the dance captain. She appreciates the feedback.

After the break we all go on to the FOP and into our counties. It has stopped raining for now. The amount of time we have left to work on the strike is minimal so we only cover some aspects, rather than managing a full strike. This was supposed to be a critical weekend, yet as it draws to an end it is hard to know what exactly we have achieved that has been so important. Only those involved in the planning and production could possibly know the answer to this.

Before finishing the rehearsal all of the inner counties perform their strikes to the music, whilst the rest of us are positioned in different areas around the FOP and perform our choreography in large packs, using our IEMs to receive instructions. It begins raining again, not heavily but enough to call upon our ponchos, although plenty of people don't bother or are already wearing a waterproof jacket of some sort. That is probably the best way as the ponchos are very irritating, especially in the wind, and they feel like they will fall apart before long as the plastic is rather thin. Toby is impressed with the strike and choreography and says it looked fantastic from where he was standing, well timed and coordinated.

Before we leave we pick up our free gift, which is an exclusive Ceremonies t-shirt. They are mostly very brightly coloured – sky blue, orange, neon pink – but there are also dark blue ones. There is only one colour per size so you take whatever you get. Medium is bright orange. I doubt if I will wear it at any point but it's a souvenir at least, issued to nobody else but us.

Wednesday 6 June 2012

We received a weekend update from Vanessa today, which I thought wasn't coming this week.

This week I have been trying to keep up with de-bibbing. This is an important factor in the sanity of lovely workforce volunteers. I ask that you follow Mass's instructions, untie your bib strings, hold them symmetrically from the top two corners, and collect them in the proper order. I know they slip and slide, but the more organised this process is the less time we spend having to organise them afterwards (It took 15 people two hours doing it full time on Sunday – a little long).

I have many emails about Oyster cards. The system has changed once again and you will be issued Oyster cards as per a schedule with varying amounts of money on them. £10 cards were issued on Sunday which will cover you for a return journey through zones 1-6. You are asked to hand in your old card, and please do not worry if there is credit left on it. As stated previously and as per the agreement, these are not for personal use, only for rehearsals.

After a lovely weekend in the rain, I saw many of you not wearing waterproof shoes or jackets. We have plastic ponchos but these take one million years to biodegrade and we want

127

to lessen our use of these (in line with sustainability) so please only take one if you really need it.

I am really hoping that the future TBA dates will be announced soon and we respect your patience on this. I would plan to take most of the dress rehearsal days off and plan to be free early afternoon for the earlier dates.

I did wonder about the Oyster cards on the way home from rehearsal and saw little sense in taking the old ones and being given ones that wouldn't even cover a full weekend of travel for me.

A few other things happened today. I received a reminder of my Games Maker role-specific training, which actually took place on 11 May – a minor error in the system. I also wrote to the security team to check that they had received my email requesting a change in shifts, which I had sent due to the early starts being almost impossible to honour. I had to finalise my annual leave soon, so I needed to know my final shift dates. It was quite convenient that this email coincidentally came:

> Thanks for getting in touch about your Games time roster.
> We have asked that all security volunteers contact us by 15 June 2012 if they have concerns about the shifts they have been allocated. In the meantime, we are collating all of your feedback and you will hear back about your rosters by Friday 22 June.

As long as they were addressing the issue it was fine by me.

Friday 8 June 2012

Yesterday marked 50 days to go until the Opening Ceremony. Today I received another email from the Security team:

> We hope you're looking forward to your role in the Security team at London 2012. We'll do our best to accommodate any requests for changes and by Friday 22 June you'll be able to access your finalised roster.
> We have also received several questions about transport to and from venues during the Games. **Please note that**

Transport for London will operate tubes and trains on an extended timetable during the Games. The full timetable is yet to be published.

In the meantime, thanks for your patience and we'll be in touch again very soon. We look forward to seeing you at the Games – 49 days to go until the Opening Ceremony!

This could mean that I wouldn't be given different shifts and will still be expected to start some of them at 6am. I was hoping to escape that but it didn't look like it would be so easy. More importantly it was now exactly seven weeks until the Ceremony. We had so much to do in such a short space of time.

23

Rehearsal 7

Saturday 9 June 2012
3.00pm – 8.00pm
1:1

Today is our first afternoon rehearsal at Dagenham. It's good to have the morning free, although when travel time is built in there isn't much time to get things done. Life goes on and errands and tasks need to be seen to but the rehearsals are taking a large chunk out of my time so I am going to have to organise myself much better.

Upon arrival at registration we received a new Oyster card so I will have enough credit to get home tonight. Steve is back today – a welcome return. I have to confess I did miss his dulcet tones last week, as he has somewhat become the voice of the rehearsals for me. He often does a roll call of counties, as he is doing now, waiting for us to acknowledge our presence with a shout or a cheer, maybe in turn replying with a "very good", as he so often does. He has catchphrases that we have warmed to. So much in Steve's world is "far out" and it now provokes more than one or two smiles or laughs. He says that he has seen the video of our strike, and how long it took us, so we need to get the time down. He mentions this with nothing but positive vibes and his usual enthusiasm.

Once on the FOP Katie, who is more commonly referred to as Katie P by her peers, briefs us on what we are going to do today and mentions some changes that have happened since the Mass Team's latest discussions. She has a plan of the entire FOP plus a larger scale map of our county, which she uses to help us visualise what she means when she talks about where we need to be, or what we are doing in certain areas, and even specific pieces of turf or rows of fences. She goes through the order of striking, mentioning the saw tooth, which is the row of interlocking triangular pieces, the dartboard, and what she likes to call the kissing gate, which is the one at the top of the fence line, or at least I think it is. In a way it doesn't concern me as I will never be the one to strike it. I just know that I am on the fence line, for now at least.

Two crucial pieces of information that she imparts is the fact that we must remember we have a chimney and a crucible in our county. These are marked out on the ground, underneath the turf, and although it is solid ground now, it won't be in the Stadium. There will be a trap built into the set, out of which the chimney and crucible will rise, so we must remember to walk around these areas once the turf is removed. Another important rule from now is that we need to walk up and down the ramp on the right hand side to make traffic flow easier. We are going to try this on our next strike to see how it works.

She asks if we have any questions and then tries to answer them. She takes on board our comments and suggestions, and then she asks us to get into our buddy lines so we are standing in an orderly fashion and she knows where everyone is. Josh is back today so I am with him again. Chris is absent again. He wasn't here last weekend either so this is his third missed rehearsal, which is a real shame as he won't be allowed back now, that is if they mean what they say about missing more than two. I do hope they won't enforce that rule too rigidly. Maybe he has dropped out voluntarily. It must be so difficult coming here from Brighton week in week out, not to mention very expensive.

As we stand in our lines, intermittent showers forcing us to either get soaked or wear those horrible ponchos, a little bit more conversation is beginning to develop, mainly between myself, Josh, Gaudi, and a few others whose names I don't yet know. It looks like we are going to be here for a while, but we are quite used to this by now. Jon does what everybody else probably wants to do by asking us all our names. So now I know who Jon, Harry and Joe are. Further back in the line is Elia. As we continue to wait we notice Danny Boyle talking to some people near Vom 5, which is the one closest to us, and wonder why he can't come and chat to us. I tell them about my brief moment with him and the photo I managed to secure. Katie tells us to get prepared for a dry run, which we are going to do shortly. This is where we walk through our county and mime the strike, but we don't actually remove anything. This is just to see the flow of people again. Dry run couldn't be more inappropriate as the showers continue.

About 20 minutes later we are still here, waiting patiently but with more than a hint of frustration. This is now translating into our conversation and there is a bit of cynicism in our attitudes, although this is really just the boredom doing its work. When we do eventually go through the dry run, even that doesn't go very well. People are still getting in each other's way and a lot of us are not quite sure where exactly we are supposed to be going. This is still not working.

Back in our buddy lines we wait expectantly for something else to happen. Katie begins to count out people towards the front of the line and takes them into the county. It looks like she is allocating people to fences, the top ones. This could finally be a positive step.

As she is doing that we see a group of volunteers in black bibs with the letters BRU written on the back. There are about 15 of them. Chris, who clearly knows a bit more about history than I do, tells us that the BRU means Brunel, who is one of the principal figures of the Industrial Revolution. He is the man we saw in the computer simulation. That seems so long ago now. Many hours of rehearsals have passed and it is but a distant memory. I can barely remember how the segment played out, only the main details.

We watch the Brunels as they walk up and down, up and down, doing their own choreography, although I do see some of our own moves in there. It seems like that is all they will be doing. I wonder how they were chosen and which I would prefer to do. At the moment we are here simply to perform a set change. The choreography seems to have been left behind and we are now unsure about where that will fit in, if at all.

When Katie returns she counts out 20 people. All of us are included. She takes us onto the fence line and allocates one between two. All of them have been covered now. Whichever fence we are standing by is the one we will strike. At least we now have a definite task. We have to remember our fence position and number, before moving back into our buddy lines again.

After another round of standing and waiting we are told that we will soon attempt a full strike. Katie confirms all of her fence allocation, of which we are the Fence 20. Other people have been allocated to hedges. On this run we need to clear all of the structures and then start to line up in pairs at the bottom of the fence line. We are going to be called on by Katie in groups, each group going to the next piece of turf to be struck. We will continue like this until it is all removed.

Another development today is that once we have removed turf from our county and have taken it past the fence line, we are to hand it over to a group of volunteers affectionately dubbed the Warriors. Steve kindly explains where this name came from. They are Group 44-FOP, but this isn't snappy enough for Vicky, their leader. So she came up with Warriors, which is also a very motivational name. They have pink bibs with CRW written on them, which I am told stands for Crew, and their job is to take care of the turf once we have removed it. As soon as we hand it over we have no more responsibility over it and we simply walk back to our lines. This should avoid the queues that we experienced last week. If these guys are only going to be carrying turf from A to B that will require some degree of brute strength so the Warriors tag is quite fitting.

The wait is not so long this time and soon enough the music is played, the same looped drum beat from the simulation, and the strike begins. The first stage is relatively easy. We just go to the fence or hedge we have been allocated and strike it in the sequence we have practised. As soon as the turf on the fence line has been struck, and it is time to go to the turf at the top, the saw tooth, and then the dartboard, any organisation slowly begins to unravel. Even though we are split into groups, it isn't clear which piece of turf we are going to so we need to work it out once we are there, which means standing in one place, possibly getting in somebody else's way as they are dragging a piece. Some pieces are clearly too heavy for the number of people allocated so we need to wait for more people.

On the dartboard, we have the same problem, in that it is unclear which way round to strike. Despite all this we somehow complete the strike, although it takes a while and it must look terrible. Steve, being the motivational expert that he is, congratulates us and says it was great, but I think most of us believe otherwise.

We are rewarded by being asked to replace all of the turf and structures in their correct places, which is an arduous task as all of the turf is in a big disorganised pile and it is hard to see which bit goes where. As it is all numbered each piece goes in a certain place. This is like completing a jigsaw on a gigantic scale and requires organisation and a lot of teamwork. We have a plan available which shows where each piece goes. Katie uses this to direct us. If the space left for a piece isn't large enough, it means everything around it has to be repositioned to make space, which could mean adjusting several pieces. There is to be no overlapping as this presents a trip hazard. The more we replace the easier it is to work out where the remaining bits go. We move on to the hedges and fences. Precise placement is key – no gaps in between. This doesn't quite work out so the entire line needs to be moved along to make space for one more. The whole process takes a very long time and it is very laborious. Removing it all is much easier in comparison. Once all is done a few counties are called out and they go on their break.

County Fife remains so we use this time before our break to evaluate the strike we have just done. It is clear that we need to allocate different numbers of people to some of the larger bits of turf at the top of the fence line. We spend a bit of time working out how many people are needed and this is noted, although nobody is specifically allocated as it all depends on who is available after the structures are struck. The pieces on the dartboard need to be removed by first dragging one piece onto the next, to create the pin wheel effect, and then dragged off. This will look particularly attractive from an aerial shot, as will the saw tooth, which we now go back to. We experiment with different ways of striking the turf. So far we have been bringing the top point of each triangle over to meet the base on each piece, thereby creating a set of teeth, hence the name. A few people take the top point and roll it towards the base. Katie quite likes this so we try it again. It doesn't always work properly. The trick seems to be to start tight and continue that way, otherwise it will end up rolling flat rather than being cylindrical, which in turn makes it harder to roll further. It then has to be lifted as we can't drag the rolled pieces. This is also difficult. It is much heavier than it looks.

Soon we are on our break so I go straight to the marquee and eat some fruit that I have brought with me, after checking my sugar level, which is fine. A coffee later and it is time to return. We are graced with a rare spot of sunshine, although puddles still remain. As we stand about waiting for everybody to return and to be instructed by Katie, I see one puddle which has the marquee reflected in it. From the angle at which I am standing all I can see over the entire area of the puddle are the bright yellow and dark blue stripes of the canvas, surrounded by the black of the tiled ground. It really is a wonderful image and I want to take a photo of it, but we are not allowed to take any pictures at all. I don't want to risk being seen and somebody saying something untoward. Those on the other side of it can't see what I can see. It is a real shame but the image etches itself in my memory and I hope I can retain it. The sun doesn't last long and the puddle soon turns black.

Katie asks us to get into our buddy lines and has a message for us. Danny Boyle noticed us rolling the turf and he rather liked it, so much so that he wants us to try this on our next strike with all of our county's turf. Well done to whoever started rolling it first. As we go through the strike we experience the usual disorientation and chaos. Maybe we are getting ever so slightly better but not enough that it is easily discernible, and the new way of striking adds to our predicament. I'm sure dragging was easier than lifting. Some pieces require several people to lift and then support them on our shoulders. Yet our Artistic Director has expressed a preference and we must comply. He even comes over and helps us out with one particularly large and very heavy piece, which he himself acknowledges as being the case. It goes from our shoulders to those of the Warriors and we are unburdened.

Eventually another strike ends and we are soon free to go. A few poor souls are charged with collecting our bibs and handing them in whilst the rest of us queue to get back inside the marquee, the coat racks now being the busiest area of our rehearsal space.

As I walk back to the shuttle buses and queue to get a place on one, I can't help but feel that we are not making any real progress. It all still becomes such a mess as soon as we have removed our fences. There is no real organisation. There must be a better way to do this, establishing a clear strike sequence, rather than seemingly improvising it. Maybe in their eyes we are leaping ahead. After all they are the ones who know, who have done this before, and probably know how to make it work. This is the Olympic Opening Ceremony and failure is never an option. They are going to make this work, but at the moment a lot of us just cannot see how. I take my seat on the bus and wonder what tomorrow will bring.

24

Rehearsal 8

Sunday 10 June 2012
3.00pm – 8.00pm
1:1

After another morning of helping with the kids and a bit of shopping, I once again make my way to rehearsals. As soon as I reach the District Line I see more and more people who are clearly going to Dagenham. Some have their Ceremonies ID clearly displayed around their necks; I prefer to tuck mine into my shirt, not wishing to reveal the very privileged position I am in. Some people are wearing their coveralls, all ready to go as soon as they register for the session. I would say that around ninety per cent of the people who alight at Dagenham East are volunteer performers. We arrive in batches, week after week, and make our way to the car park where a bendy bus is waiting to transport us to the rehearsal site. Dagenham is our host and is now regularly visited by thousands of people who may never have happened across this quite unremarkable part of the host city of the Olympic Games. It is from here that our segment of the Opening Ceremony originates in earnest, and for this Dagenham can be proud.

Just like at every rehearsal, I find a memorable place to put my bag and I get dressed. A coffee follows, plus a bottle of water that goes into the deep pocket of my coveralls. There are large stacks of bottles of Abbey Well water, a sponsor of the Games, at various points around the site. Thousands of bottles are made available every weekend, some left in the sun's path so you need to reach underneath a pile to find a cool one. Up until now the rest of the catering has been the now familiar burger van, which always has queues stretching from it during breaks. Today somebody else has been brought in to capitalise, setting up shop in the coffee tent and selling a selection of sandwiches, salads and snacks. At least there is now a choice and more food available, which will lighten the pressure on the burger van, and the queue time for performers during our rather short break.

After my usual milling around inside the tent and absently watching the same sequence of slides on the overhead screen, Steve announces his presence and welcomes us back for another session. He does a roll call of each county, this time including the Warriors, who give the loudest shout by far. Their camaraderie is conveyed in their collective cheer, and it is easy to discern their sense of pride in the job they are doing.

Following on from yesterday's experiment, the main announcement is that rolling is the new dragging. This has come directly from Danny, so this is how all counties will strike turf from now on. I do remember hearing Danny say that it looked so much better when he was observing yesterday. We therefore have to perform some strikes this afternoon with this as the main focus to see how it will work across the FOP.

Out we go into our counties and whilst everybody is arriving, people dotted around our area, I take the opportunity to re-familiarise myself with the layout of our fences, hedges and turf. I feel that I should know the number sequence at least, even though I only strike one fence before moving on to turf.

After a quick walk round Katie asks us to gather in the usual place, just to the right of the fence line, for a briefing and to maybe take a look at the plan again. I am beginning to grow quite fond of Katie. There is no shortage of opinions and ideas of how we could or should be doing this. But as with most things there needs to be a leader and Katie is that person for us. She is the one who holds the pieces together, more than a hundred of them, and although some of us may beg to differ, I know I couldn't do what she is doing. I wouldn't want to be in her shoes. She has a very difficult task and I respect her for her efforts.

Soon we are in our buddy lines again and the long wait begins before we go through our usual routine of dry runs and full strikes, with more need for patience in between. Whilst the rest of us wait, me included, Katie takes a group of people on to the dartboard to go through who will strike what and how exactly. To ease our boredom we chat and play games on Jon's iPhone. There is little else to do. A shower here and a shower there adds to our frustration, even more so because by the time those who wish to have put their ponchos on, practically fighting with it in the wind, the shower is over. It is difficult to tolerate them if they serve no other purpose than to flap around in the dry wind. So it's best not to bother, defeating the purpose of having them. A minor dilemma that is heightened in the current state of affairs.

We are going to do a strike soon. We have heard this before. Soon means anything but. A few words of cynicism offer scant relief to this stagnant monotony. Something of more interest is that Josh has heard there will be live drummers encircling the entire Stadium. They will get to play for the duration of the Ceremony. How incredibly fortunate they are. I feel just a little envious as I stand in this car park in Dagenham waiting for something to happen, just as Chris arrives. I thought he would have been told to leave, as he has missed the last three rehearsals. He says that he spoke to them and explained his unavoidable situation and they relented, although it wasn't actually such a big issue for them. Is this fair to the hopefuls on the reserve list? Is that list in fact as healthy as they have claimed? I don't give it too much thought – I'm glad he is back. Clearly the threat of being thrown out if more than two rehearsals are missed was an idle one. The further we go the less likely they are to fulfil their promise. If too many people from the reserve list join to replace those who have been here since day one, we may never pin our segment down.

The strike we were promised earlier does finally happen, but it's just a dry run. It does seem strange to mime rolling turf and then picking it up. If somebody was to look out of their window now, they would see hundreds of people walking in lines with one arm raised up at shoulder height. But we go through the motions, they see how it looks, and they make their notes, leaving us none the wiser on how we are doing. Back to the buddy lines.

Diane turns up and takes the opportunity to give us some haka practice. Even though we spent some time on this last week, it still seems like too long ago. She tries different things – falling in, taking our cue from the person in front, and staggered starts. She tells us that we must always be on the beat, even when we are stationary, so our feet are always moving. Whenever we are queuing to go back on to the ramp, as long as there are a few of us in the group, one of the people at the front should begin Work Prep, doing it twice, and the people behind fall in. The same goes for when we are in our county and waiting to strike a piece of turf. Just go into Work Prep if you are caught standing still. I personally think that will just add to our confusion, and she acknowledges what I have just thought, but we just need to go into the routine if appropriate, without thinking about it.

Before long the instruction is given to standby for a full strike. The music is cued and we filter into Fife, taking our positions as usual. Structures are cleared with little fuss, but that's the easy part. Rolling is the new dragging, I remind myself as I walk back up the fence line, keeping to the right, and stepping over a roll of turf as I do so. The piece I do with a few others is more flat than it is cylindrical once it's been rolled, or rather folded. The short intermittent showers have dampened the turf enough to make it much heavier than usual and as we lift it onto our shoulders it drips all over us. This is not only difficult and disorganised, but also dirty now. It doesn't take long for our yellow gloves to get soaked. At times a queue forms as we wait to hand over to the Warriors, but the turf doesn't get any lighter. They have their own organisational issues and we are left to carry the burden quite literally.

When returning to our lines to wait for a clear path so we can go and strike another piece of turf, not a single person takes the initiative and begins Work Prep. This was expected. Amidst the chaos and confusion, Diane's words are all but forgotten or ignored. Nobody plucks up the courage to just go into the sequence. So we continue, rolling and striking, until a couple of minutes of Hail Mary sees us to the end.

That was not great. Time for a reset. There is no time to dwell on what we could've done better. As we are putting the turf back on to the fence line, the three very long pieces, the middle one of which is no longer peeled back, but rolled like the rest, somebody makes the very valid and obvious point that these pieces are far too long. Katie says that if we want to cut them in half, then she can arrange it now. Easy. By next week, there will even be Velcro in place where it's been cut to keep it together and stop it from sliding about before we strike it, as it will be on a ramp of course.

Once we have reset we are allowed to go on a break. Although they are supposed to be 20 minutes and no more, this rule is seldom followed by all. People are still queuing to buy food when we should be back on the FOP, as announced by Steve. But as if fully acknowledging that we are giving up many hours of our time for nothing, and that without us there is no show, he is as patient and as courteous as ever.

When most of us have returned we are asked to gather round a guy who is introduced as Pete. He is a familiar face, getting involved in a lot of the directing of traffic, but we haven't had any contact with him yet. He is going to give us a quick tutorial on setting up and operating ratchets, although only a few of us will be required to do so as there are only four in our county, two people per ratchet. They are not real, just replicas, so are very light. They do look very impressive. There is a bar on both sides. Each person needs to pull the bar out, slot it into a hole on the short ends, and then it is ready to operate by moving the bar back and forth. They are going to be positioned on all four sides of the chimneys and the idea is that we will ratchet these towering structures up out of the ground.

Back to our buddy lines now and more waiting. We are told we are going to fit in one more strike today. We have our IEMs on now as the music is going to be played through them. Steve comes on and asks us to move to the outside of what is known as the M25, which is the path that runs all the way around the main set. We have to move to that area and then crouch down, or make ourselves small, as he puts it. This is going to be our creep position. At the beginning of the strike, before we move on to the ramp, we hear the sound of a tree being uprooted all the way up on the Tor, which has hitherto been of little significance, just something that we were told the position of in our second rehearsal at this site. It is more or less on the opposite side to Fife, and it is towards this that we must look when given the cue from our creep positions. As we slowly stand up, all eyes must be on the Tor. We are wondering what the sound is and there is bewilderment on our faces, as we fall into our buddy lines, still looking in the same direction. We go through this once or twice, before making ourselves small again. This time we are going to go from our creep positions, into our buddy lines, and straight into the strike. This is an exciting development. There is now a touch of drama to what we are doing.

By the time the music plays on our earphones, the tree has been uprooted and the Warriors are making their way down the Tor and round to the counties, except that here it is as flat as a pancake. We begin our strike. Josh and I take our fence to the dolly and place it as directed, then walk round the back of it and join the line that has formed, before returning to strike some turf. On this occasion it rolls a bit better and this in turn makes it a lot less cumbersome when lifting. I am right behind him still. The Warriors take our turf and we walk back again, only this time we are asked to pick a ratchet and take it to where we are told by Pete. Now this is interesting and indeed different.

When given the cue by Pete, we set up the ratchet as instructed earlier, and we begin to operate it. In theory this is when our chimney will begin to rise out of the trap, causing more than a few jaws to drop

I imagine. We are both on different ratchets, but we spend the rest of the strike just pushing and pulling the lever, back and forth, back and forth. All around me turf is being struck, chaos ensues, green turns to black, and still I push and pull. A group of people are directed to do their choreography on the side. The rows increase as we move into Hail Mary and only a few pieces are left, requiring fewer people.

Another strike ends. That was much more enjoyable. Pete asks the bib numbers of all of the ratchet operators and jots them down in his notebook. All of us ensure we see our numbers with our own eyes before we are satisfied that he has us down. If I can't be on top of a chimney then operating a ratchet is the next best thing. At some point surely all eyes will be on them, or so I believe. I do now recall seeing people doing something beside the chimneys in the computer simulation. This is what they must have been doing and Josh and I will be one of them. That has heightened our moods immeasurably, and we now feel like we are definitely doing something worthwhile, rather than just moving a fence and some turf.

We both discuss how the strike went. It wasn't great by any means. At one point I heard somebody (Lucy, I learn later) exclaim "absolute chaos". She wasn't far wrong. We all want to believe that this is beginning to work, that we are making progress, but the turmoil belies the dream of perfection and utter spectacle. Nonetheless we somehow manage to clear the FOP yet again; it just looks and feels terrible, plain and simple.

After bib collection, this time more organised, Fife is announced as one of the counties that will be issued with boots today. We must queue for them in the marquee. They come with a friendly note from the costume team:

> In this bag is a pair of boots matching the size you were fitted with. We are giving them to you early so you have time to break them in and make them as comfy as possible.
>
> These are your show boots and are very precious so look after them – however, we need them to look as 'distressed' as possible so please do the gardening in them and really scuff them up!!
>
> IT IS NOW YOUR RESPONSIBILITY TO BRING THEM TO ALL FUTURE REHEARSALS AND PERFORMANCES.
>
> Many Thanks and Happy Industrialising!
>
> Love from the Costume Team x

25

A Secret Out And A Secret Kept

Tuesday 12 June 2012

I don't have a garden at home so I couldn't muddy my boots that way. On Monday it was raining so I decided to begin breaking them in – maybe I could get them a little dirty at lunchtime in the park near work on the way to buying my lunch. They were quite comfortable for the first few hours in the morning, but this soon changed as the day progressed. By the time I arrived home in the evening the bottom of my right leg, just below my shin, was rather sore. The left leg was fine. Any attempt at getting my boots dirty had failed. I decided that I would have to just suffer more to break them in, otherwise it would take longer, and so I wore them again on Tuesday. My right leg got worse today. I was finding it increasingly difficult to walk in them, and by the time I was on the walk home, every single step I took was painful. At one point I was thinking that I wouldn't make it home, or would at the very least have to remove the boots and walk in my socks. Somehow I did make it back and took the decision to not wear them for the rest of the week. I had a 10K run to do on Sunday.

Earlier in the day an event of quite some significance took place. Danny Boyle revealed to the press the set that would comprise his Green and Pleasant Land for the Opening Ceremony, as he called it. This was rather unexpected and I discovered the news second hand. He had given much away: the use of farm animals, some of the activities that would be taking place in the set before the Ceremony proper, the ringing of the bell, the representation of Glastonbury Tor, the moshpits, the real grass, clouds that would produce rain. It seemed like nothing had been left out. Initially I felt quite disappointed at this revelation to the world, but of course he was the Artistic Director and he knew best. It was his show, his baby. He could do whatever he wished.

This did now give me a license to talk about it a little with my friends and family. I emailed a link to the story on the BBC website to members of my family, showing them the set I would be performing in. My sister asked if I'd met Danny Boyle. I said I had done briefly and he was very friendly. Some of my work colleagues speculated about what the show could entail, they questioned me, tried to tease information out of me, but I revealed nothing. I have to say I rather enjoyed this scrutiny.

One girl found the whole idea ludicrous and a recipe for disaster. It was the use of animals that worried her: 70 sheep, 12 horses, 3 cows, 2 goats, 10 chickens, 10 ducks, 9 geese and 3 sheepdogs. I revealed that we still hadn't worked with any animals, with a little over a month before the Ceremony, which she found hilarious and only added to her disbelief. She also offered my favourite reaction from every comment I'd read and heard: how on earth were they going to clear that set and get the Stadium ready for the Athletics a couple of days after the Ceremony.

That did indeed offer me some comfort. Of course people now knew what the set would look like but they had no idea what we were going to do with it. I'm sure nobody suspected that we were going to remove the entire Green and Pleasant Land and make way for chimneys and industry. That was still our secret and that was going to cause enough wonder to silence the sceptics, of which there were many. Lots of people concluded that rural England was the main image we were going to project to the world. We knew that they would be proven wrong, but we still had to make it look impressive and awe-inspiring. We were a long way off at present.

Wednesday 13 June 2012

Today I received an update about my Games Maker role:

> You have recently been invited to Venue-Specific Training at the IBC/MPC. This invite was sent in error, and you do not need to attend this event.
>
> All the security volunteers who work at the Main Press Centre also work in the Common Domain, where the demand for volunteers is greatest. You will need to attend venue training for the Olympic Park Common Domain for which you will have received an invitation. We have put together a special blended training session just for MPC Volunteers.

The Venue-Specific Training in the Common Domain will be held in the Copper Box, one of our fantastic new venues, where Modern Pentathlon will be held. Since you also work in the MPC you will receive a separate tour of that venue and a specific briefing about your role in the security screening area.

Friday 15 June 2012

As a subscriber to Underworld's mailing list, I received a long overdue newsletter from them today. Well, they'd been rather busy, as they explained in part of their mailer:

"As work continues at a frenetic pace on the Olympic Opening Ceremony, it feels like the thing that is dominating our lives is the one thing we can't really talk about – so here's Danny talking a bit more about the show on Tuesday."

There was a link to an interview on the BBC website with Huw Edwards, which had been posted with the article about the set. They went on to say:

"With around 6 weeks to go, Rick and the Underworld team are flat out dividing their time between the studio and various rehearsal sites. Full-scale production rehearsals with thousands of volunteers are already under way and from next week the Olympic Stadium becomes home.

It's been quite a journey so far – one we hope to be able to tell more of once all is said and done, but for now, Mum's the word and it's back to that dark room (at least it's keeping us out of the rain!)"

They included a couple of photos of the Stadium from the outside and it did give a tantalising look at what was in store for us.

26

Rehearsal 9

Saturday 16 June 2012
3.00pm – 8.00pm
1:1

This is our final weekend in Dagenham, and it's going to be a busy one. I finally managed to go for a short run on Thursday after work in training for my 10K run on Sunday morning. That's not exactly good preparation – I only did about 15 minutes in total – but that is about as much as I have been able, or willing, to fit in amongst rehearsals. I need to try and get some sponsorship money today from the guys in Fife. I'm sure people will be happy to sponsor me; at least I hope they will. I just have to ask – something that I am absolutely not good at. I already know I will probably crumble when faced with the incredibly difficult challenge of asking somebody to sponsor me. I can't let this opportunity pass me by, however. I'm also hoping I can get talking to Danny Boyle to see if he would be willing to make a donation. Surely he couldn't refuse. It would be bad PR! Exploitation for a worthy cause. So I set off for rehearsals with my sponsorship form in my back pocket, wearing my boots again, despite my run tomorrow. I reckon they will be okay today as I may just have broken them in. My leg has settled back down so I'm no longer limping.

Out of Dagenham East station for the penultimate time. We all cross the road and pass the same volunteer who is always in position on the island at the crossing. I spare a thought for this selfless person whose job it is to simply prevent people blocking the traffic when the lights go green, for hours on end, every weekend. He watches us go past without a word of thanks from most of us for giving up his time to perform such a mundane, but necessary, task.

There are volunteers who stand outside the station and are responsible for even less, no longer needing to direct people as we all know where to go. Yet they give up their weekend to do just that. The volunteers who direct us onto the buses, the ones who welcome us to

145

the site, those who line the route to registration, asking us to keep to the path, often being ignored, the people who register us, who would surely love to change places with us, watching us go and rehearse to be a part of Olympic history, the ones who re-staple our laminates to our bibs, a service which I once needed, the issuers of our bibs, the lovely people who prepare our hot drinks, pre-fill the cups with powdered coffee, tea and hot chocolate, re-fill the hot water, clean up the mess that some of us make even though there is ample space in the bins which are within arm's reach – they are all the unsung heroes.

Steve once asked us to thank anybody who is wearing a luminous yellow bib, as they are volunteers getting paid nothing to help make everything we see possible. This was at 3 Mills. I wonder how many of us have ignored this request, or have long forgotten his words. I am no better than any of those who have thanked nobody. We all too often take for granted these selfless people. We forget to give to them what we would love to receive if we were in their place. We have given up a lot of time too, but we are going to get so much in return. They will have very little to show for their time, except a claim that they were somehow involved. They will remain unsung heroes. I must thank them from time to time, as often as it crosses my mind and I am presented with the opportunity. Even a greeting would be nice rather than absent-mindedly walking past without even two simple words. I will be better from now on.

I enter our marquee and today one side of it has been taken over by children and their parents. Members of the Mass Team are directing them. I hear they are part of the NHS section. I immediately recall the hospital bed in 3 Mills during our first rehearsal there. Apparently they are going to be on the other FOP this afternoon, rehearsing their own routine. There are lots of hospital beds, just waiting for their occupants. I'm not quite sure what their segment is about but I do remember seeing lots of women with NHS bibs in previous rehearsals. It looks like they are going to be shown looking after children then. This must be incredible for the kids, being part of the greatest sporting event in the world at such a young age. I go outside to catch a glimpse of what is happening on their FOP but there is not much to see at the moment. I will try to take a look later.

Most of today is spent in much the same way as usual. At the beginning each member of the Mass Team took a count of how many people were present in their counties, and then proceeded to move people around to even out the numbers where there were too many absentees. It took quite some time, but in this fashion we had some guests in our buddy lines. Joe hasn't turned up for a couple of weeks. It looks like he won't be back. Poor guy just has too many work commitments. He may have just bowed out as a result of the frustration that a lot of us have experienced over the last few rehearsals.

The first strike we do is as chaotic as usual. We just need to go through the motions I suppose and do the best we can. The Brunels now make a regular appearance, although they stick to the M25 going around the main set. There are also a group of women who I believe are Suffragettes, carrying a large banner around with them and chanting. They often rehearse whilst we are waiting for something to happen, walking around the set in their group. The music played is now more of a track, not just a beat. There is a section in the middle which is mainly a whistling melody when we have to all stand still and stop what we are doing. It lasts one minute. When the full music begins again, so do we.

As ever we reset when all is completed. We encounter the same problems with the piles of turf and not knowing where each piece goes, all of them in random heaps. Some people nominate themselves to only consult the map and direct those of us with turf in our hands, which works quite well. We have a system! I'm not sure how long it takes us but it seems to be quicker than last time.

Later on, just before we do our next strike, some of us are called over to help out another county with their beam engine. A few people have already been briefed and it's up to them to explain. Jon and Harry are with me, but before either of us can get a full picture of what we are supposed to be doing, we are called back into our buddy lines to prepare for the strike. All we know is that once we have done the first of our turf we have to break from our usual path and take some traffic cones and lengths of wood, representing guard rails and tracks, to a designated area of our neighbouring county. That is where the beam engine will rise out of a trap. What we have to do once there, we have no idea, but we will just have to improvise.

We begin in our creep positions, making ourselves small, and then falling into our lines as the tree is uprooted. Everything that follows is the same as ever, except for our brief diversion to help with the beam engine, although most of us don't quite know what we are doing, except setting down whichever piece we are carrying. We spend the rest of the strike doing choreography. I am a bit concerned about the ratchet now. I thought I was going to be doing that every time. Pete took our names. I should have been on a ratchet. Concern becomes disappointment as I realise that I may have been replaced as quickly as I was chosen. Two strikes now without a ratchet, and no coincidence.

The rehearsal is more or less over and I haven't asked a single person to sponsor me. I knew this would happen. I did mention my run to Elia during our break and she offered to sponsor me without me prompting her so that is something. She also thought I was crazy. That could be true. I probably won't get back home until around 10pm tonight. I have to be in Regent's Park no later than 9am, travelling all the way across London on a Sunday, to meet and coordinate the team I have organised, made up of some of my print contacts, who have very kindly agreed to run with me and raise money for Macmillan Cancer Support, the charity I work for.

I have no idea how the run will go, how difficult I will find it, or indeed how easy it will be to get everybody together. I'm going to have to take tomorrow morning in stages, as I often do when faced with something that takes me out of my comfort zone. Sitting on the train and contemplating this, I am surrounded by a sea of Ceremony performers, some of them obvious, some of them not so, but all of us sharing a common secret about what will happen to the Green and Pleasant Land. It's nice to be in the know.

As soon as I arrive home I have to get my kit and race information together and pack it for the morning. The kids are asleep so I've not been able to spend any time with them since leaving for my rehearsal today. Ever since the afternoon sessions this has been the common trend, every single weekend. This is indeed a sacrifice of time spent with my family. I am usually the one to tuck my kids in, put them to sleep, yet I've been missing this all too often of late. I wonder how many more mums and dads have missed their children today, all in the name of the Opening Ceremony of the Olympic Games.

My mind returns to the task at hand as I consider everything I need for tomorrow: running kit and extra Macmillan T-shirts for the team, coveralls, no boots as I'll wear my running shoes the whole day, waterproof jacket just in case, a few snacks to keep my sugar levels up, and a couple of books to do some research for something I am doing in my spare time. Having somehow squeezed everything into my bag, I catch up on my daily prayers. By the time I make it to bed it's past midnight. I feel exhausted. It doesn't take me long to fall asleep.

27

Rehearsal 10

Sunday 17 June 2012
3.00pm – 8.00pm
1:1

Waking up all too soon I silently acknowledge that this is going to be a long day as my feet swing round and hit the floor. I am in no mood for a run but there is no escaping this. Besides it is all my doing. One stage at a time then. I take comfort from the fact that by midday it will all be over – just a few hours away. There is, however, lots to do and achieve in those short hours.

Outside the weather is glorious. It is warm and sunny, just perfect for a run in Regent's Park. My regular commute by cycle is the only thing that is going to get me through this in one piece. Though I have no business doing so, as I have barely trained, I set myself a target of under an hour. If I can do that I will be very pleased indeed.

Fast forward to 9.55am and I am standing in the starting group with my fellow runners (and walkers, bless them), all ready to begin, having found and assembled everybody, and arranged for a group photo of the six of us in our Macmillan T-shirts. The photo will hopefully be published in Print Week, accompanying a short bite-sized article reporting on our efforts, in the hope that it will raise awareness of my charity within the Print industry. I have at least been promised this after a speculative email I sent to one of the editors.

This is the reason why I am standing in this place at this time, waiting for a horn to blow which will kick start the event. I am in for three laps round one of the less busy areas of the park. I have no idea how this is going to go as I have never run this distance before. Maybe my knees won't be able to take it. My lungs could well explode. I'll just have to stop and rest. What more could I possibly expect. The horn blows. After exactly 59 minutes and 45 seconds I pass the finish line, having stopped and walked just once for a few minutes. My commute clearly does more for me than I could ever imagine. With a sprint finish included I am really rather pleased with myself. Three of us finish together, another soon follows, and the two walkers are heroically battling on. I take the opportunity to relax after my efforts as I wait for them to finish, a great sense of relief engulfing me now that it is all over and I can reflect on what I have achieved in putting together my small team. From an expectant email a few months ago to the finish line today. This reminds me of another activity I am heavily involved in at the moment, although the finish line is a long way off and we are currently undergoing an intense course of training. The team is exponentially bigger and media coverage on an infinitely larger scale is guaranteed. It is safe to say that most of the people within my field of vision at this precise moment, made up of spectators, runners, organisers, marshals, park-goers and their families, could well be watching this other event next month. And I will be part of it.

My thoughts are interrupted as the final two members of my team approach the finish line, two hours after they started. Their families are waiting and they deserve every ounce of applause and praise that they receive. It is time for me to express my gratitude and continue my day. After getting changed I make my way to the nearest park exit and walk to Camden where I find a coffee shop that has seats available and enjoy a well deserved latte whilst I do my research.

A couple of hours later, feeling revived, I grab some lunch, which I eat on the walk to Mornington Crescent, and I go directly to the last rehearsal at 1:1 in Dagenham – the final stage of my busy day. So far the sun has held out but it is getting very slightly cloudy now. I hope we are not going to experience a meteorological descent into the wet and cold after such an auspicious bout of sunshine. Any negative thoughts are soon dispelled upon reaching the overground portion of the District line where a trainload of Ceremony performers feel the sun's rays shining on their faces.

I arrive a little late today, and although I know I won't have missed anything, I feel the urge to hurry along and go through my usual routine, not feeling completely relaxed until I am ready and have a coffee in hand. I have my camera today, mainly because I wanted to take photos at my run this morning, but I definitely have a mind to take some pictures at the rehearsal. It is the last opportunity I will ever get at this site and it will be a shame to walk away with no visual memories at all. If other people take photos, I will definitely do so too, so I keep my camera with me.

During Steve's introductory portion today, we get to see an

exclusive time lapse video of our set being prepared in the Stadium. With less than a week before we are due to move in, as it were, they have a lot to prepare but they are getting there and I am sure they will serve us well before we take up residence. The end of the video is met with cheers and applause, and this is repeated as we go through the now customary roll call, the Warriors always a few decibels above the rest of us.

Today the performers in the Green and Pleasant Land segment, which comes before ours, are present as we make our way onto the FOP. Their bibs are lime green and have GPL printed on them. They are about to finish and the team wants to take the opportunity to go through the transition from their segment to ours. This is what we will concentrate on at the beginning. Some classical music plays on the PA. The voice in our IEMs tells us that we are only going to go until we are told to stop, which will be very early in the strike. I'm wondering when we will see the sheep, as they are supposed to be exiting through our fence line. Surely we need to get used to them being here.

Just as we walk onto the FOP, the GPL performers leave, taking a few of their props with them. As soon as we all reach our fences or hedges, we are told to stop, the transition complete. The GPL volunteers have finished and now our rehearsal begins in earnest. By now we know that there is little point in bracing ourselves for anything as people are scattered about and chatting amongst themselves.

There are lots of volunteers with cameras, and they are freely snapping away. Groups of people are posing in full view of the Mass Team and other officials. I am not the only one determined to get a visual record of our time here. With safety in numbers I follow suit and take a few shots of the FOP and various key aspects of the rehearsal site like the shelter, marquee, and viewing tower. Josh takes a couple of photos of me with the FOP in the background. It's a shame that puddle, which I can still remember, isn't here today! Over to the side I see our ratchets. Not only do I take a photo of them, but I also think that I only got to operate them once. Just another rehearsal memory. Katie eventually asks us to gather round for a quick briefing, which she gives, before being called away.

After some waiting we are asked to move into our counties and find a space somewhere. We are going to do a warm-up. Steve explained last weekend that from past experience they have been able to keep injuries at a minimum by ensuring people are suitably stretched and prepared for lifting. One of the dance captains or Mass Team stood in the centre of the FOP atop one of the platforms and gave us directions through our IEMs. I couldn't actually see her so was just following the people in front of me. I found the exercise just a little tedious, but I suppose the reason for it was perfectly valid.

On this occasion I really don't feel like I need a warm-up after my run this morning. My calves are aching a little, but not as much as earlier. We begin with stretching and just loosening up our muscles, just like last week, only this time there is music on our IEMs. I don't recognise any of the songs played, until I hear the opening groove of 'Are You Ready (Do The Bus Stop)' by The Fatback Band. Excellent choice! Now I'm beginning to enjoy this. She has us nicely warmed up so we are just going to have a bit of a dance, which she teaches us step by step as the track plays. It is very simple, but a lot of fun. For the entire duration of the track we all repeat the routine and by the time we are on the third or fourth round, most of us are having a good time. I don't think I will ever forget all of us gathered in County Fife listening to and performing to the funk and groove that is the Bus Stop. I'm sure this is all I will be able to think of when listening to the song again. Another lasting musical memory. The steps we are taught are already imprinted in my brain.

After the warm up we are told we are going to do a full strike soon. Some of us take a seat on the turf and wait for something to happen. I chat to Jon, just small talk about what we do when we are not rehearsing. We are interrupted by the sound of drummers. It looks like we have more company this evening. The same drummers that Josh mentioned a few rehearsals ago are now descending upon us and lining the entire circumference of the FOP, just like they will be doing on show night. There are 1,000 of them, made up of men and women of varying ages. I am told that a lot of them are not musicians of any sort, yet they have somehow been given the huge responsibility of drumming throughout the entire Opening Ceremony. I am once again envious of these people who are banging out a repetitive beat on upturned plastic and metal buckets, even large garden bins, all hanging from their necks. Whatever happened to nice shiny drums? Surely this is going to look cheap and nasty – in front of the world. Maybe they haven't been supplied with the real drums yet. I find it hard to believe that bins and buckets is the choice of instrument.

Regardless of this, the sound they are producing is quite incredible. Listening to 2,000 sticks forming a rhythmic perimeter around us all is an experience I can't wait to relive in the Stadium, which is not so far off now.

We move into our buddy lines, only a loose formation, and I finally see Gaudi, my new buddy after the change in numbers. He asks if I picked up my accreditation for the Stadium this week. I haven't received any emails about this. In talking to other people I learn that the emails are being staggered, so plenty of people haven't picked up their accreditation either. Some people also mention an email about the Stadium rehearsals, giving us all of the information we need for next week, but I haven't seen it. Something to look forward to when I get home if I have time. As we wait, the drummers rehearse, playing their beat over and over.

Soon we are asked to move into our creep positions. We sit here for quite some time. I take the opportunity to finally mention my run this morning and ask if anybody could sponsor me. Not many people hear me, although this is entirely my fault. A less reserved person would go round individually and ask, or shout out to everybody. I get four people to agree. Such a wasted opportunity, especially since I have come to rehearsals after doing the run this morning – a perfect way of trying to win favour with those reluctant to part with their money.

All thoughts are cast aside as the same classical music we heard yesterday plays on the PA and in our IEMs. As the sound of the tree being uprooted is heard we break from our creep positions and slowly form our buddy lines, always looking towards the Tor, wondering what is happening. The drummers around us are going to be part of our strike today, providing the backing for the track on our ear phones. A few quick, sharp bangs of the drums and the full beat kicks in. The music is also undergoing development and we are slowly moving towards something more complete. It is quite special to witness firsthand the stages the music has been through, from a basic beat to what we are listening to now, the backdrop for our strike.

This time I have neither beam engine nor ratchet duties, so after my fence is off, it is turf all the way for me. The section in the middle, where the music breaks down into a slow whistling melody, begins and we are cued to all stand still and put down any turf we are holding. This section will represent a minute's silence, and it is at this point that the soldiers will make their way to the poppy field, which is in a neighbouring county. Going from the cacophony of the drumming and music to this whistling is quite powerful, the motionless silence of every single volunteer enhancing the poignancy of the moment,

153

despite its relative brevity.

When the drums begin to blare around us again, we continue our work. By this time we should soon be approaching Hail Mary. It hasn't been a complete disaster so far, although we are still nowhere near being able to claim that it has gone well. We are still encountering problems which soon lead to relative chaos, but I think we are improving ever so slightly. Steve, as always, thinks we are all great. He is far too kind.

After the strike, which also signals the end of the very relaxed rehearsal, I take a couple of photos of the FOP. I now have before and after shots. Soon we will be leaving this place, never to come back again. I need to get some more photos.

After gathering my things, I take a quick walk around, snapping various things to help me remember the Dagenham rehearsal site: a pile of turf, the IEM trolley, the inside of the marquee. In doing so I notice Danny Boyle talking to somebody just past Vom 3. I am about 20 metres away, far enough to get a decent photo unnoticed using my zoom. I turn to walk away but realise that this is the perfect opportunity to ask Danny to sponsor me. He is still chatting to the volunteer and nobody else is vying for his attention, nobody seeking an autograph or photo. Without thinking I walk over and linger nearby, not wishing to interrupt. Somebody else has thought the same, but he only wants a photo, which he is granted. As Danny starts to walk off I get his attention and he turns back towards me.

"Hi Danny, I'm Nadeem," I say, offering him my hand, which he shakes.

"Hi," he replies, an expectant look on his face. This is not the time for hesitation. He has lent me his ears, even though he must have far more pressing matters to attend to. Our rehearsal is over, but his day is surely not going to end just yet. He wants me to get on with it.

"Is there... any chance you could sponsor me?" My hands are clasped as I await a response.

"Oh? Who's it for?"

"For Macmillan Cancer Support."

"Oh, right, I know them," he says in a positive tone. This is promising. I have his interest. "What are you doing?"

"Well, I actually did a 10K run this morning." A marathon would have been much more impressive, but 10K it is.

"Really? Go on then, how much do you want?"

"Well, whatever you like. Just £1 if you want." I mean this

wholeheartedly. Every penny is important to us. "It's up to you. I've got my form with me…"

"OK, let's do it now then."

This is great. Enthused, I quickly get my form out of my bag along with a pen, and hand them to him.

"I feel a bit cheeky, asking you like this, but it's all for charity."

"How much did you do again?"

"10K." He deliberates for a few moments, repeating the distance to himself, considering an amount to give.

"Er…I'll give you _____." That's great, I think, as he starts to fill in the form. All of my sponsorship so far has been done online so his will be the first name on my form.

"I'll just put 3 Mills," he says, as he comes to the address.

"That's fine, I don't want your home address!" It's so cool that Danny Boyle is sponsoring me.

When filling in the amount he mulls over this, confirming with himself the money he has promised to give, before writing _____.

"Do you want the money now?"

"Well, you can give it to me later if you like."

"I may as well give it to you now." He reaches into his pocket and pulls out _____, handing it over with the form, which I take a quick look at. I have to ask him this.

"Are you a UK taxpayer?"

"Yes." he replies.

"Could you tick this box?" I indicate the Gift Aid box which will give us more money at no cost to him.

"Oh, it's getting a bit dodgy now," he says in a humorous tone. I laugh at this, as does Toby, who has seen what is happening and is looking over.

"No, no, it's all legitimate," I assure him, smiling. He ticks the box and I thank him more than once, before leaving him to his business. I walk away feeling very pleased with myself, carefully securing the sponsorship form and the money in my pocket. What a nice man he is.

After taking a few final photos, I leave 1:1. The site is still teeming with people. Already it feels like we have reached a milestone in our rehearsals. Next week we move to our final venue. The one everybody is excited about. Saturday couldn't come soon enough.

When I arrive home it is dark, even though it is the height of summer. It has indeed been a very long day, but a very eventful and rewarding one. The kids are both asleep. I haven't seen them since yesterday afternoon. It naturally hits me more so than it did yesterday. They have been testing Misbah's patience, as putting them both to sleep is no easy task. I peer into their bedroom and watch them in their deep slumber. Holding the door open I think about how great it will be to one day tell them about rehearsals for the Opening Ceremony. Hopefully they will feel proud that their dad was part of this incredible event and with a bit of luck they will be able to see me in the Ceremony, maybe only for a split second, but it will be me. For this I am missing them all too often.

Tomorrow evening after work I have some errands to run, so I will be back late, probably after they are asleep, meaning I may not be able to spend any time with them until Tuesday evening, more than three days after I saw them yesterday. Misbah tells me my eldest was asking where I was today. I smile a guilt-ridden smile. I tell myself that it's only for a few more weeks. I leave them both to rest and spend some time with my wife who is getting used to me not being around for most of the week. On Saturday I have an all day rehearsal. That is going to be salt in the wound for her. I have no time to reflect on this as I go to bed feeling spent. I fall asleep almost immediately.

28

Updates And Tickets

Monday 18 June 2012

Whilst at work the following day I managed to find the time to read the email that had been sent late on Saturday night about our move to the Stadium. This was a significant stage in the rehearsal process, and something that everybody had been waiting for. The email contained very clear directions to the Olympic Park through Westfield, plus other relevant information:

> We have finally reached that moment where we take the show to the Stadium! The following information is very important. The Stadium security is very tight and we cannot admit anyone who does not have their ceremonies ID, and then the additional Ceremonies accreditation after 16 July.
>
> There are two phases for accreditation:
> 1. 18 June – 15 July: You will be able to use just your CER pass as per your rehearsals at 3 Mills and Dagenham.
> 2. 16 July – 27 July: You will also need your Games Time accreditation. You will be sent information about how to collect this in a separate email from UDAC.
>
> Your ceremonies ID and accreditation will allow you access to the Olympic Park only for your scheduled rehearsal times. If you do not bring your Ceremonies ID and accreditation you will not be allowed into the Olympic Park. There are no exceptions to this. You will be sent home to retrieve it so you may miss your rehearsal.
> A PSA is a Pedestrian Screening Area located at your Stadium entrance. When you have shown your accreditation you will enter the search area, similar to airports.
> Any bags you have will be x-rayed.
> You will pass through a metal detector.

You may be subject to additional random searches.
Do not bring any food with you.
Meal packs will be provided to all cast when they attend a rehearsal at the Stadium. Tea and coffee will be available during the breaks. Bottled water is available at all times.

The rehearsal schedule now looked like this:

DATE	TIME	VENUE DETAILS/NOTES
Sat 23 June	09:00 to 17:30	Stadium Orientation + Rehearsal
Sun 24 June	09:00 to 13:00	Stadium
Fri 29 June	17:30 to 22:00	Stadium
Sat 30 June	09:00 to 17:30	Stadium
Sun 01 July	09:00 to 13:00	Stadium
Sat 07 July	13:00 to 22:00	Stadium
Sun 08 July	09:00 to 13:00	Stadium
Tue 10 July	17:30 to 22:00	Stadium
Sat 14 July	09:00 to 17:30	Stadium COMPULSORY
Wed 18 July	12:00 to 22:00	Stadium COMPULSORY
Fri 20 July	TBC to 22:00	Stadium COMPULSORY
Sat 21 July	TBC to EOS*	Stadium Dress Rehearsal COMPULSORY
Mon 23 July	TBC to EOS*	Stadium Dress Rehearsal COMPULSORY
Wed 25 July	TBC to EOS*	Stadium Dress Rehearsal COMPULSORY
Fri 27 July	TBC to EOS*	Stadium SHOW DAY

*EOS – End of Segment – Group 44 performs early in the show which has a scheduled start time of 9.00pm. When your segment has finished performing, you will get out of costume and be released.

There were now no timing gaps in the rehearsal schedule. Some very long sessions were planned in the last few days, which was not only exciting but also made me wonder if that would simply mean more waiting. For those people who were not entitled to paid leave, it must have been frustrating to miss a day's work and then only be called upon to do anything of use for a few hours. I know some people already felt this way.

The same afternoon I received an email from April Doty, Security Team Leader, confirming that we only needed to attend one Venue-Specific Training session since some people had expressed an interest in attending sessions for both the Main Press Centre and Common Domain. As far as I was concerned, if one session was going to cover both venues then it would be pointless to go to two events so I kept my booking the way it was – Wednesday 11 July. I was beginning to look forward to it.

Tuesday 19 June 2012

With just 38 days left until the Opening Ceremony things were beginning to take shape. The chat I had with Elia about the dress rehearsals in Athens came back to me when I received this email from LOCOG:

> The Opening Ceremony of the Olympic Games is less than six weeks away, and we hope you're as excited as we are!
>
> If so, you'll be pleased to know that we're offering all Games Makers the chance to win a free ticket to one of our Technical Rehearsals for the Opening Ceremony, taking place on 23 and 25 July.
>
> The Technical Rehearsals provide a unique opportunity for you to play your part in the final preparations for the Ceremony. With your help we will create a live audience atmosphere to help test elements of the big show. You will be able to experience both the Olympic Park and the Olympic Stadium too.
>
> Please note this event is a rehearsal and as such will not accurately reflect the final content of the show. To assist with our testing, the show may also involve regular pauses in performances.

For a chance to win a ticket I had to answer a very simple question: how many applications were received for our Games Maker programme? The answer was 250,000. All I had to do was click a link and then give my preferred date. I opted for 25 July for no apparent reason. As I was in the Ceremony I could just give my ticket away to a friend or a family member. The same was true for Games Makers who would be on a shift on those nights.

I'm not quite sure why it had to go to ballot as there were 70,000 Games Makers and two of the three dress rehearsals on offer, so a total of 160,000 seats. It seemed unfair that some people would have to miss out, especially since this could be the only chance for some of the Games Makers to visit the Olympic Park and Stadium. I suppose there must have been a reason.

Thursday 21 June 2012

A couple of days later the Ceremonies cast received an offer for a pair of tickets to the dress rehearsals, only this time there was no ballot. We were going to be given the tickets:

> It's hard to believe that there are only 36 days to the Olympic Opening Ceremony. With your talent and dedication we are well on the way to delivering the finest Ceremonies in history.
>
> As a small token of our appreciation we are pleased to offer you two free tickets to the Opening Ceremony dress rehearsal on 25 July. As you will be performing in this rehearsal you are free to give these tickets to friends and family to use instead. By the time you have returned to the holding area, changed out of costume and been released, the creative segment will be over and the audience on their way out.
>
> Ticket distribution will happen during one of your scheduled rehearsals. You must personally pick up and sign for your tickets. Any party found selling their tickets will have them deactivated. No tickets can be reprinted under any circumstances.

So that was two tickets secured, with a possible third. I was glad I chose 25 July for my Games Maker ticket now. It went without saying that I

would give one of my tickets to my wife. She deserved more than
anyone to know what I'd been up to all this time. The other one or
two I was undecided about.

Friday 22 June 2012

I couldn't wait to get inside the Stadium tomorrow. It was going to be
amazing to finally see our set properly and get an idea of the place we
would be performing in. It didn't seem so long ago now that we were
auditioning for the privilege now bestowed upon us. As if in
recognition of my eager state of mind, we received one final email
before the rehearsal:

> Hello lovely 44s
>   Please take a few minutes to read and absorb the
> information in this e-mail – it will make things easier for you on
> Saturday.
>   You should have received the Stadium arrival information
> with map earlier this week. There is no parking at Westfield
> Mall or the Olympic Park. Bicycle parking (at your own risk) is
> very limited around Stratford Station and Westfield. Bicycles
> will not be permitted through security.
>   The walk from the tube to the Ceremonies Compound
> takes about 20-30 minutes. Check in at the Compound begins
> at 9am but please give yourself extra time. Head to John Lewis
> in the outdoor section of the Westfield Mall. You'll see a large
> "Olympic Workforce" sign. At the end of the walkway you will
> see the white security tents.
>   You DO NOT need your LOCOG accreditation to access
> the Olympic Park for the next few weeks. Thousands of
> Ceremonies participants (including us) have not yet received
> the invitation e-mail to go to the UDAC. Just show your
> Ceremonies ID at security.
>   Airport style security is in effect. If you can't take it on a
> plane, don't bring it to the Olympic Park.
>   The route from security to the Ceremonies Compound is
> marked with the Circle/Triangle/Square logo signs you are
> familiar with. Stay on the designated pathways because
> construction works are still going on.

You will receive a meal pack upon arrival to the Compound, but if you have specific dietary requirements a small amount of food will be permitted through security (no liquids except for medication).

Be prepared for all types of weather. It's been particularly cold, wet and very windy like Dagenham. You will be outside and exposed to the elements the entire time. There is no big top at the Stadium; you will be held and briefed in the seating bowl.

- OTHER NOTES -

PHOTOS/VIDEO: There has been an unprecedented amount of people reported and observed taking photos and video during the last couple of rehearsals (bib numbers are being tracked). You may only use your phone as a communication device when you are on a 'break' outside the FOP and seating bowl. Anyone using a phone outside this time may jeopardize their participation in the show.

CIVILITY: We have been getting pockets of complaints of people not being that nice to each other. There is no excuse for this. We are all someone's mother, sister, father, brother, friend or partner. Please treat each other with this in mind.

We really appreciate your massive commitment and we are super excited to see you in the Stadium this weekend!

So we didn't quite get away with taking photos during the final rehearsal in Dagenham, although there were no real consequences for most, but that was a warning indeed. I had no intention of taking my camera to future rehearsals, or taking any photos on my phone. There were always so many staff members around that it was very difficult to do anything unnoticed by at least somebody.

During the week I'd ordered some Macmillan Thank You cards to send to all of the members of my team who had taken part in the run on Sunday. I'd written everybody a personal message, and posted them in the week. I had some spare, one of which I was going to give to Danny Boyle with a message from me. It was an excuse to write him a note, I suppose, but I also wanted him to receive a reminder of how he had helped my charity. Part of the Macmillan experience for our fundraisers is not being forgotten after the event. We also like to thank our donors personally. That was exactly what I was going to do. I hadn't written his card yet, but I planned to do so tomorrow on the train.

Later that evening I received a Games Maker update about my shifts:

> We received more than 2,000 emails asking for shift changes. We've tried to accommodate as many of your requests as possible, but given the scale of our operation, we haven't been able to agree to them all. Some of you who did not request changes to your original roster may notice alterations to your shifts because of changes in operational requirements at your venue.
>
> We know some Games Makers had concerns about transport arrangements for early morning/late evening shifts. Transport for London and National Rail will publish extended Games timetables.
>
> If you have an early shift, please just get here as early as you can – we accept that some people will not be able to arrive precisely for the start of their shift.
>
> The Opening Ceremony is now only 35 days away, but our shifts start even sooner when athletes and media start to arrive on 16 July.

Soon afterwards I received two more emails providing me with links to my shifts at each venue. I logged on and discovered that all of my shifts had been kept as they were. Like it or not I was stuck with some very early starts. I would just have to do my best.

WAVE FIVE

THE STADIUM

29

Rehearsal 11

Saturday 23 June 2012
9.00am – 5.30pm
Olympic Stadium

I get up early today. I've already decided that I am not going to be late, even though I know there will most likely be lots of waiting. I want to get to the Stadium as soon as possible and beat the queues that will no doubt build later on. The timetable says Orientation and Rehearsal. We haven't been told what the former will entail, but I am hoping that we will get to see the computer simulation again, as a refresher, but also because it will make more sense now. Maybe Danny Boyle is going to welcome us and take us through some key elements of the venue and set. He gave a talk at the end of a rehearsal a couple of weeks ago in Dagenham, but already I have forgotten much of what he said. It was mainly motivational though.

On the journey to Stratford on the Jubilee Line, having made the connection at London Bridge, a fairly simple journey for me, I take the opportunity to write the Thank You card to Danny. First and foremost I want to thank him again for kindly sponsoring me. I've already handed my sponsorship form to the Events team at work, although they got a photocopy; I kept the original. I also want to say a few personal words about what this all means to me and how fortunate I feel to be working on one of his productions. I once read something about how he was influenced by Indian films about crime when working on 'Slumdog Millionaire', some of which helped him to capture the gritty reality of life in the Mumbai underworld. To now have the opportunity to maybe speak to him personally about this is something that I really hope will materialise. I'd also like to ask him what it was like to work with Irrfan Khan, one of my favourite Indian actors. It takes me a while to compose the card as I can only write properly during stops at stations, due to the bumpy ride. I also make a copy for myself.

The train reaches Stratford and terminates. I make my way through the station, heading towards Westfield, and the John Lewis that was mentioned in the directions in the email, which I have already consulted more than once. I find an entrance up a fairly steep and rather long flight of steps, and the John Lewis is just around to the left, not far at all. Once outside again I take a right and walk along The Street, and now I can see where the entrance to the Park is, owing to the amount of official looking personnel in the vicinity. As I reach the entrance I can see the top of the Stadium. I show my Ceremony ID and I am told to join the queue, which isn't very long, just beginning to snake around the first line of barriers. I am on time and it looks like it won't take long to get in.

The PSA really is like being at an airport. This is the sort of place I will be working in when I am on my Games Maker shifts. My bag is checked and I am frisked, but it is all done very quickly and soon I am walking away, following the small crowd to the left and round to the right. The Aquatics Centre is now in full view on the left, in all its glory. And it looks absolutely amazing. I haven't made a point of looking at images of the Olympic Park on the internet, but I have some idea of what the main venues look like from maps I've seen in my Games Maker manuals. I've always been rather intrigued by the Aquatics Centre, the shape of it, so to see it now is something quite special. The bit that juts out is simply awesome. It's such an unusually stunning piece of architectural design.

Over to the right is the Water Polo Arena, which isn't quite as aesthetically pleasing as the Aquatics Centre, but the giant crayons in the water next to it look superb. That's a nice touch. I've always had a great appreciation for simple, everyday objects sculpted in giant form. I remember seeing an enormous bicycle in Deansgate, Manchester when I was a student there. Although it had been reduced to nothing but a very simple frame it was still so effective. The crayons are brightly coloured and arranged in a long row at intervals. Across the water from the Water Polo Arena is an embankment with deep orange flowers that I couldn't begin to name. The landscaping is quite sparse; there is still a lot to be done.

One thing that has struck me as I've been walking across the bridge over the river is the sheer tranquillity and serenity surrounding us. It is so quiet here. I suppose the Park is a very big place and aside from us and some security staff and marshals scattered about, there is nobody around. I feel so lucky to be here at this time, when the many,

many thousands of spectators who are expected during the Games are not allowed anywhere near where we are now. We are so privileged and I will never lose sight of this.

Over to the left the Orbit towers above us. I'm not quite sure what exactly I think of it at the moment, but I certainly don't hate it, as some people have said. I agree that it looks odd, but there is something about it that makes me want to like it. I think about where the Main Press Centre is, having seen its location on a map. I don't even try to work it out. I'm not even sure which side we are on, or which way I would need to walk to reach the rest of the venues. I certainly can't see anything else, except of course the one thing that has been in full view ever since I walked round the fence, back at the Aquatics Centre: the magnificence of the Olympic Stadium.

I'm sure some people will describe it as an eyesore. I think most modern architecture provokes an intense division of opinion, but this architectural wonder before me has won me over many times already. In short, I love it. I love the shape of it, and the triangular patterns and lines surrounding its outer perimeter. As I admire it I keep walking towards it. I can't wait to get inside. A marshal checks our ID passes and we continue, past a very clear and large sign informing us that photography is forbidden. I wonder how long it will be before somebody takes a photo of the sign and posts it on the internet. We quickly come to another marshal who checks our IDs again. There is no way somebody without one of these exclusive passes will get in. Security has been very tight so far.

Walking into the area on the outside, we are directed left and along the perimeter, the Stadium circling round on our right. On our left are merchandise and catering stalls, all closed, but seemingly ready to open, when the time is right.

Now that we are so close to the Stadium I notice that the triangular shapes around the side of it are in fact derived from sheets of tarpaulin, long and rectangular, but twisted to one side to create the effect I have seen from a distance. One side of each sheet is brightly coloured and as I walk round I see that the colour changes every so often. Some of them have block numbers written on them in large black figures.

Past the stalls we bear left slightly and then come to yet another check point, showing our passes again, and walking through a barrier to the right. A few paces on and we walk past a flight of stairs on the left, and are directed down another set of steps on the same side, into a building, which I soon see is the registration area. That was quite a walk from the PSA. We go through the usual routine of scanning our passes and picking up an IEM, which we now use at every rehearsal.

Beyond this there is a queue for a snack: either a Dairy Milk or a flapjack. I choose the latter as it will be more filling. They did say they will be providing us with lunch. I have no other food on me so the more the better. We are specifically told that we can have one or the other, but not both.

Onwards we go, through a set of doors and up a couple of flights of stairs, through a costume area at the top, and then out once again down another set of steps, the same ones we passed on the way in, so we have come full circle through the building. Turning left at the bottom we take a few paces and come to another set of marshals who once again check our passes. This is the final check before we reach the inner concourse encircling the Stadium. We are directed towards the entrances, which are really just gaps in between the sheets of twisted tarpaulin. There are four of them allocated to us, one for each of the 44 Groups. Heading to the one marked B, I come to a table which is positioned directly underneath a set of steps that lead to the upper stands. Our bibs are laid out, ready for collection. The number 461 is by now so ingrained that the request for it needs no thought whatsoever. The volunteer hands it to me, I thank her kindly, and I turn towards the top of the lower tier which is only a few paces away.

With each step I take I can see more and more of the far side of the auditorium, which very quickly becomes the set. The sun has decided to shine at the most opportune moment, rendering the sight before me almost breathtaking. The set is smaller than I'd imagined, but it still looks fantastic, and I take the opportunity to just lean on the barrier at the top of the stands and take in as much detail as possible.

Except for on the Tor on the far side, there is no turf laid out so it isn't quite ready for a strike, but all of the structures are in place. It looks just like the now familiar model that has made it into the press, just not as green. We could only imagine the Tor at Dagenham, but now it is right before my eyes and it looks incredible. The terraces rise quite steeply to the oak tree which is going to be uprooted at the beginning of our strike. The barn, represented by a shed at Dagenham, is now in place, and our ramp is no longer flat.

All around is the M25 which is wider than I thought it would be, and more open too. For some reason I thought we were going to be out of the audience's view when in our creep positions, but we will in fact be out in the open. The auditorium looks great too. The top rows in the upper level are rather high up and the seats are coloured black and white, arranged to make what initially look like random patterns all around the arena. The voms are clearly visible at intervals, cutting holes into the lower seating stands, and over to the left of where I am, between two blocks of the upper level, hangs the bell, the world's largest harmonically tuned bell, no less. It is yet another feature of this place that looks simply amazing.

There are tea and coffee points to the side but they aren't ready yet, which is a shame as I was rather looking forward to a caffeine hit at this early hour, but I will have to wait. Instead I walk into the seating area, which is filling up gradually, and see Josh in one of the rows. I join him and take a seat. He introduces me to Alex, his girlfriend I assume from the way they are talking to each other. How nice for them to both be in the Ceremony together. I momentarily wonder how great it would have been if Misbah and I could have done this together, but she didn't actually have any interest in doing so in the first place. Josh points out the LED lights that are on the back of every seat in the Stadium – large square panels with rows of small lights. They were not lit when I was surveying the auditorium just now, but suddenly they are flashing on and off, seemingly randomly, and changing colour. It looks like they are just being tested. I have very little capacity for technology but even I can appreciate how incredible it could look if all of these lights are lit up in different colours after sunset.

Whilst chatting with Josh I observe various aspects of this magnificent structure: the enormous speakers that are seemingly floating below the non-existent roof; the amount of wires and cables criss-crossing the entire circle of air within the circumference formed by the partial roof, which only covers the very top rows of the upper stands; the giant triangular frames that house the floodlights, one of the few parts of the Stadium that are visible from the outside. There are lots of workers in hard hats and hi-vis jackets, busy with their assigned tasks, moving something here, driving a trailer there, or carrying a vital piece of equipment from A to B. Directly beyond our seating is an area for the instructors, Mass Team, dance captains, and other personnel, a lot of whom are present, no doubt going over the plans for the rehearsal, talking about what we are going to be doing. I can't see our Katie but she must be here somewhere.

I take a moment to contemplate that this entire arena will be filled with people and all of us sitting in these seats now will be down there, in that set, performing the most ambitious set change ever attempted.

I can't believe I am involved in this so directly. Even after all this time, it doesn't quite seem real, but I take great pleasure in knowing that it is indeed very real. I am here, where very few people on the planet are allowed to be right now. I can't help but smile.

After overhearing that the drinks counters are up and running, I get myself a drink and return. Sipping my coffee we reconvene something that is by now so familiar to us all: waiting. More and more performers are arriving as we do so. This is the longest rehearsal so far and we are in a new venue, so they are taking their time today.

Eventually the very distinctive voice of Steve Boyd is addressing us and giving us a warm welcome to the Stadium, which is met with applause and cheers. After some standard housekeeping points he gives us a very serious reminder that we are on what is officially classified as a construction site, since there is still a lot of work going on, as can be observed quite easily, so we must exercise plenty of care and attention. This is especially so when walking around as there are lots of uneven surfaces across the tiles that are being used to protect the track and field underneath. We are then invited onto the FOP by county.

I can see Fife round to the left. Our ramp is a clear indication of where our patch lies. When our county is called we make our way down to the bottom of the stand and bear left towards the opening, stepping over bags and belongings on the way. There are plenty of hazards to negotiate before reaching the relative safety of the M25. After being up in the seating for so long, it is nice to be down here, to get a view of the auditorium from where we will be on show night, looking up at the spectators, rather than looking down at the performers, as is usually the case for most of us.

Everybody is free to walk into and look around their respective counties. The ramp, and the entire FOP, is covered in what looks like random strips of black, white and grey gaffer tape, although the thick lines are actually painted on, or maybe even printed onto the surface. I'm not quite sure what this is supposed to represent. Immediately to the left of our ramp is a large waterwheel, which is being fed by a rock pool, although it is not quite finished yet. Tests are being done as we explore our county. There are flower beds and plants, which won't be struck, along the edges. They need thickening out, but there is time yet. The same is true of the hedges in their troughs on wheels. Even at this early stage, and without any of the turf in place, it all looks fantastic. Katie arrives on the set and quite rightly points out that the traps for the chimney and crucible are at least real now, which means

Our audition venue and site of our first two rehearsals

Audition numbers – my very first souvenirs

Our secret directional sign

With Wenlock and Mandeville at Orientation Training

Cast marquee at Dagenham

My passport to rehearsals

The team at Dagenham could assess our strikes from here

With Danny Boyle in our holding area

Experiment in turf rolling and lifting

After our first full strike

A full reset meant unravelling large piles of turf

Danny Boyle giving direction in the Stadium

An early rendition of the set, before a full strike…

*…and afterwards. Sometimes the chimneys
wouldn't go back down*

After clearing the FOP the tech team took over

Waiting to strike during a rain-soaked rehearsal

Fife pin badge designed by Chris Savage

Members of Fife at the Skybar in Stratford

*Polly and Diane, my two
dance captains*

*Katie P, County Fife's Mass
Movement Coordinator*

Working Women of Fife. L-R: Dia, Fiona, Elia, Jan

First time in full make-up

In full costume. L-R: Gaudi, Josh, Chris

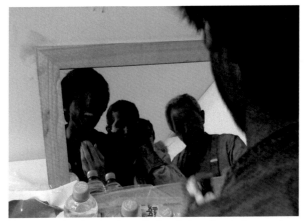

Getting made up before dress rehearsals

Our holding area at Eton Manor

Jay's dance class during hours of waiting

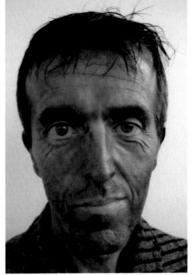

This spread and overleaf:
Working Men and Women –
An Attitude

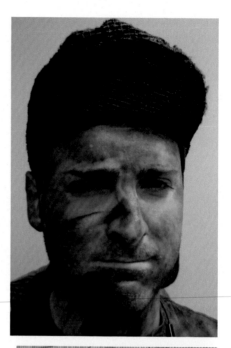

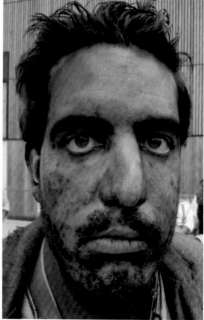

The Kingdom of Fife

*Walking to the Stadium on show night as the sun sets
over the Olympic Park*

*The landscaping in the Park added
an amazing mix of colour*

During a break on a Games Maker shift

The Park in full flow

We endured a lot of this as we rehearsed

that we won't be able to walk over them, as we so often did during rehearsals in Dagenham. It is easy to see their outline cut into the set.

After some time Steve is back on the PA and asking us to make our way into Hampshire, where we are going to see a chimney rise. A few checks are made, some talking into radios, and then lo and behold a chimney does indeed rise up out of the FOP, and continues to rise. Cheers were inevitable – it is quite a moment for us to see this column of faux solidity rise so high. It is clearly inflatable, but the illusion that it is solid as it reaches for the sky is successfully achieved. We now witness another chimney from a neighbouring trap. This one is taller than the first, and as it reaches its full height, it begins to sway quite heavily from side to side. A few teething problems maybe, but they do look rather majestic in their full glory. The material they are made from has a charcoal coloured brick design to help them look real. Looking into the traps we can just about see that there are workers underneath the set, clearly there to help with all of the very technical operations in the segment like the chimneys rising, beam engines emerging from below the FOP, and many other aspects that I have no knowledge of. I would love to take a look around underneath, but sadly that is one privilege that I will not be afforded at any point.

We are now asked to move towards Cornwall or Devon, I believe, where they are going to bring out a large loom. This will be used at some stage during the segment. Out of the vom on that side several people are pushing this enormous piece of machinery onto the M25 and up the ramp. It is a very impressive looking prop and it is only now that I am getting a sense of just how big our segment is. We couldn't fully appreciate this at Dagenham, and still can't do so now, but more and more aspects of our section are seeping in and it is slowly growing into something quite incredible.

After a couple more less spectacular demos, we move into our buddy lines. So was that the orientation? We didn't get to see the video again, as I had hoped. A missed opportunity, I feel, as it would have been good to put it into the context of the Stadium, and there are some large screens around the perimeter, which would have been an ideal way of viewing it. Still, they haven't deemed it necessary and they know best.

Lunch is announced for 1pm, around an hour and a half away. We are reminded that no photography is allowed. I think some people haven't been able to resist the urge to get their camera phones out, despite Vanessa's warnings during the week. It does seem that rebellion is on the rise as some of the Warriors, who are positioned by the Tor, begin to climb up it, despite receiving no such instruction as announced by Steve on the PA. They are kindly asked to come back down.

After Katie has organised us and counted how many people are present, she begins to allocate specific people to fences and hedges. This is a positive step forward as the people she allocates now will be set in stone. Jon and Harry are absent today, so unfortunately they will miss out. I will definitely be with Gaudi on a fence, and Josh will be with Chris, who arrived not too long ago, on the fence to the left.

With all of the structures allocated, Katie moves on to the turf on the ramp, and the priority turf at the very top, consisting of three very large pieces that cover up the traps for the crucible and chimney, which need to be freed as soon as possible. Six people are needed for the second piece of the three. Myself, Gaudi, Josh, Chris, Elia and Nancy, three sets of buddies, are given the task of removing that section, again set in stone. All of us are happy with this. We are finally making some real progress today with definitive allocation of specific jobs.

At 12pm we are granted a tea break. It is actually quite difficult to find where my bag is as we are occupying about three blocks and the rows of white seats look so similar. After locating it I see that lots of people are forming a queue, which I quickly realise is for our lunch, so I join the end. It doesn't take me long to reach the building where we picked up the flapjack or chocolate earlier on. They have piles of brown paper bags containing our lunch. There is a choice of meat, vegetarian and halal, which is a nice touch. Having grabbed my bag I make my way back to the stands. Lots of people are tucking in but I distinctly remember the announcement being made about lunch at 1pm, so despite the time already, I only go as far as examining the contents: halal chicken sandwich, a bag of crisps, a clementine, and a granola bar, which I do quite like. Not such a bad free lunch. I quickly drink a coffee and by 12.30 we are being called back to the FOP and into our buddy lines.

For the next half hour we do absolutely nothing, and then as promised, we are given a one hour lunch break. Lots of people have already eaten their meal but I now start on my sandwich, which is not too bad at all. Danny is evidently not here today so I won't be able to give him the Thank You card I wrote for him. Maybe tomorrow. At the other end of the Stadium somebody has decided to climb to the top of the upper stands to get what will in effect be the best view of the FOP. Steve calls out the guy's bib number and politely asks him to come back down, his voice never once betraying any possible frustration he may be feeling at some people doing just as they please in this construction site without any regard for safety.

After lunch we are back on the FOP. We have done relatively little today and it has been rather frustrating, especially since this is an all day rehearsal. Katie now comes down our buddy lines, calling out bib numbers. Gaudi, Josh and I are in her number range, as are Jon and Harry. She gives us a new laminate which she staples to our bibs. I keep the old one as a memento. The new one shows that we are going to be smelters on the West Side. I have no idea where this fits in but it is obviously a specific role so I am grateful for having been chosen for it, randomly it seems. Some of the ladies are given roles as weavers. They are going to operate the looms.

All of the traps need to be surrounded with barriers, or guard rails, before they can be opened, for safety reasons. Some people have been assigned the role of taking these rails onto the FOP and placing them into the holes around the edge. Whilst they are going through that the rest of us are left to just chat and stand around. One guy, whose name I don't yet know, has decided to teach a couple of people how to juggle using the yellow gloves we wear. Other people take the opportunity to sit on some vacant trailers. There is no sense in standing up as we have no idea when we are going to be called to do something. We don't actually have to wait very long.

Now that all of the railings have been fixed in place they need to be taken off. I'm not quite sure why the same people didn't do them, but we are all a team of course, so I have no problem with helping out. They are quite heavy so it's two to a railing. I get paired up with Paul around one of the beam engine traps. They are difficult to remove as they are slotted in quite tightly, but we manage it eventually. They are indeed heavy and, due to their shape, quite cumbersome. I see one guy, Julian I think, carrying one on his own! He'll need to be careful or he'll get injured – the last thing he will want. Some counties don't have a ramp to go up and down, but a set of steps, and it is down one of these that Paul and I go, with a little bit of difficulty. These very heavy rails are surely not the best idea. I get the impression that I'm not the only person thinking this.

Once we have placed our rail where it belongs, we are back on the FOP, just wandering. I manage to catch a conversation between a few people and Pete, the prop guy who allocated me to a ratchet and then forgot me, although I am now a smelter which has softened the blow. He acknowledges that all of this waiting around must be incredibly frustrating for us all, but we are in fact doing them a great service by helping them establish what is and isn't working. I suppose this does make sense, as we have made plenty of changes so far. In putting together any large spectacle, as he has done many times in the past, the initial stages are the bane of everybody's life, but they are also vital, and they couldn't do this without our patience and resilience. In just a few generous sentences Pete has made everything we have done so far make almost complete sense. Despite what we inexperienced folk may think we have helped them immensely. It is at that precise moment that I decide I will no longer complain in any shape or form about having nothing to do. Just go with it, as they know better, and enjoy every moment of being in this wonderful structure. I intend to do just that. In the words of Steve, uttered a few rehearsals ago in Dagenham, "welcome to show business". Indeed.

The rest of the rehearsal is spent doing a bit of work with the structures, practising the removal of fences and hedges according to the allocation that was confirmed earlier, and looking at flow once again. It's been a long day and I can only hope that tomorrow is more productive, even though we will only be here for half the time.

30

Rehearsal 12

Sunday 24 June 2012
9.00am – 1.00pm
Olympic Stadium

Another early start today, but it's only four hours so an early finish too. It's actually the shortest rehearsal we have had since we left 3 Mills. I'm not sure how much we are going to get done as it takes an age for everybody to arrive and for the team to start organising us. The main drawback today is that it's been raining and showers are expected, so the Park and Stadium won't look quite as attractive as they did yesterday when the sun was shining for most of the day. When we were at Dagenham I often wore my waterproof cycling jacket underneath my coveralls when it was raining, so I make sure I have this with me today just in case.

Getting through security is fairly quick again. On the walk to the Stadium I see Harry walking ahead of me so I catch up with him. He couldn't come yesterday as he had other engagements. After registering we pick up lunch instead of receiving a snack. I go for the halal option again. I think I'm just going to save mine until after the rehearsal. Some people have already started eating theirs.

After picking up our bibs we walk towards the seating, across the podium level, and if I thought the set looked amazing yesterday, it is without a doubt breathtaking today. All of the turf is in place and it is now at least as complete as it was in Dagenham, with a few added features. From where we are standing we can see almost all of it laid out before our eyes. It absolutely multiplies the magnificence of the Stadium. Looking over towards Fife, my eyes follow the outline of our perimeter, the now familiar P-shape. Today we are surely going to do a full strike.

We find some seats and put our bags down, and then I go to get myself a coffee. I have drunk so many of these now that I have grown quite accustomed to the taste, although it has taken me a while. The toilets allocated to us are a few blocks along from our seating area. They seem to be at regular intervals around the perimeter. Today we are asked to use the ladies for some reason, the large globally recognised image of a lady being replaced with a makeshift gents sign. This is something I definitely won't be allowed to do during the Olympics!

On the way back I notice a couple of boxes to the left of the steps that lead down into our block. They contain large plastic bags for us to put our things in, to stop them getting soaked, as most of the lower tier is not covered. There is also a new allocation of ponchos. Upon examination these are much more durable than the Dagenham ones, made of heavier PVC. They are also bigger so don't fit into my pocket as easily, but they are at least built to last, unlike the other ones which would tear quite quickly in strong winds, which we have endured a lot of. I suppose the idea is to give one to whomever wants it, and then hopefully they won't need another one. Sustainability is a large part of these Games so having a plastic poncho in the first place isn't ideal, but faced with one of the wettest months of June since records began, they can at least minimise how many they go through. I take one of each and then make my way back to my seat, drink my coffee, and wait patiently whilst staring in wonder at our set and everything around it. The same activity that I observed yesterday is in full swing. Workers are going about their business, preparing our set so that we can all go in and pull it apart, piece by piece.

After a while, not as long as yesterday, we are invited onto the FOP. They are clearly conscious that we are short on time today. We go through the usual routine of standing around next to Fife on the M25 before Katie asks us to get into our buddy lines so she can see who is present and who is absent in Fife today. There is always somebody missing, but two people who are now regretting not being here yesterday are Jon and Harry, who have been made swings, as Katie puts it, so they will just be slotted in wherever they are needed, as all of the fixed roles were allocated yesterday. In some ways this means they could be performing a variety of tasks but receiving a definite role yesterday was a plus point and they have missed out. As we are drawing near to show night – just over a month left – we are pinning things down at the start of our strike, and we are possibly getting slightly better too, as we have to move on to the final waves, after Hail Mary. We are still none the wiser about these.

I tell both Jon and Harry that Katie was allocating smelters yesterday and they were both in her list. Initially disbelieving me, they go to find her and return with a laminate just like mine, Josh's and Gaudi's. At least they have this, and they thank me for telling them. It was a pleasure.

Soon we are going to do a full strike. Those of us who are on priority turf go and familiarise ourselves with our piece and work out how best to roll it, as it is very large. We soon work out that just rolling it will not work, so we will need to fold one corner over first, and then roll it from the top of the triangle. We unroll it and put it back in its place before returning to the buddy lines.

There is some talk of a group on Facebook for people in County Fife, which Wasif has set up. I haven't spoken to him since I met him on the way home from 3 Mills. He is several bib numbers before me so he is always further down the buddy lines. I think most people interact more with the people around them. These are the people we strike with and spend more time with. I make a mental note of the name of the group and will request membership to it during the week. I don't use Facebook very often, but it will be good to be part of the online community of Fife.

As we are waiting the Suffragettes walk round chanting and waving their banners. I'm not sure yet where they fit into our segment, but they are always on the M25, never on the FOP. A steel band walks round too, sounding great. Some people, including Liz, take the opportunity to have a dance. I again wonder how they are a part of this; I have no idea. I do know that they wouldn't be here just to entertain us. The Brunels are also doing their thing in their groups, going through choreography, some of which differs from our hakas, some of which is done at double time like we once did in Dagenham. They often wear hats and smart black coats now, which is part of their costume. Some of them have begun to grow beards. This reminds me about the message we received quite some time ago now. I think I am going to leave it about a week and then stop shaving. Around three weeks of growth will give me a decent enough stubble. The longest I've ever gone is two weeks in my teens. I have to say I am not going to miss shaving every other day. It will be a welcome change in my routine.

The first strike of the day begins in the usual fashion now, with the classical music. We now also hear a speech from The Tempest playing on our In Ears and on the PA. I vaguely remember this from the simulation. Beginning in our creep positions, we get into our lines and then the music begins. As ever structures are first and that bit goes smoothly. Trying to find a clear path round the back of the dollies and back up the ramp isn't always easy; due to the sheer amount of traffic, we inevitably find it hard to make it through at times. Pete is often at the bottom of the ramp, directing people to stop as others pass. We have done a lot of work on flow but it is never going to be perfect since everybody walks at different paces so some form of direction is needed. There are too many factors in this that can affect when something will happen, or will have a knock-on effect elsewhere, so we need to know how to react to unavoidable situations.

When I reach our turf, with Gaudi close by, Elia, Nancy, Josh and Chris are already there. It is already being rolled so Gaudi and I join in as the roll gradually grows wider, taking one side each. My gloves are already soaked through. Chris counts us down to pick it up, ensuring we all lift in unison. It is very wet and therefore very heavy. It hasn't rolled perfectly so is difficult to hold on to. Still we begin to walk down the ramp, which now has all turf removed from it, making it slippery. This is no idle observation as I do slip on the way down, but I somehow manage to keep my footing. With such a heavy piece of turf on our shoulders that could have been a lot worse.

Once down we walk over to the right and the Warriors take the turf off our shoulders and onto theirs. From here we all walk back and it's now a case of clearing whichever piece we come to. Katie is at the top, calling out numbers required for the next piece along. I end up on a small and much lighter piece with one other lady. On the way down the ramp for the second time, the lighter weight makes no difference as I slip again and this time end up in a sitting position, still holding my end of the turf on my shoulders. I get back up immediately but I already know I have pulled a muscle in my back. It isn't painful but does cause me some discomfort.

Soon the music slows down and we are into the whistling portion where we all have to stand still and look towards the poppy field. My back is now causing me some pain. Clearly it won't be a good idea to carry any more turf so when the main music resumes I join a group on the side of the ramp who are doing choreography with Diane leading. The strike is almost over and not everybody is needed to clear the remaining turf.

When we finish we are asked to do a reset. Instead of joining in I find somebody who can point me towards First Aid. I do not want this to develop into something bigger and end up missing rehearsals. The pain is growing. It's directly behind my chest, to the left, so I can walk fine, but with every breath I am taking I feel a sharp pain in my muscles. I find Vanessa who gets hold of a First Aider, who then asks me to go and see somebody at the top of the seating area. I can't see anybody so Vanessa gets on her radio, to no avail. She is very helpful, insisting more than once that the First Aider finds somebody to help me promptly. I don't know why the man standing right next to me can't help. He probably just needs to give me a quick massage and push the offending muscle back into place.

In the end he does ask me to follow him into Vom 4. They are clearly not very organised. I'm not one to complain, and have suffered more than a few back aches, but at the moment every inhalation is painful. I extend my breaths as much as possible as we walk further into the vom. At least I have seen what it's like backstage. There are a few trailers and curiously a house which is clearly not a permanent fixture. It looks more like a hut but with a red brick exterior. Not far from where this is, there is a First Aid trailer, which is where I am being taken.

The medical team there give me a couple of painkillers and apply a heat pack to the sensitive area for a few minutes, handing me a spare one in case the pain continues when I'm at home. They can't give me any kind of massage as that could in fact make it worse. In the meantime I just have to endure the pain, which is still getting worse. The heat pack hasn't made any real difference. Another guy walks in with blood trickling down the side of his face. He managed to split his ear when picking up some turf, but he is okay. He just needs something to stem the blood flow. After taking our details, to record the injuries officially, we are both free to go. I am advised to take it easy and to definitely not do any more heavy lifting.

I find Katie when I'm out of the vom and tell her that I'm going to have to sit out for the rest of the rehearsal – doctor's orders. She asks me to stick around though, as there may be developments that I need to know about, which is fine. As almost everybody else is putting our set back together again, to enable us to fit in one more strike before the session ends, I can only watch, which I am not comfortable with, but there isn't much I can do. Eventually I go and sit down on one of the trailers on the side and try to stretch my back. Complete rest may have been prescribed, but in my experience of back injuries this is the worst method of recovery. I care not what the medical staff say, I know that this just needs a bit of stretching and massage. At least I strongly believe so. A couple of girls are sat close by. We speak about how dangerous the ramp is as more than a few people have reported slipping on it. If they don't address this problem they are going to have lots more injuries, something they are trying hard to minimise.

Once the reset is complete, we are asked to get into our buddy lines again. Now that I am back and still standing, a few of the guys ask if I am okay, and then begin to taunt me for doing nothing during the reset. It's all in good humour of course, but I've already decided that I can't just sit and watch. The painkillers seem to have begun to work so when Steve asks us to get into our creep positions once again, I do so too. It is now close to 1pm so for the first time we are going to over run, but they want to get one more strike in. We definitely need the practice. Although the last one wasn't that bad, we still have a long way to go to make it look and feel good, with only a month and two days to go before it has to be perfect. We haven't even completed our segment yet.

Into the same routine yet again – classical music with The Tempest speech, tree uprooted, Steve cues us to begin the strike, and away we go. My fence is a light one so this is no problem. The priority turf is as heavy as it was on the previous run, but we manage to roll it tighter so it is easier to handle. I make sure I lift on my right side, away from the affected area, so it goes fine. On the way down I slipped yet again, despite trying hard to keep from doing so, but I manage to remain standing. I make a note to not wear these shoes again. I have avoided my boots in recent rehearsals, but they do have good soles, so maybe it is time to break them in properly. On my next run I feel very nervous walking down the ramp but this time there is no incident at all.

Another strike ends and this time there is no reset as it is time to go home. It wasn't great, but as always we managed it and when we have finished there isn't a trace of turf remaining on the set.

Once again it is difficult to see my bag, even though I pulled my very bright yellow rain cover over it before putting it into the issued plastic bags. The stands are a sea of similar looking personal effects, and since there are now hundreds of people filling the blocks, it is harder to scan the rows. I'll have to be less absent-minded about exactly where I sit at the next rehearsal. Another no show from Danny Boyle today, so I still have my Thank You card. Maybe next time.

On the way out of the Olympic Park I eat my lunch as I walk. Some people are stopping in their tracks to take photos of the Orbit or the Stadium, ignoring the sign that was always going to be ignored. There will be plenty of time for this as we have many more rehearsals here before show night. I'll take the opportunity later to create some lasting memories. As I walk out of the final exit, I am already keen to return and continue rehearsals. I am completely absorbed in this and it is now an essential part of my routine, almost like a fix. I often look forward to rehearsals during the week as I perform my duties at work, so often thinking about this incredible spectacle that we are working so hard to perfect, before the world will be our audience for night only.

31

Ticket Allocation

Wednesday 27 June 2012

The results were evidently in for the Games Maker ticket ballot and I'd been successful:

> We're pleased to confirm that you have been allocated a ticket to the Technical Rehearsal for the Opening Ceremony of the Olympics!
>
> The process for getting your ticket is in three stages:
> 1) Fill out the online form. Once you've completed this, your ticket is guaranteed. The deadline for doing this is 1pm on Friday 6 July.
> 2) You will receive an automated confirmation email from Ticketmaster. Please keep this for your reference. Your ticket will be emailed to you in due course.
> 3) Ticketmaster will email your ticket by 20 July. Once you have received it please print it out and bring it with you on the night.

So that was three tickets I had in total now, although one of the tickets would be for a separate seat of course. For me the obvious recipients of the tickets were my very deserving wife, and my parents. They would love the experience and spectacle. After securing my ticket I spoke to my wife, quite excited that she would have the opportunity to witness live what I'd been spending so long rehearsing. I wanted her to see it. Knowing that she would be in the audience would make me feel good and very proud. Unfortunately it wasn't going to be so simple.

I had thought about this a few weeks ago but recently I'd been so occupied with everything that was going on that I'd quite forgotten that Ramadan was due to begin on 20 July. The Ceremony was on 27

July. By rights I should have told Ceremonies then that I wouldn't be able to perform. I should have pulled out for religious reasons. Yet I was in too deep even then and I'd found it impossible to do so. I would never get this opportunity again.

In recent years my religious inclinations and proclivities had consolidated, but obviously not as much as I may have hoped. The month of Ramadan is one in which Muslims dedicate their time to worship, prayer, and fasting in the name of God, and forego entertainment, music, TV and other impious acts, of which performing in the Opening Ceremony of the Olympic Games was definitely one. As a Type 1 diabetic, I am actually exempt from fasting, even though I attempt to do so, and I usually succeed in getting through the daylight hours without consuming a single drop or crumb, whilst at the same time keeping my blood sugar levels within a safe range. This, however, was beside the point. Fasting or no fasting, around the time when that bell was going to be rung, I should have been at home either preparing to break my fast, or at the very least getting ready to recite my evening prayer. The fact that I had consciously opted to be doing nothing of the sort when the sun set on 27 July was an act that I knew I would be judged upon one day.

My parents and my wife would have loved to see me perform in the Stadium but for them there was never any question about what was more important. They would have to stay at home. I even asked my parents, knowing that they would say no. I had to ask at least, just for my own peace of mind. The only other person in my family who would be prepared to go was my older brother, the one who had declined to apply to audition many months ago. He never gave it a second thought when I asked him. He also knew who he would be going with, if she could make it down to London during the week. That was two tickets allocated. I decided to hold a raffle for the third ticket at work, with all proceeds going to Macmillan Cancer Support.

Thursday 28 June 2012

Having joined the Facebook group for volunteers in Fife on Tuesday, it was good to discuss rehearsals and anything else that people wished to talk about during the week. Wasif, who also set up the group, was busy organising an afternoon meet up at the Sky Bar, which gave good views of the Stadium, on Sunday 8 July. He had somehow managed to secure the upstairs private area for nothing, just for us performers. Unfortunately I had to decline the invite as it was after a rehearsal and I was ever conscious of what Misbah was doing. It just didn't seem fair for me to be out having a good time whilst she was sat at home with the kids, especially since every weekend was being taken up by rehearsals. I also had my Venue-Specific Training the following Wednesday, so that would be another evening without me around.

After some thought I visited the Games Maker zone online and saw that there were still places available on the Sunday, in the afternoon. It fit in perfectly with the morning rehearsal, and it would give me a few hours at the Sky Bar in between the two. By now I could easily tell that there was no problem with attending both the rehearsal and Games Maker training on the same day. They were both very different activities, run completely independently, and there was no way somebody would realise that I was doing both. It was no longer such a big issue as far as I could see. I booked myself on the training and accepted the invite to the meet up. I was now in for a long day. Rehearsals were to begin at 9am and the Games Maker training was scheduled to finish at 9pm, with four hours in between, but at least I would get it out of the way whilst I was already in Stratford.

Later that evening we received an email from Vanessa ahead of the biggest weekend of rehearsals so far. The main points covered were the timings and accreditation. Only 44% of people had received an email from UDAC so several thousand cast members were yet to pick up their accreditation.

There were going to be rehearsals on Friday, Saturday and Sunday, in the evening, all day, and in the morning respectively. This marathon weekend meant that I was only going to be spending around 18 hours at home, not including time spent sleeping, between Thursday night and the following Monday evening. I was spending very little time with my youngest daughter, who was only 15 months old, and would often be asleep when I was at home. When going back and forth between rehearsals and work, it didn't feel like I was spending so little time at home, but when I sat down and really reflected on what was happening, it did at times weigh heavily on my conscience. There were so many husbands, wives, mothers, and fathers, who were making the same sacrifices as I was. For so many of us, our spouses were the ones who made rehearsals possible, and deserved as much thanks as any of us for giving up our time.

32

Rehearsal 13

Friday 29 June 2012
5.30pm – 10.00pm
Olympic Stadium

Whilst at work today, I receive an interesting email from Ceremonies:

> As the sections of the show that you are starring in are in period costume we need to pay similar attention to detail to your spectacles. The easiest and most cost-effective solution is not to wear them if you feel you are safe. If you have contacts, could you wear them?
>
> We need details or a photo of your spectacles so we can assess if they could pass as a period item, plus your prescription so that we could look at providing a pair if we have to. As you can imagine, this will involve a great cost so we are only at the enquiry stage.
>
> Please email your scanned or written prescription with your full name, group number, and bib number.
>
> Costume Team

I haven't thought about this, but of course a modern looking pair of glasses caught in a close-up will look anachronistic. I would probably prefer to wear my glasses as the lighting could cause me issues, so I decide to find my prescription when I have a chance, although it does sound like they won't be able to fund lots of requests for period glasses.

So another working week comes to an end and this means a weekend of volunteering. This is the most intense stage in the entire schedule. I leave work at the usual time and make my way to Stratford once again, only this time it is in the height of the rush hour. I take a different route through the station, just following the signs for the Olympic Park that take me through a passageway which has a series of large posters on the walls on either side, advertising some of the roles the Games Makers will play in the Olympics, in an engaging way. I can't help but feel that I've drawn a bit of a short straw with my Security role, stuck in a PSA all day, although I know it could have been worse. It just wasn't what I'd been hoping for and I wondered how somebody who will be smoothing out the sand for the long jump inside the Stadium got that role.

Walking through Westfield to reach our Stadium entrance it is almost possible to imagine the sort of atmosphere that will engulf the entire area once the Games have begun. It's a nice place to be even now, simply because the Olympic Park is nearby and the bare beginnings of the Games are apparent through the signage and personnel dotted about, giving directions to those who are lucky enough to be on their way to the Park.

We don't have a sunny evening tonight but it isn't raining. I still carry my poncho with me as the time of year is currently no indication of the expected weather pattern. The turf should at least be dry which is good.

The FOP has been reset since our last rehearsal so we can just go straight into a strike. We only have four and a half hours, so that probably means around three hours of actual rehearsal time. The voice of Steve is soon sounding out around us as he talks on his microphone, welcoming us to this long weekend and confirming that we will be starting with a full strike once we are invited on to the FOP. Before that, however, he introduces Danny Boyle who wants to speak to us as a group.

Now that we know what we are doing in the strike, in terms of how we are removing everything, he wants to talk about why we are doing it, even though he feels we are beginning to get to grips with this already. The Industrial Revolution, he feels, is probably the single most important event ever for mankind. It brought about such change that life as we knew it could never be the same again. There was a good side to this as well as a bad side. The negative aspects were things like child labour, the abuse of working men and women who had to endure horrid conditions in the factories and mills, warfare being industrialised which created machine guns, tanks, bombs, and artillery. On the plus side there was such economic growth and creation of wealth that society benefited from improved education, better healthcare, which would eventually lead to the creation of the NHS, and more widespread equality such as women's rights represented by the Suffragette movement. Some of these things are depicted during the Ceremony.

One of the aspects of the Industrial Revolution that we are showing is transforming the Green and Pleasant Land, the age of agriculture, to the "dark satanic mills" of industry. This is what our segment is about. Isambard Kingdom Brunel is enticing us to rip up the land and make way for the machines, the smoking chimneys, and the factories spawning mass produced goods. We are raising hell, ousting the farmers and their animals, ripping away their fields and crops, and it has to be convincing, which is why we have been through relative hell in our rehearsals. This is the first time our segment has been given its full context, and it is truly motivational.

We are executing the most ambitious set change ever attempted, yet it is much more than that. We are demonstrating a revolution, one that required intense hard graft and an unprecedented level of change. It was an historical milestone that altered the world, so we should be proud of what we are attempting to show and convey to the world, from the tiny island where it all began, which is all the more appropriate.

After his talk we are invited onto the FOP. I walk down the steps but before going round to the left, I see Danny talking to a volunteer briefly. I have my Thank You card in my back pocket. Another guy approaches him and asks for his baseball cap to be autographed, which he does with pleasure. Once again I wait patiently, before grabbing his attention:

"Hi Danny, can I just give you this? It's a Thank You card on behalf of Macmillan for sponsoring me a couple of weeks ago."

He reflects for a second, and then remembers.

"Oh, yeah, did I give you the money?"

"Yeah, you did indeed."

"I probably should have given you some more; you're the first person to have asked me."

"No, no, that's okay. I actually thought afterwards that I should have shown you the front of the form, as that indicated that I did do the run that day, just so you know I wasn't pulling a fast one!"

I hand him the card, which he puts into his jacket pocket.

"I just wanted to say thank you, and wrote a few more words. Hopefully you'll enjoy reading it. Thanks a lot."

We both turn away at the same time, in opposite directions, me towards Fife, him towards a colleague who is waiting for him.

Conversation over. I am conscious that I should be with the others so I hurry along and find my little group. New conversations begin.

One guy who I don't often speak to is beginning to find the whole experience a little tiresome now, not happy at the amount of waiting we are put through at every rehearsal and the apparent lack of organisation. There is no denying that we do have to exercise a lot of patience. It would be interesting to know how many hours we have spent idle of all the time spent in rehearsals. That could be quite a shocking ratio. I can only recall what Pete told a few of us last weekend. With that in mind, and with my own reflections on the position we are in, I am glad to be here. I have the right to feel frustrated, but I no longer feel I have the right to complain, even if this guy feels otherwise. He is visibly not happy. Maybe he is just having a bad day. Either way we are being called on to the set to go over our priority strikes once more. It is vital these go smoothly.

The six of us who are on the second piece have a conversation amongst ourselves about what we are going to do. We need to tighten this up. I suggest allocating people to the same part of the piece, so we always go to the same side or end when we arrive from the ramp. That will make our movements smoother and reduce confusion. Josh is going to fold over the large end, every time. I am going to start rolling from the pointed end, making sure that it is kept tight. Gaudi and Elia will join me on either side, followed by Nancy and Chris, who will then count us down to lift. That is now decided and we have to stick to it. We spend a few minutes practising this. If I start rolling tight, it is indeed possible to roll the turf into a nice solid cylinder, which makes it so much easier to lift.

Back in the buddy lines, we are told that we are going to be striking in stages today, so that they can look at certain aspects more closely. They will cue us to stop and then cue us again to continue. I get the feeling that they are really trying to cement this part of the strike now, or at least as much as they can do, so that we can move on to the rest of it. There are only four weeks to go and we surely need to start moving on. We still don't know what the smelters are going to do, except that we will be around the ring in the centre at some point, with the forgers behind us. They are going to wear fire retardant clothing. This was probably all shown in the computer simulation, but I can't actually recall any of it.

More waiting ensues and then Steve asks us to get into our creep positions, crouching down and making ourselves small. The classical music and the "Be not afeard..." speech sound out together, one over the other. The rumble of drums is next with the sound of the tree being uprooted. I imagine what this will sound like when all 1,000 drummers are here. I honestly can't wait. We are now in our buddy lines, looking towards the Tor. The Warriors are making their way down and onto the M25. A few booms tell us the strike will soon begin. Steve cues us to strike, the full beat thunders around the Stadium, and we begin.

When we reach our fences we are told to stop. The music is cut. The Mass Team spend some time conferring and then we are off again, with the music cued back in. We continue like this for the entire strike, although the pauses are not quite as frequent. Our priority turf went well. Once it is rolled I step over it to the other side so I am lifting on my left, with Elia and Gaudi either side of me, the roll on their right to keep things even.

Sometimes there are no Warriors available to take the turf off our shoulders, so we have to stand and wait if we are in a queue, or just go and drop it onto the pile ourselves. Once we do that it is no longer our problem and we go back to continue striking.

It is still chaotic once we are back on the FOP, but it is slowly becoming more organised, and we are in a position now where we can use our own initiative. Sometimes it is clear a few people need help with a particularly large piece of turf, so that is where we go, being careful to step over other turf being rolled. With so much happening it is sometimes to our advantage, the chaos concealing our confusion and, at times, lack of direction. Hopefully the audience will always be focussing on a part of the strike that is going well! There is indeed a lot to focus on, and this is only a small part of it.

The poppy moment is always very powerful – going from such turmoil to a complete standstill. The whistling is very emotive and I am sure this single minute will capture the hearts of many when we do it for real.

We finish on time but it is already late and it will easily be past midnight before I can get some rest before an early start tomorrow. I feel like we have made good progress tonight and it looks like we are going to get plenty done tomorrow. It's another full day; hopefully it will be put to better use than last weekend.

33

Rehearsal 14

Saturday 30 June 2012
9.00am – 5.30pm
Olympic Stadium

Today we are told to make our way to the upper stands once we have collected our bibs. I need a coffee before doing anything. I was here less than 11 hours ago and within that time I've only managed a few hours sleep. There are cups of Cadbury's hot chocolate available today. Maybe later but first I need caffeine.

The view from upstairs is so much better. These are probably the best seats for our segment as the stage is raised and from here you can see most of the set rather than just the side you are sitting on, which is the case with the lower tier. All of the turf is in place and it all looks great from here.

The weather is cloudy with the occasional light shower. When we are called onto the FOP it has dried up so at least the turf will be normal weight and there won't be any chance of slipping on that ramp. Katie gets us into our buddy lines, as ever, and counts us all, in the process reminding us which of her groups we belong to. She asks us if we have any points we wish to raise, goes over what we are going to do when we perform the inevitable first strike, and mentions anything else worthwhile. The usual chatting and banter ensues until we are told we are going to be doing a strike, but only a dry run initially.

Most of the morning is spent doing that dry run, then a full strike, resetting, and doing another strike. It has become such a routine now that we reel them off with relative ease, although there is always a question mark over how well it flows, and more importantly, looks. It is hard for us to know how well we are doing as we cannot see it, but the feedback is always positive. We can only accept this at face value as it never feels that way, not even now. Nevertheless we always get through it and we are clearly improving.

Earlier on Katie was talking to us in our county and she was feeling

192

a little upset about somebody who had told her he was leaving as he had had enough of the whole rehearsal experience. It was the guy I was chatting to yesterday. She knew it wasn't her fault, but felt somehow responsible that he was having a bad experience, to which we reassured her that it was not at all her fault.

I can now see that he is not here, whereas he was in the buddy lines earlier. I think it is a real shame, but clearly he felt very strongly about what we spoke about yesterday. That said, to up and leave after all this time is beyond my comprehension. This is definitely a once-in-a-lifetime opportunity, especially since all of us were originally chosen by ballot to audition. We are so close to show night, and whatever happens, we will pull this off, because we are working with professionals who have done similar things many times before, and because absolute success is the only option we have. We are going to make this happen, no matter what, and it is going to be beyond incredible. I cannot understand how you could walk away from that. A few of us speculate that he will be back once he has had time to calm down and think things through. In the meantime, however, we are a man down and it makes a difference, so a reallocation has had to occur.

Just before lunch Toby asks all of the smelters and forgers to gather around the ring in the centre for a briefing on what is expected of us. He tells us that the forgers will encircle the ring, whilst the smelters will be positioned along the trough that extends out from it. We are going to have a smelting shovel, which we will pick up from Vom 4, and the forgers will be issued with a large hammer or mallet, as they will be forging the ring. At some point the crucible will be used to pour molten metal into the trough, we will use our shovels to feed it along and into the ring which will be forged into the central ring of the five. This is an important role we are playing and I am indeed very pleased to be one of the lucky few to be so privileged. I suppose I would have preferred to have been a forger, but I can't complain. Toby then takes us through the actions we all need to do in our respective roles – an overarm swing for the forgers, timed so that is done in unison, and an extension of the arms and a pull back for the smelters. We all practise this, before it's the end of the briefing. We are going to be cued in to go to Vom 4 and collect our props, but we are told it will be after the poppy moment.

After an eventful morning we have an hour for lunch. Instead of returning to the registration area like last week to collect our lunch pack, it is distributed just outside one of the blocks. A very long queue quickly forms but I manage to get within two minutes of the front. We have the usual meat, halal and vegetarian options for the sandwiches, with the remaining contents more or less the same. We are told to move to the lower stands but not everybody does so at the same time, some preferring to eat their lunch first.

The FOP is now clear of all turf. The only thing left is the one ring in the centre. There are four others just like it, suspended above the upper tier, two at one end and two at the other. The hundreds, or probably thousands, of lines on the stage are visible – a sea of black, white and grey streaks. There is one wide channel that meanders from one end to the other. It looks suspiciously like the River Thames. Finally I realise what is underneath the Green and Pleasant Land: a representation of London seen from above. All of the lines are the thousands of roads, streets, lanes, hills, avenues, ways, crescents, terraces, approaches, closes, rises, and other thoroughfares that together make up the transport infrastructure of London. Once we clear everything this is what will be revealed for the remaining performers. It is a work of art that I can appreciate much more now that I know what it represents.

Around the FOP there are trailers loaded with real turf, piles of Astroturf, sections of corn, dollies stacked with fences, groups of hedges, all positioned wherever each county happens to dispose of them during our strikes. After the break we are surely going to have to reset once again, trying to make sense of the random mess we have left. Every single piece has a specific place, part of an enormous 3D jigsaw that we have solved so many times now, and will continue to do so.

I dispose of the remains of my lunch in the recycle bins provided. These are in abundance on the podium level and come in threes: one for food waste, one for paper and plastic, and one for non-recyclable. After moving my things down to the lower tier and finding a seat I notice a queue forming up the steps. At the bottom Danny Boyle is chatting to a few people. It looks like they are getting things autographed. It's a long queue so I don't join it. There will surely be other opportunities, and besides I don't have anything to get signed, aside from my bib maybe. I've seen plenty of bibs over the weeks bearing Danny's signature.

I bump into Daniel who is some way along the queue. He is holding a photo of him and Danny at Dagenham which he has developed. I wonder why he happens to be carrying this around with him. He explains that an announcement was made on our IEMs late last night that Danny will be signing items during lunch today. I completely missed this. I must have removed my ear phones by then. So this is an official signing session. Maybe he has decided to do this now, before things get even more hectic, and he won't be able to accommodate every single person who approaches him as he seems to have done thus far. I may as well get in the queue and not miss this chance.

I make a hot chocolate and join the end of the line which is still stretching just beyond the top of the steps. People have brought DVD covers, photos, cards and other such items. I have nothing. I could get my Ceremonies ID card signed, as others have done, but I would prefer to keep that intact. Looking in my wallet, the only thing I can find is my British Film Institute membership card. It is film related and Danny has been there a few times. I remember when he did a Q&A, with Cillian Murphy too, after a preview screening of his film Sunshine, an event that I unfortunately missed.

The queue is moving slowly and lunchtime is almost over. A few steps from the bottom one of the members of security politely asks those of us remaining to return to the rehearsal as there is no more time left. Steve has already asked us to make our way into our counties, but Danny is still there, signing items. Some people disperse but a small group of us, including James from my section of our buddy lines, try to persuade the security guard to let us remain as we are so close. He is having none of it, but we hold our ground. Danny is still there so we can't see what the problem is. It takes a lot of persuasion and insisting from us, but eventually the poor guy gives in. One girl in front of me has a paragraph pre-written, which she wants him to reproduce in a card. Some people get a bit uptight about this, as it's really only supposed to be a signature, but as ever Danny politely does what she asks. When it's my turn I hand him my membership card.

"This is the only thing I could find. You're familiar with this place."

"I certainly am." He turns it over to the reverse side but I ask him to sign the image side, which he does. I also ask him to sign my bib.

"Pull it really tight," he says. "You have to do that with the bibs." He has signed a lot of these.

As he is signing his name on my back, I ask him about the card I gave him, not surprised that he hasn't recognised me.

"Did you get a chance to read the card I gave to you?"

"Oh, you're the one who I sponsored?" He now faces me, having signed my bib.

"Yeah, that was me."

"I did read it. That was very sweet of you."

"Would be nice to talk about what I wrote in there, about films and stuff."

"Yeah, that would be good."

As always I am conscious of time and the fact that other people are still waiting. I thank him and walk away. I would love to spend more time chatting but I always catch him at an inconvenient time, when other things are happening. In truth, I must admit that I do always feel just a little shy in his presence, not because of who he is, but because that is part of my nature. I also find his overly friendly approach slightly overpowering. Strange as it may seem, I have always found other people's kindness and affability a source of discomfort and I often feel the need to walk away from it. I almost welcome the fact that Danny Boyle is too busy to give us more time individually.

Ultimately though, that's not why I'm here and I am always aware of this. I have a job to do, like any other. Any time spent with him is a bonus for anybody who gets the chance, but certainly not a right bestowed upon us, even if it is his vision that we are here to help realise. I've almost definitely been filmed by him once, spoken to him a few times, been sponsored by him in the process, shaken his hand, had a photo with him, and now have his autograph twice. I think I've had more than my fair share. I don't think there will be other opportunities. He will be too busy. He did this signing session for a reason.

By the time I reach Fife the sun is beating down and it is just a few hours before we are due to finish. In order to continue our rehearsal we need to do another reset, which is already under way so I join everybody else and pitch in wherever needed. Turf always comes first. We usually try to make sense of the pile, trying to work out which piece is which number, and therefore where it is positioned, but what invariably happens is we just take everything to our county and work it out as we go along. There is no clear system, nor is it possible most of the time. Lifting it off a large pile, as opposed to off the ground, is twice as hard too. Still, we are getting more used to doing this and it is becoming a somewhat dreaded part of our routine due to its regularity.

Once the set is back in place, around 40 or 50 minutes later, we are ready to pull it all apart again, our hard work destroyed in about a third of the time. We are told that we are taking it from the top and will be doing it in stages again, the stoppages cued. We are also going to incorporate our choreography into it at the beginning of the strike as we walk onto the FOP for the structures. This will also be cued, on a certain beat, when we will go into our combination minus Shut Boot/Sliding Doors.

Whilst we wait Diane explains to us that we need to pin down the performance aspect now. We know the strike and what we have to do, even if it doesn't always go perfectly. That will come with more practice. We do, however, need to begin performing the strike, rather than just going through it. Our facial expression is deadpan, we have to look straight ahead, no looking around, we are absolutely focussed on our work, and we are walking with determination and a clear purpose, heavy footfalls. The click track that always plays in the background on our IEMs, behind the music, is to help us move rhythmically and on the beat, each click representing a footfall. If we are ever stationary for any reason, we must still be moving to the beat, remaining deadpan and focussed straight ahead. Diane demonstrates and asks us to always keep this in mind from now on. She also goes over when we will be cued to begin our choreography.

The strike soon begins, right from the top. Classical music and "Be not afeared…", tree uprooting, drum roll, bang & shout, percussive, rhythmic beat, slowly builds to another drum roll, bang & shout, percussion repeats, drum roll builds, moving on the beat, standby strike, bang & shout, strike go, bang, standby for levers pull/chisel hammer, bang, moving forward, bang, one, two, three, bang, and…boom, choreo, on the beat, click, click, click, click, drums pounding, go and rip this land apart. This one strike, with the choreography and Diane's pep talk about performing and focussing, plus the music on the PA, has an incredible effect and I think for the first time I am absolutely charged and determined to remove this Green and Pleasant Land and make way for chimneys and beam engines and looms.

With a few complete stops incorporated, we go through our structures as usual, followed by the priority turf, which goes well, and then manage one more piece of turf, before the poppy moment. Everybody stops. If people have some turf on their shoulders, they put it back down. Everyone looks to the poppy field where the soldiers have gathered. For one minute we are all silent and motionless, no jerking of the head, no hands moving, no eyes wandering. Admittedly not everybody manages this. Not this time.

When the music kicks back in, whilst everybody else continues into Hail Mary, the smelters and forgers go to Vom 4, in our case, to pick up our props, which are not actually there, so we do without and walk back onto the FOP via the M25 and our own ramp, over to the trough that leads into the ring. There is a lot of traffic to negotiate so we don't find a clear path, having to stop in our tracks on the way to let people pass. With this momentary pause I look at our chimney towering above us, positioned to the right of where we are. I scan the FOP and can see other chimneys in neighbouring counties. One of the last ones is still rising. It looks amazing.

The passage clears and we move off towards the trough. Josh, Gaudi, Jon, Harry and I, plus Daniel too now, are amongst those who are on the west side. A separate group from other counties are positioned opposite us, on the east side. Without our shovels, we just perform the action when cued. The forgers are now forging the ring, swinging and hammering together. Everybody else is slowly moving in, having cleared the FOP, getting closer and closer, all around us. The smelters stop, and the ring begins to rise. It doesn't actually happen this time, but Steve is talking us through it, helping us picture what will be happening. The smelters are then cued to turn about, giving the forgers plenty of space, and then everybody, except for the forgers, walks out to the edge of the FOP, doing our combination, including Shut Boot/Sliding Doors. For now we just have to find a space wherever we can, and then continue our combination, until we are cued to stop and turn around for a pyro shower.

Steve congratulates us and declares, "We have a segment." Much of it was cued and we were really just following instructions that we hadn't known about before, but we somehow managed it. The Mass Team and every other member of the crew are applauding us. It feels great. As I look around I see Katie. She looks very impressed, and there is an overwhelming sense of how far we have come since the disjointed strikes in Dagenham, the chaos which is still apparent, but is now much more organised, the many hours of waiting and waiting, the changes we have made, all of which have culminated in this: a complete segment. I think the entire FOP has, for at least one second, felt this too. We do still have a long way to go but at least we now have a complete segment and we just need to rehearse, practise, fine tune, and perfect. It has been a fantastic rehearsal, and we have achieved a lot. Even better, we don't have to reset! Soon enough we are free to go. Day two of this rehearsal marathon is over. Back tomorrow, nice and early.

34

Rehearsal 15

Sunday 1 July 2012
9.00am – 1.00pm
Olympic Stadium

Today we have a short rehearsal to bring to an end a rather long weekend. After yesterday I am looking forward to another full strike and complete segment. We have moved a few steps forward and reached a real milestone. Upon arrival at the Stadium we are greeted by the military, so this is a change. They seem friendly enough, but are still just a little intimidating. It's a high security area after all. My bag is checked but I have no problems getting through.

Once I've collected my meal pack and lunch I go through the usual routine until Steve invites us onto the FOP. The turf is all back in place so we are going to start from the top once again. Whilst the crew are preparing and having their briefings, we just wander about and chat amongst ourselves. The set is always being improved and embellished, tested and adjusted. As we stand on the set there are all manner of operations occurring underneath us, some of which we see through the traps, but only ever a glimpse of what is happening: the rails that the chimneys are brought out on being tested, a strap pulled here, a rope tightened there, team leaders giving instructions, all of them just working around us.

Since yesterday the rocks in the pool next to our fence line have been fully painted and textured. They are of course just large chunks of sculpted foam, yet they look incredibly realistic, complete with algae and dirt. Somebody has spent a lot of time on these. Josh lets curiosity get the better of him and lifts a large rock with one hand, this specimen weighing a hundred times lighter than its solid counterpart. The water is often allowed to flow freely, before being drained and discussions held about its functionality, or other such issues that do not directly concern us, yet are an integral part in making our set as credible and as visually arresting as possible. It is a joy to see it all unfold, long before the eyes of the world will fall upon this fine display of flamboyance.

Before too long we are in our buddy lines and getting ready to do a full strike, just like yesterday. One difference today is that we won't be doing any choreography at the beginning, just after we are cued to strike. We will, however, need to do our Work Prep when cued. This makes more sense as we are of course going to be working. Another difference today is that the drummers are here, so they will be playing whilst we strike. This is the first time they have been present with us in the Stadium. Hearing them practise their drum patterns and beats is incredible. Their rhythmic banging is reverberating around the entire Stadium and it is just a tantalising taste of how they will contribute to the atmosphere on show night.

As we wait and chat in our lines, some of us opting to sit on a nearby trailer instead, Chris is doing a round of Fife with a large bag of red sweets, in celebration of Canada Day. He is also wearing a pair of very cool looking red-rimmed sunglasses.

Katie does her rounds and informs us of any updates that we need to know after the Mass Team's discussions last night. When we go home they continue, rehearsing with another group of performers, or they wrap things up, discuss changes, de-brief before the next rehearsal, working late. They are all paid staff but they must be giving their entire life to this. I can only wonder how they find time to do anything else.

When I saw Katie, and everybody else, applauding us yesterday I was rather humbled. We mustn't forget just how much they all deserved the applause too. They have led us to this point, each and every one of them. In our case Katie, who is our leader. She has organised us, guided, briefed, and listened to us, acknowledged our thoughts, taken suggestions, accommodated our shortcomings with never a bad word, divided us into groups, directed us this way and that, allocated tasks, been there with us in the rain and the wind, always with a smile, always a welcome, has made changes, been patient, understanding, enthusiastic, upbeat, she has helped us visualise on her map, explained and clarified, time and again, tirelessly led us to where we are now. And she so humbly applauded us.

With these thoughts pushed to the back of my mind, I focus on what we are about to do. This time we are going all the way through to the end with no stops, just following the cues. Diane quickly explains when we are going to do Work Prep, just as we move out of our creep positions, before we slowly form our lines, but it will be cued. She also explains that whenever we are walking back to continue striking, we must do so in groups of two or three, ideally, but never alone. This shouldn't be difficult as we never strike anything alone.

As the drummers pound their drums, we begin our strike in the usual way. I am now constantly trying to stay focussed and only look ahead, or at the very least not turning my head. When striking my second piece of turf, I am with Gaudi. The Warriors take it from our shoulders, we walk a few steps forward, and then the poppy moment kicks in. As ever everybody stands still until we are cued to continue. We both walk together towards Vom 4. This time there are smelting shovels waiting for us, all lined up outside the entrance. Josh, Harry and Jon are there ahead of us. We all take a prop and rest it on our shoulders. They are rather long so we need to take care not to knock somebody with the handle. By the time we walk up the ramp we are more or less in a line, with others having joined us.

At the trough there is a bit of confusion with the cues. Some people begin smelting immediately, some of us wait for the cue and when it doesn't come we join the others. There is a lot of space along the trough. It slowly fills up as more smelters arrive, but it hasn't worked very well with the initial gaps. When the cue is given we all turn and make our way to the perimeter, doing the combination, except we can't do so as we are still holding our smelting shovels. I just keep moving on the beat. I make a mental note to ask Diane what we should be doing here. Steve has been on our IEMs throughout the post-Hail Mary portion, describing to us what is supposedly happening so we can picture the scene, the rings all converging behind us as we perform our choreography, facing the audience. Eventually the music stops and we are told to turn for the pyro shower. The middle ring has fully risen today and we all look up at it as Steve explains that we are "the luckiest one thousand people on the planet, to be so close to the pyro shower." This enormous ring is just hanging in the air above our heads. That alone looks awesome, maybe because we haven't seen this before, or maybe because the idea of five enormous rings hanging there is almost incomprehensible at the moment. We wait until the music fades out, all the time just staring up at the ring, transfixed at the sight above us. Once again the underlying feeling is of how far we have come.

Yesterday was no fluke – we have managed our entire segment again and now it really is just a case of perfecting it. Steve is always so enthused at our performance. Every single strike we have ever done is met with nothing but positive vibes from him. It so often feels like anything but the praiseworthy display we are told it is, yet it is impossible to discern what it really looks like from down here, so maybe it does look that good. Whatever it may be, the strike is over and we now have to do a full reset. Everybody breaks formation and it is back to work.

After the reset we have a short break and when we return Katie wants to go through a few things with those of us on priority strike. She speaks to us against a backdrop of drumming as they continue to practise around the Stadium, some of them lining the perimeter of the podium level, others in small groups around the FOP, evidently being told which beat to play via their IEMs. It is a real pleasure to be here in this environment, so many groups of performers working independently in the same space. The Brunels and the Suffragettes are doing their thing, us Working Men and Women are dispersed throughout the Green and Pleasant Land, having briefings, going over strike patterns, practising hakas, the tech team are testing their equipment, and the drummers are providing a thumping soundtrack of beats, bangs, and boshes. There is so much going on. The atmosphere is amazing.

I manage to grab Diane to ask her about the smelters doing the choreography at the end. She says that since we have shovels over our shoulders, we just have to walk to the perimeter and then continue to move on the beat whilst everybody is doing the combination. This therefore means that we won't actually do any choreography except for Work Prep at the beginning, which is a real shame. All of that learning from Polly and Diane, and subsequent practice, will come to nothing. It doesn't quite seem right, and I am rather disappointed. There have, however, been many changes so far, so who knows what could happen. I hope we find a way around this.

One development has just been announced. We are to get into bib order and move into the voms, in the case of Fife, into Vom 5. Organising this takes some time as it isn't a question of us all just piling in. We have to maintain our lines and as more people enter, we are moved back, which happens several times, until we are in the vom and round the corner to the left, out of sight of the entrance. On the way there we see a wonderful period horse-drawn bus with no horse, clearly a prop for the show. There are also some hospital beds lining the walls. The inside of the vom is actually quite vast, with doors leading into corridors on the sides, and further back a sort of outer corridor, presumably encircling the arena, which is where a lot of us are now standing, the line running along the wall. At various intervals there are doors leading into rooms, press areas and photo labs. I try to imagine the hustle and bustle in this backstage area on show night, with the roar of the crowd as we are getting ready to exit and begin our segment. It has been confirmed that this will be where we exit from, and as soon as everybody is in place we are going to do just that and go into a full strike and complete our segment once again.

There follows the customary waiting of more than a few minutes before we begin to trickle out of the vom and into our creep positions, making ourselves small as Steve likes to describe it. Unlike the first time today, there is less confusion about when to do Work Prep, on which beat, and it goes more smoothly this time. So begins another strike. It is almost becoming robotic, at least the fence strike is. There is a bit more improvisation involved in the turf strikes, but we all know what to do and we are gradually clocking up a very healthy tally of complete strikes so it is increasingly a case of going through similar motions, and so we continue.

This time I find myself split from the smelting group before the poppy moment, due to too much traffic crossing my path, so when we resume I have to walk solo to Vom 4, which isn't ideal, but I remain focussed and walk on the beat, synchronising my foot falls with the clicks on my IEM. Our shovels have once again been laid out neatly, ready for us to grab and sling over our shoulders. I manage to join the line and we walk to the trough, once again stopping at the top of the ramp to let people pass. Turf is still being cleared in some counties. When we reach the trough I manage to find a place very close to the ring itself, with the rest of it extending out to the right. A clear cue is given to begin smelting. The forgers are all hammering in unison. I wonder if we should be smelting as one too. I'm sure this will be confirmed once somebody notices that we are all over the place, sometimes our shovels clashing as they crisscross from east to west. It's just something else that doesn't look or feel very good. What does look great, however, is the view from here as everybody slowly walks in towards us. My eyes should be on the trough, but I can't help but steal a glance at the hundreds of people surrounding us before the cues to stop, turn and walk out are given, all of us leaving the forgers around the central ring, which has already begun to rise. It does feel odd to be walking on the beat whilst everybody is shutting boots, pulling levers, chiselling and hammering. That is, however, what the smelters have to do, as I've been told. For the second time today we turn and see the ring suspended in the air – just the central one again. It's a nice way to end the long weekend. We have made a lot of progress and it's all beginning to come together with just 26 days remaining and only a handful of rehearsals.

35

A Letter From Danny, A Note From Vanessa

Tuesday 3 July 2012

Dear Volunteer

As we move into the last three weeks of rehearsals I want to thank you for your hard work, patience and dedication – seriously, you're an inspiration to all of us on the Ceremonies team and a huge credit to the whole idea of the Olympics. These last few weeks are critical for us all so please stay focussed, continue working as hard as you have been and I know if we do so we will put on a Ceremony that will make a few jaws drop!

I know many of you have been dismayed by the media scrutiny on the show – helicopters, newspaper leaks, etc. Some of you have asked why we agreed to the two media briefings we have done when 'open season' continues on trying to reveal every aspect of our work to the public ahead of 27 July. We thought they would be a good way to satisfy the media's curiosity about our show but, in the case of certain papers, it hasn't quenched their desire to be the first to reveal every detail possible.

I am sorry that, despite our best efforts, we appear to be unable to stop these stories appearing in the press and realise that this may make it hard for each of you to safeguard our show. Don't let it get to you. Stay virtuous! I believe we all share the desire to protect the show so our audience, in the Stadium, at home and in the media, can discover the surprises for themselves on the night and piece together the puzzle with their friends and family.

Again thank you from all of us for everything you are doing to deliver a fantastic show on 27 July.

Danny Boyle

There had been a few stories in the press which speculated about some of the details of the Ceremony. Some of the information was close to ridiculous and sadly some of it was painfully accurate. One article even included an overhead photo of the FOP after we had completed a strike, revealing the fact that the Green and Pleasant Land was not there for the duration, although there were no details of how that would happen.

We had invested so much time in the show, and fully believed in what we were trying to convey and achieve, that most of us felt extremely frustrated at some factions within the media who were trying to ruin the surprise. For the time being it was our show and our secret. We all wanted to hold on to that and preserve the surprise upon which the wonder that was going to unfold was so reliant. Some of us thought that Ceremonies had taken measures to enforce no-fly zones and impose embargoes, but this had not been the case. Dismay was absolutely what we felt, and when we received no official reaction about the leaks, that soon became disbelief that the media was being allowed to get away with it unchallenged. Most of us were not seasoned professionals and simply not used to this happening.

Danny's message finally acknowledged that, and in some ways, coming from the top, that was all we needed to allay our concerns. We had built the show together, and we all continued as one.

It was quite comforting that some of my colleagues at work had no desire to log onto the internet and search for the stories. They didn't wish to spoil the surprise for themselves either.

Friday 6 July 2012

Hello WMW & Warriors

21 days to go!
We are coming to the last few weeks and have been asked to add a Contingency Rehearsal on 16 July to your schedules. This is a possible make-up day, or a day for camera angles and working through transitions. It's also possible that only certain groups will be asked to attend to get further direction. The Contingency has not been activated so please DO NOT attend unless we ask you to.
We sent everyone an SMS last week before Sunday's

rehearsal (about increased security). We will be using this method of communication for last minute changes and reminders. Please don't respond to these messages.

So far we have been rehearsing your segment individually. Next we will start putting the Ceremony together, so we will rehearse the transitions from what happens before you and after you. Also we will be rehearsing how you leave your holding area and get onto the FOP. With a cast of 10,000, what happens backstage is very important and we need to get it right.

We will soon be able to give you better refined times for when you need to get to the Stadium for all dress rehearsals. Please be aware that we will not be running the entire show for our audience. We are asking the public to leave at 10.15pm so they can get to public transport.

During dress rehearsals, you will wear your costume and make-up. You will also start rehearsing your walk from your holding area to the Stadium according to what happens before and after you. You will have to get into the Park before the doors open to the public. For these reasons, we have asked you to come to rehearsals very early. You will spend several hours waiting, so be prepared for this.

As you probably understand, such a complex show – made up of many different and complicated segments – is a huge machine. We are all part of this machine, and we have to act and move at exactly the right time for the machine to work as a whole. As all dress rehearsals are conducted as per show day, after your performance you will be led back to your holding area to change out of your costume and then leave the Olympic Park. Unfortunately, there will not be an opportunity to watch the show.

Show Night: the hard work, the sweat, the laughs, the frowns – we promise it's all worth it, and it ends with the World's Biggest Show, an 80,000 person live audience and a billion people watching around the globe. Like the dress rehearsals, unfortunately after you have completed your role it won't be possible to view the rest of the Ceremony. At the conclusion of your performance you will return to your holding area to change and then exit. This way you can get safely away on public transport before 80,000 members of the audience, dozens of coaches, and 10,000 athletes all leave at the same time. In this way it is like all other shows: as a participant you do not get to watch. We recognise this is a hard thing, but experience has shown us over many ceremonies that this is the best way to ensure that the cast has enough time to get off site safely and home. It is a night to set the video recorder and watch it later with a glass of something special.

The schedule was now as follows:

DATE	TIME	VENUE DETAILS/NOTES
Sat 07 July	13:00 to 22:00	Stadium
Sun 08 July	09:00 to 13:00	Stadium
Tue 10 July	17:30 to 22:00	Stadium
Sat 14 July	09:00 to 17:30	Stadium COMPULSORY
Mon 16 July	18:00 to 22:00	Stadium CONTINGENCY
Wed 18 July	12:00 to 22:00	Stadium COMPULSORY
Fri 20 July	10:00 to 22:00	Stadium COMPULSORY
Sat 21 July	10:00 to Midnight	Stadium Dress Rehearsal COMPULSORY
Mon 23 July	10:00 to Midnight	Stadium Dress Rehearsal COMPULSORY
Wed 25 July	10:00 to Midnight	Stadium Dress Rehearsal COMPULSORY
Fri 27 July	10:00 to Midnight	Stadium SHOW DAY

I couldn't quite believe that we were going to be required until midnight during the dress rehearsals, when previously it stated End of Segment. That meant 14 hours. I could only assume that this was simply time that they wanted us to set aside and then a tighter schedule would be issued later. However, to spend that long in the Stadium rehearsing did sound exciting, especially since everybody would be buzzing with the pending spectacle so close. The length of the schedule itself, the days gradually getting deleted, was a nice depiction of just how the Ceremony was creeping and creeping.

36

Rehearsal 16

Saturday 7 July 2012
1.00pm – 10.00pm
Olympic Stadium

There has been a lot of discussion on our Facebook page recently about being allowed to watch the Ceremony, or what is left of it, after we have finished our segment. Brian has been brilliant in expressing to the Casting team what this would mean to us, why we wish to do so, and even suggested ways in which this could be achieved. Most of us, including myself, cannot understand why this isn't a given since we have granted so much of our time to the Ceremony. After Vanessa addressed the issue in her update this week, I am beginning to understand that this is possibly just the way things work. We are going to be performing our segment and will then be asked to leave. We are not even going to be permitted to remain in the Park for the fireworks. Not being seasoned professionals, a lot of us are having difficulty grasping this. I am not sure how we will say goodbye to the Ceremony so easily. Yet we will simply have to accept this as part of the experience.

With all these thoughts in my mind I arrive for another rehearsal on another Saturday afternoon. Walking to the Stadium through Westfield I occasionally spot a fellow performer, either because I know them or because they are wearing the tell-tale lanyard around their neck. Newly installed Olympic-related signage is appearing regularly, the final touches being put in place to welcome the world. So many Games Makers have already begun their shifts, even as I am due to have my venue training the following day.

Today I am met with a longer queue than usual so it takes some time to reach security, which is now much tighter, the airport-style checks in full swing. For the very first time I am asked to show my diabetes card on account of my needles being taken on site. With no further checks required, I am soon on the familiar walk to the Stadium. It is always a pleasure to walk past the Aquatics Centre. Sometimes I gaze up at the 'wave' as I walk underneath it. At least I believe that is what the design represents. Soon I am collecting my bib, just helping myself now, having already picked up my two snacks from the registration area.

The weather is quite pleasant this afternoon. The FOP looks much better in the sun, and of course makes for a much nicer environment to rehearse in, although by now we all know it could rain at any time. As I make myself a coffee (the Cadbury's hot chocolate is no longer available, as spillages were apparently causing stains to the seats) Massive Attack's 'Teardrop' starts to play on the PA, perhaps a clue to the final soundtrack selection on show night. As Liz Fraser's angelic voice fills the Stadium, I sit back and enjoy the experience. They are testing the LED lights again, as they often do, except this time they are testing the entire auditorium. Sometimes the lights are used to flash randomly, or make large blocks of colour that could travel around the auditorium, and sometimes they are used to create words and longer messages. The possibilities are endless and I'm sure they will be used to full effect on show night.

My thoughts are lost in the music and light display, although this short spiral into sun-tinged bliss is interrupted by the sound of an extremely cheesy 80s-style pop song. I have no idea who this is, but I am suddenly in fear that this will be part of the soundtrack on the night. I can't do anything but sit and listen to this and wait for it to end. It is so bad I feel very relieved when it is over.

Over on the set the stage team are setting the FOP, just adding the finishing touches, positioning hedges, straightening the fence lines, and making it ready for us to tear apart yet again. After a short respite we have to sit through that horrible song again. Why have they chosen this? It is beyond me. We actually have to endure the song for a third time before Steve welcomes us to this long rehearsal. Aside from the usual introductions and information, he addresses an issue that some people have complained about, that of the railings that go around the traps being too heavy. I can certainly vouch for this as I helped carry one during the first rehearsal here, although haven't done so since. They have sourced new railings that are much lighter and a demo is given where a railing is lifted with just one hand. Those who are responsible for carrying these applaud their approval.

Soon we are on the FOP and in our counties. We are going to begin with just a priority strike today, in order to make way for the bellows, which will be used to blow smoke onto the set to help create the industrial scene we will move into after Hail Mary. As soon as the required turf is removed and the bellows have been tested, we stop and replace the turf. Now it's into Vom 5 where we line up for a while, waiting to strike.

Toby talks to us through our IEMs about the haka routine. He has decided that we will do Work Prep immediately before we strike our first structure. He will go through it later with us. Rather than doing a full strike, as expected, we are told to have a short break, so it's back into the seating area for a hot drink and a snack – there isn't much else to do. We are, however, treated to a run-through of the opening scene, just before we come on. There are two horse-drawn carriages, the same one that we saw last week and have just seen today whilst we were waiting, exiting Vom 3 and Vom 5. They make a round of the FOP on the M25, meet and then return into the voms. The classical music, which I have learnt just this week is Nimrod by Edward Elgar, plays on the PA at the same time as Brunel's speech from The Tempest. Demonstration over. It was quite special to witness that – our first taste of the actual show as it will happen, or at least it seems to be.

After the break we are back on the FOP to do a warm-up. I'm not sure why we do this at some rehearsals and don't do so at others. Whoever it is leading us is on the Tor, but I can't quite see her so I just follow the others. It's only a few minutes before we are deemed adequately stretched, and then it's back into the voms. Our county is directed into the corridor on the right this time, lining up against the wall, lowest numbers at the front and working our way backwards. We are held here for some time, presumably so that everybody can be shown into similar areas around the Stadium. Standing with one ear phone plugged in, I wait with the others to be told to standby. Unfortunately there is very little to see here – just white walls and grey carpet, and the occasional doorway that leads somewhere unknown. The corridor stretches far back, curving to the right, so it probably encircles the Stadium like the exterior pathway we were in yesterday.

The sound of Nimrod eventually tells us that we are going to be striking soon. Steve joins us in our ears and we are led outside via the door we came through, turning to the left to exit the vom. Into our creep positions, we wait for the cue to form our lines, this time not beginning with Work Prep, as we are going to do that just as we approach our first structure to strike, in mine and Gaudi's case our fence. This means it will be staggered and seemingly random, with some people preparing for work before others have even reached the ramp. We both do the routine but it is clear that we are going to have to establish a cue if we are to be in sync with each other, as we are supposed to be.

The strike continues in much the same way as last Sunday. We pick up our smelting shovels with no problems, still arriving in small groups rather than all together, and taking our place along the trough wherever we happen to be in the line. I had to step over some turf this time, before reaching the trough. There was also turf left at the edge, where we are smelting, which I had to just shove aside. It was soon removed. I notice at least one of the beam engines in my peripheral vision that has made it out of its trap. Some workers are stood around it performing the Dials routine. Within a few minutes, with the middle ring rising behind us, we make our way to the perimeter. I take a place near our waterwheel and move on the beat, shovel held in one hand, whilst almost everybody else is in the combination. Overall I don't feel the strike has been quite as good as last time, but we did add a few bits and pieces, so it's been slightly different.

When we turn today and look up to what will be the pyro shower, I am amazed to see that all five rings have converged. The ubiquitous Olympic symbol is floating above us, an enormous representation of the five interlocking rings. I think this has taken everybody by surprise and it looks incredible. As the final bars of the music play out on our IEMs, and as Steve, in contrast to my own opinion, declares the strike "unbelievable", I can only stare in awe and wonder at the sight above us. Last week I was amazed to see one ring hanging so high. To see all five has made the entire journey so far worth every single minute. I have no interest in whether we could have come this far with less waiting around, or fewer rehearsals even. We have given so much time but we are being rewarded handsomely now. And it is only going to get better.

When the music stops and our focus breaks I notice a few people suspended in the air on ropes. They are the ones strapped onto the chimneys as they rise out of the traps. For now the chimneys are back inside the traps and the guys on them are left hanging.

Steve announces our dinner break. A rush to the registration area to pick up our meal pack ensues. I wonder what's in store today. We changed from Walkers crisps to Pringles last Sunday and an apple instead of a clementine. No change in the granola bar, however. As I open the brown paper bag I am faced with the same combination of items and wonder if this is what we are going to get at every rehearsal.

Except for the sandwich it is all the same. Taking a seat next to Harry we both eat our meal. He tells me it is his birthday today, although doesn't elaborate on how he feels about spending this day rehearsing for the Opening Ceremony. Maybe he has a night out planned afterwards, but I don't ask, instead looking at the LED lights being tested again. This time they are using the different colours available to them to make flags. We see the Union Jack, the Stars and Stripes, and others that I don't recognise. I am sure they will be very warmly received when the Stadium is packed with people from all over the globe in a few weeks' time, pockets of cheers erupting as people spot their nation's flag.

After the break we are called onto the FOP to see a pyro test. This isn't as grand as it initially sounds when we are treated to nothing but a few sparks emitting from the trough where we smelt. For the next 90 minutes or so we go through the end sequences, once we have completed the Hail Mary portion of the strike, which is essentially how the FOP is set at the moment, not a single piece of turf to be found on the set. As we begin to smelt and the forgers play their parts, everybody goes into the combination as soon as they have finished striking. All of us, forgers and smelters included, practise this, facing towards the centre. Now something new is introduced: when the cue is given we all go into Shovel/Pickaxe, slowly advancing forward with the moves, and then we gradually walk towards the ring when cued.

We go through this a few times, building up to when we turn and walk to the perimeter. Each step is cued and counted in, so we all move together, going into the full combination as we walk out. This we also practise more than once. Again, they are clearly attempting to pin this down so we can move on from practising it and concentrating on the performance aspect. We are now asked to stand on the perimeter, like we have been doing for the last few strikes, but trying to keep it consistent and even all the way round. The aim is to form a large ring that runs all the way around the FOP. Those of us at the top of the ramps have to keep our lines, which are a few rows deep, as even as possible as we don't have a railing to guide us. This requires some adjustment, but once established we have to remember exactly where we are standing, and ideally walk towards this precise position every time we break out from the centre to form our very own ring, just as the real rings are converging above us.

All the while the drummers are establishing their own positions. Some of them walk to the inner edge of the M25 and form rows, facing the audience, whilst others work their way onto the Tor, making sure their route doesn't clash with our movements. The flow is once again under scrutiny with up to 2,000 of us being directed and positioned. It all takes practice but we eventually get to where Steve and his Mass Team want us. Finally we establish our exit points. Those of us who take a rail onto the FOP at the beginning have to remove it as we finish, before exiting. The rest of us are going to be leaving via the aisles in the stands, walking through the audience. That is going to be quite an experience. Steve predicts that they are going to be applauding us, patting our backs, shaking our hands, maybe even wanting our autographs. I'm just a little sceptical about his latter belief but whichever it is, it will be awesome.

Back to the present and it is time for a full reset. We escaped this earlier, but now it is upon us. I don't mind the hard work involved here or the heavy lifting; it is mainly the difficulty in unravelling the large pile of turf and working out where it all goes. Structures are quite easy as they are placed relatively systematically when struck. To alleviate the arduousness of the task, they are playing music on the PA, mainly dance. This gives rise to a bit of a dance-along amongst the group, led by Katie, on the dartboard once that turf has been replaced. There is one guy in our group, Mikele, who is somewhat of an eccentric to put it mildly. Crazy he is, and I told him as much when we were in Dagenham. He duly agreed with me. He can often be heard singing in the buddy lines. He is full of life and this now comes to the fore as more and more people take the opportunity to have a boogie whilst we await instructions. The assumption is that we are resetting for another full strike so a bit of light relief isn't going to go amiss. With the reset more or less complete, people are either watching the dance competition, as it has sort of become, or just sit on the turf, relax and chat whilst watching the LEDs being tested yet again, colours randomly flashing and words being spelt out. A massive WELCOME fills one side of the auditorium.

At around 8pm, with just a couple of hours to go, we are granted a quick ten minute break. Considering the rehearsal will have been nine hours today, we haven't done as much as we might have, although we have still made some good progress. Just one full segment and a reset so far.

When we return we are back inside our corridor in the vom, lined up for another strike, as expected. On our IEMs we are told that there will be no creeping this time. They have decided to abandon that idea, so we are going to exit the vom and walk straight up the ramp. This will all be cued so we just need to listen for the instructions. The changes have been coming thick and fast of late.

Once again the music eventually begins and we are cued to strike. For the first time I really notice the section of the auditorium that will be visible as we move out of the vom. That is going to be packed with spectators. Such an amazing sight it will be. I'm not supposed to be looking around so I re-focus. With the incredible sound of the drummers surrounding us, we walk straight up the ramp. This works much better than creeping. It is more direct. Gaudi and I have worked out a better way of doing our Work Prep at the fence: I do a count of two and on three we both begin, ensuring we are in sync. On the ninth beat we both grab the fence and then wait until it is time to walk down the ramp with it – just a few seconds.

When we reach our priority turf a couple of minutes later we have to wait a while to get more people to help us as there are only three of us. I have no idea what has happened to the others but it makes no difference who strikes the turf. Katie eventually finds a few people to help. When these things happen there is nothing we can do and we just have to wait rather than breaking our backs as it is so heavy.

Within around 17 minutes after beginning, it is all over and for the second time today we are looking up at the full set of rings just floating high above us. It looks superb again. After our toil and the chaos of the strike we receive our just reward. This without the pyro shower. During the minute or so that we are standing there looking up, I think about how the strike went. It wasn't great. The smelting itself wasn't bad, but we need better cues for when we pick up our shovels, when we move off and when we begin smelting. It isn't quite working yet and probably doesn't look very impressive. Toby confirmed earlier on that we are not smelting in rhythm, like the forgers, otherwise we will resemble a group of rowers. That aspect has been resolved, but the rest still needs some work.

Before we leave for the day we have to do another full reset. It's almost 9pm and we are busy piecing together this enormous jigsaw puzzle. I wonder how many pieces there are. However many there may be, within around 35 minutes we have put the set back together and we are free to go, half an hour early. Tomorrow will be another busy day: rehearsal at 9am for four hours, then off to the Skybar for our meet-up, and ending the day with venue training until 10pm.

215

37

Rehearsal 17

Sunday 8 July 2012
9.00am – 1.00pm
Olympic Stadium

There are no showers forecast today. Instead we have heavy rain. By the time I reach the Stadium every part of my attire not covered by my poncho is drenched; only my socks survive, protected by the boots we were issued with. We are directed to the upper stands once we have registered and collected our meal packs and bibs. Hundreds of volunteers have already arrived as I am late today. Getting out of bed was such a struggle. All of the lower rows have been filled so I climb to the upper ones. As I am doing this Steve gets on his mic and asks everybody to sit with their own counties. Most people tend to sit with people they know, so it follows that a lot of us are already with people from our own county. However, Steve's very simple request is anything but in practice. A different kind of chaos to what we are used to ensues: firstly deciding where everybody from Fife will gather, and then everybody getting there, whilst all of the other counties are doing the same. We manage it in the end.

The weather definitely requires coveralls today as it is also far colder than it should be. As I struggle into these in the limited space available, Danny Boyle addresses us. He has some important information to impart as well as a vital request. Before getting to that he expresses his complete joy at Bradley Wiggins winning the yellow jersey in the Tour de France. He is clearly very pleased and wanted to share that with us.

He begins by addressing the news from a couple of days ago that the actor Mark Rylance has had to withdraw from the Opening Ceremony due to unforeseen circumstances. He was drafted in to play Brunel, reciting the "Be not afeared…" speech from The Tempest at the beginning. It is very unfortunate, but unavoidable. This does now mean that Kenneth Branagh will be taking his place, something that hasn't been announced yet so we are the first to hear about it. Kenneth has recently been awarded a knighthood, and Danny tells us that people in the business are already talking about him being offered one for his services to the Olympics. He goes on to tell us that should that be the case he won't accept it. There is what appears to be spontaneous applause at this. Whether or not this will transpire as just described in the coming weeks and months remains to be seen.

He now moves to the more serious business that concerns us directly. Firstly he congratulates us for getting to where we are. Without any cuts in the planned segment, we have pulled off what so many people said would not be possible. It is the largest single set change ever attempted, and we have managed it, not just once but several times. We have nipped that firmly in the bud and he has no concerns over that. The performance aspect is a different matter. They have been watching the videos of our recent strikes and there is an underlying concern that not all of us are performing as we should be: focussed, determined, eyes straight ahead, no smiling, no talking. We absolutely must be in the moment throughout our segment. Some of us are doing it, some of us are not. Those in the latter category will tarnish the overall performance and make it look bad, which will affect the performances of those who are fully focussed on the task. We are the Working Men and Women. The audience needs to see us working, they need to see the attitude that is a requisite to digging up the countryside and working in the mills and the factories, engulfed by the steam and the grease and the dirt. They need to feel the hard graft, all the work that has gone into this, part of which symbolises the work required to build the Stadium, all seven years of it. If we adopt this attitude they will believe that we are those people in our past, the working men and women in the dark satanic mills. Past ceremonies have been spectacular, which is great, but it is also expected. What isn't necessarily a given is a spectacle that will have drama in it. He wants a dramatic spectacle and it is our collective performances and hard graft that will achieve this. And as with any drama on a stage, he has decided that we are going to get a curtain call. We will face the audience as they applaud us and we will then applaud them back. It's going to be a very powerful moment, he promises us.

His words are very inspirational and I think this talk has really affected us as a group. We have supported him so far, he has endeared himself to us with his friendly manner, his approachability, and his total belief in us. I imagine this is the sort of talk he gives to his cast members on his film sets, maybe not to the outright professionals, but to those for whom acting is new. We are his actors and it is his job to get that performance out of us. I certainly want to give to him what he so rightly demands, and I am not the only one who wants this.

He goes on to explain that he understands we are not all actors. We can't all give a performance. However, we can help ourselves by at least walking in rhythm to the beat with heavy footfalls, remaining focussed throughout and not looking around or losing sight of that attitude and hard graft. He says there will be lots of cameras on the FOP. They are going to try to get all of us onto TV, not just wide shots but close-ups too, which means we have to be in character as much as possible. As an aside he adds that all of our names will be in the programme, although we will still have to buy it for £15; they couldn't negotiate a free copy for us. With those words hanging in the air, and with a lot for us to think about, he passes us on to Toby.

The rain has been relentless so far. They have given us ponchos but they are not so heartless that they will make us rehearse in this. We are stuck here for the time being. Toby has his own agenda for us, that of the poppy moment when everybody stands still. He wants us to sing along to the whistling: la-la la la la la-haaah, and so on. We either do that, or we whistle. I've never been able to whistle. As a child, when I couldn't master this skill that seemingly comes so naturally to the rest of the world's population, I abandoned all attempts and decided to live whistle-free. I therefore have no choice: I have to sing.

He makes us all stand and takes us through this, playing the whistling track on the PA. Evidently by the lack of sound, a lot of us are feeling rather reticent, myself included. Gradually the singing and whistling becomes louder but it still doesn't sound very convincing. Toby moves on swiftly, cueing us into the full combination that we will eventually fall into as soon as we have finished our turf, although not the smelters and forgers. All of us go from Shut Boot/Sliding Doors to Levers/Pull and then to Chisel/Hammer. We repeat this over and over, countless times. Around 1,000 of us are stood here, row upon row, a massive block of people, and we are doing the same moves at the same time, all in rhythm. It is the hand clap and thigh slap of Chisel/Hammer that has the biggest impact, even more so since we are all in sync, 1,000 claps becoming one. It sounds very special indeed. I resist the urge to look around me, instead remaining focussed as we all perform the choreography, but this must look spellbinding from the FOP. All of the dance captains are down there, in their ponchos, and they are in a very enviable position right now. Some of them are jumping with joy to see us so effortlessly perform what they spent so long teaching us. They should film this and play it back to us. I would love to see it, as I am sure a lot of us would. Steve congratulates us on our IEMs, acknowledging just how far we have come as a group. Still we continue. By now my movements require no thought, no anticipation even. I could close my eyes and remain in sync, all of us moving like clockwork.

Toby then cues us to move into Shovel/Pickaxe. Although this is supposed to be done whilst moving, we do it stationary in the stands, just doing the hand actions. Even this seems natural, although we have never done it like this before. We do this a few times and then stop, although the music continues. At this point, just as we are supposed to be walking to the centre, turning and then walking back out, with the rings beginning to converge above us, a boat that is split into thirds and carried by people underneath each section, and several other groups of people who I cannot identify, walk around the FOP on the M25. They have to rehearse their part in the rain. Even at this stage some turf will still be getting carried off. The parade has the right of way at this point; the M25 is their domain, so whoever crosses paths with them must give them priority. This is going to get cued when we are striking. In the meantime we are given a half hour break. The rain is beginning to clear up so we are going to get a strike in before the rehearsal ends.

After the break, we are told that we won't be going through the whole segment as it is so wet and therefore hazardous. There is no music and we are not being timed. All we have to do is remove the structures and the terrain, as that is how the FOP must be left for the next rehearsal group – the NHS. The turf is completely soaked and dripping wet, making the large pieces very heavy indeed. We don't need to strike the ramps otherwise they will be very slippery and more than likely cause accidents. I certainly know about this. Steve repeatedly asks us to be careful and not to rush. When rolling one piece of turf with Chris, the guy from Canada, my poncho gets caught and starts to get rolled along, taking me with it. A couple of shouts from me and we stop, roll back and laugh at what just happened. Although the ponchos keep us dry they can clearly present hazards themselves.

The full strike takes us a while but we manage to safely clear everything, and then we are directed into the voms. We are now going to do a full dry run of the complete segment, just miming the structures and terrain, with the music playing. When exiting the vom, just before we walk up the ramp, and whilst the tree is being uprooted, we all gather just before the M25 and form a bulge, as Steve calls it. From here the audience will be able to see us, getting ready to strike, although they won't know what is about to happen. Our focus needs to be on the tree until we are cued to strike. We must be in character before we bulge, and then remain that way until the end. We begin and walk up the ramp with nothing to guide us into position. My fence is just before the waterwheel – that is mine and Gaudi's marker which we established a few rehearsals ago. Even though we have nothing to place, we still have to walk to the dolly and mime putting our fence down, walk round the back of it, then go to mime rolling our turf, and hand it to the Warriors, just as we would do if it was real.

This time the smelting duties work a bit better: collecting our shovels, forming a line, and the route to the trough. We do still have our props so we smelt when cued, our shovels almost interlocking at times as there are so many of us, so timing is still important and there does need to be some kind of rhythm, just not completely regular. The rest of the segment goes quite well, the rings converging yet again, and they do still look amazing up there. We are cued to remain facing the rings when the music has stopped, and after a few seconds we turn and applaud the audience, who are applauding us. End of segment. End of rehearsal. The weather has been preventative today, but we have still made progress and of course Danny Boyle's speech was a highlight, as was the choreography in the stands. I thoroughly enjoyed every second of that and the sound of the collective hand claps is still in my mind as we gather our things.

Those of us who are attending Wasif's meet-up at the Skybar have to make our way there in our own time. I have four and a half hours before I need to return for my venue training. As I walk out of the Olympic Park with Mikele, who isn't going to the Skybar, the sun is shining. He asks a Games Maker where he got his uniform from as he would also like one of those t-shirts. I say nothing, preferring to keep my secret just that. By now there is no danger that anything untoward will happen, but I prefer to stay quiet about what I am doing. I do feel quite lucky to have one of those uniforms packed away in its original packaging at home, waiting to be worn for the first time one day before the Opening Ceremony. I even consider offering him one of my two t-shirts when my shifts are over, but I don't mention it in the end. An act of kindness never to be acted upon.

On the way to the bar the sunshine gives way to the heavens. I see a guy called Steve, who I met a couple of weeks ago, and follow him as I don't actually know the exact location of the bar. A lift takes us up to the top floor where Wasif has so skilfully organised access to the VIP bar and lounge for nothing. It would usually cost a small fortune to hire. There are certainly some perks to being a performer in the Opening Ceremony. It is a very nice space with great views of the Stadium. There is also a balcony which gives us the opportunity to take as many photos as we wish. I have made a point of bringing my camera today, so finally I manage to get some photos, albeit from afar, of the Stadium that has almost mesmerised me ever since I laid eyes upon it. I fully intend to take more photos on my walk through the Park later on.

Having bought a diet Coke, I take a seat in the lounge where Wasif has arranged for the Wimbledon final to be shown on the big screen they have available. Andy Murray has already made history by reaching the final – the first British man to do so since 1938 – but the question on everybody's lips is whether he can win. Whatever the outcome it's going to be a great match, and after our work today it is nice to sit and socialise for once, and get to know some of the people who I recognise but am not yet acquainted with.

Over the next few hours I manage to meet Mark, Tim, Russell, who was the guy giving juggling lessons, Brian and Suzanne. For the most part our eyes are on the tennis, cheering as Andy Murray secures the first set. This is exactly what he needs. He is looking good in the second set too. Can he actually do this? Brian has created some cards for people to sign. One for Katie, one for Diane, and another for Pete. He has put photos of each of them during rehearsals on the covers and more inside. With everybody's comments they will make a very nice gift for them. As they do the rounds I notice a photo in one of them with Danny Boyle giving a talk with some of us around him listening. I spot myself in the background, just my head visible. It's a great photo and a nice memory. With today's smart phone technology Brian emails the image to me within minutes. It was quite brave of him to take the photo as they have been rather strict about photography, so I am grateful to him for capturing a moment like this.

The second set goes to Roger Federer after he breaks Murray in the final game. It looks like the downward spiral may have begun. I pray that I am wrong. He can't possibly squander this golden opportunity. Please, Andy! The roof goes on and play continues, now indoors. Suzanne is taking payment for some pin badges that a guy called Chris has designed and arranged production of. He posted his design on the Facebook page during the week – very good it is too. Apparently Fife is a kingdom, so he thought that at least deserved some kind of recognition. No other county could claim such a title. A lot of the counties have arranged a common dress such as t-shirts or hats. We are going to have badges to wear, which will of course make nice souvenirs afterwards. I have requested two, one just for safekeeping.

Soon it is time for me to leave. Before doing so, however, we manage to get a group photo of Fife, around 30 of us, on the balcony. The visual mementos are beginning to grow. And I am glad to be part of this one. I say my goodbyes with the third set being played, and make my way back to the Olympic Park, this time on different business.

38

Venue-Specific Training

Sunday 8 July 2012
5.30pm – 10.00pm
Olympic Park Common Domain

For this I have to go to the Copper Box. Walking over the bridge from Stratford Gate I have my camera at the ready and take a few photos before asking a steward the way to the venue. I have to turn right, along the river, with my back to the Orbit, the Stadium on my left. This is new territory. I eventually come to a carpeted area with hundreds of brightly coloured overlapping circles. Another photo opportunity. Nobody says a word as people are freely snapping away. It is a bit of a walk to the Copper Box. I am now beginning to get some idea of how big the Park is, although I've seen very little of it. It begins to rain as I walk over another bridge past a McDonald's.

Once inside the venue I register and get directed to the auditorium where we are seated. It is rather cramped, very little leg room. I hope we won't be here for long. I have a couple of forms to fill in so proceed with that before occupying myself with just looking around and taking in the second venue I've seen from the inside. The seats are the most striking – row upon row of randomly coloured chairs. There is no pattern here and I quite like it.

After waiting a while, we are introduced to a couple of Games Makers who take us through the format of the training. The first half is going to be spent here for some information to be provided on screen. No chance of a quick exit and stretching of legs then. We also do introductions, much like I am used to by now. Some facts and figures follow. The best part of this half of the training is a very quick-paced video montage of athletes doing all sorts of amazing things in their respective disciplines, set against an extremely inspiring track that I don't know. This is what the Olympics boil down to: these incredibly fit and lean individuals pushing their bodies to their absolute limits in the hope of securing a metallic disc on a ribbon and, for them, the ultimate accolade. When all is said and done the Opening Ceremony is simply leading up to these moments. I wonder how many more such shots will occur during the events that will take place here and in every Olympic venue. For a moment I still cannot believe that this behemoth of sporting excellence is coming to London. And I am so deeply involved in it. Yet it is indeed real and it is happening. Video over. That was amazing. It is time to file out and get into groups.

All of the Main Press Centre (MPC) volunteers are gathered together by April Doty. It's nice to put a face to the name. She has always been friendly on email and is equally so now. She speaks with an American accent and explains that we will be visiting the MPC and taking a brief tour of the Common Domain – just the sections that are open at the moment. One of the guys in our group confirms that Andy Murray has lost the final. For a moment I feel deflated but this is very quickly dispelled when prior expectation is in fact acknowledged as true. Always so close but never over the winning line. Doing what the English are such experts at, I convert utter disappointment into recognition that he has done his nation proud and probably did his best. For once I don't think we could have asked much more of Andy Murray except for maybe a hold of serve at a vital point in the match. Still, he was playing one of the very best there has ever been and he couldn't quite do it today. I haven't seen the whole match so maybe he gave everything he had, which is as much as you can do. Maybe next year he can go just one step further.

Outside it is pouring with no sign of the rain abating. I pull out my poncho and fight my way into it, as others resign themselves to getting soaked, since waiting for it to stop is not an option. We walk towards the MPC first. It's maybe ten minutes away, walking at a fairly slow pace. Within a couple of minutes the pouring becomes torrential and almost everyone does indeed get completely soaked. Somebody comments on the fact that I just happened to bring a poncho. I say nothing, preferring to keep the reason close to my chest.

Our accreditation is checked before we are allowed into the media complex, which is made up of the Main Press Centre and the International Broadcast Centre (IBC). This is the building we are walking along, its grey and white panels reaching several storeys above us. First we go inside the MPC building which is already open and fully functioning, although there is a lack of press people at the moment, so they are gearing themselves up for the influx in a couple of weeks. A large lobby with a Reception area, flanked by a coffee shop on the far left and a seating area on the right, leads into the main press area where the journalists will come to report on the day's events. There are rows and rows of booths stretching far away on both sides, each one equipped with the necessary leads for a laptop. In the centre of it all is a wall of pigeon holes, each of them marked with a symbol that represents the Olympic sports, symbols that I should by now have memorised. Whenever there is a press release, or event results for a sport are issued, they will be put into the pigeon holes and the symbol illuminated to tell the journalists about the new information, which they can use in their articles. This place will be teeming with personnel in a couple of weeks, yet today there is almost total silence reaching into every corner of this enormous room. Somebody asks if we are allowed to take photos and April answers with a yes, as long as we don't upload them onto file sharing sites. For some reason, I don't take out my camera and do exactly what I would love to do. The second we enter a lift to go to one of the upper floors, leaving the vast space behind us, I bitterly regret not doing so. I will not get the chance to be here again with nobody else inside and just hope that we have to pass through here in order to get out.

Upstairs we are shown the conference room. This time I do take some photos. On the wall outside a London skyline is painted in purple with London 2012 written beside it. The sun is shining again and through a large window we are treated to a rare image of the Orbit, or the portion of it that is visible above the IBC, with a rainbow beside it.

Going back downstairs we are shown a rest room for the journalists. There are loungers inside – a place where they can come and rest for a while after the long hours they will surely be putting in. Apparently this facility is in response to feedback that the press people never have somewhere to go and relax whilst they are working. Walking down a corridor we are back in the main lobby area, just past the coffee shop. Photo opportunities missed.

Outside we walk past a series of shops that are provided specifically for the press – a bar and restaurant, a bank, post office, dry cleaners, pharmacy, newsagents, and hair salon, amongst others. It is a mini village where everything they need is within a few paces. Now we enter the area where we will be working – the PSA. This is accessed by an escalator and is located inside the car park. In order to enter the main complex the journalists and other personnel will need to go through the security area after parking their cars. We are shown what we will have to do – scanning passes and loading trays. That is it in a nutshell.

In the car park. This is not quite what I wanted. There is nothing remarkable about this PSA. I will be surrounded by dreary pillars and walls. I am now glad that I only have three shifts in the MPC. I would prefer to be in the Park. Three sessions here will be ample.

After a look at the staff catering facilities, which is inside the same building where the journalists will eat, except that our area is tucked away in one corner of the top floor and will offer less choice than in the main dining areas, we leave the press complex the same way we came. For the next hour or so we are taken on a tour around the Park. Mercifully the rain has not returned. We are shown the Athletes' Village, the Basketball Arena and the Velodrome, all viewed from afar. Some areas are not yet accessible and are cordoned off.

One thing that catches my eye is a sculpture made up of large rectangular panels or sheets, all laid on top of, over and around themselves, interlocking to form an enormous mishmash of red and white. It is certainly different, at least in my limited experience of modern sculpture. We are told that it has been commissioned by Coca-Cola, hence the colour scheme, and is in fact a building with the panels surrounding it. I can't actually see beyond this outer shell into the centre. There is definitely not a building in there. Perhaps April meant something else. I am left intrigued and make a note to find out more about it when next given the opportunity.

The only thing left to do now is to be shown our registration area, called Cherry Park, where we will need to go before each shift to be signed in and allocated to a team for the day. We walk back through the Park, the same way I approached the Copper Box. This time the Stadium is over beyond the bridge and the view of it from here is quite special. The McDonald's I went past on the way in is apparently the largest one in the world. Some people are speculating about what the Stadium is like inside. I cheekily ask if we are allowed to take a look inside before we go – I couldn't help myself.

One of the girls in the group I recognise as the one who was on my table during role-specific training. Lucy was her name. She reveals to April that she will be in the Closing Ceremony as a dancer. Over the multi-coloured carpet we see something that wasn't there before: a row of trailers with piles of turf loaded on them. Somebody remarks that they must be for Danny Boyle's country set, ready to be put in place. She has no idea why this turf is on the trailers, and not for the first or last time. Within the Stadium music is being played on the PA. Rehearsals are still in full swing. I see one of the rings in the corner above the partial roof and smile to myself, reminiscing about the afternoon's session.

On the way to Cherry Park we take a bee line to the Orbit, getting right underneath it. From here it looks enormous, its red framework towering above us, with some of it jutting out farther than seems comfortable. There are lots of photo opportunities here, every angle presenting a unique perspective. I feel lucky to have seen so much of the Park today. We walk past the Aquatics Centre, through the main PSA and on towards Cherry Park, which is essentially just a set of Portakabins where the Games Maker security staff will register. We are told that on all of our shifts where we are in the MPC, we needn't register here, instead find the MPC team leader who will take us to the press complex and we will register there. We finish early, before dusk. We are free to go and another long day has ended, although I still have to get home, which will take at least an hour. With the bitter disappointment of Andy Murray's defeat still hanging over me, I walk through Westfield and into the station.

39

Rehearsal 18

Tuesday 10 July 2012
5.30pm – 10.00pm
Olympic Stadium

With just a day between this and the previous rehearsal, and with just 17 days to go, things are beginning to hot up even if the weather is anything but. We have light rain this evening, but nothing to worry about as we are used to this now. Even so, we are in the upper stands tonight. It doesn't take Steve long to call us onto the FOP. We are going straight into a full strike fairly soon.

Whilst we wait in our lines, only loosely formed, Josh mentions receiving an email asking for the smelters and forgers to attend the contingency rehearsal on Monday 16 July from 5pm until 10pm. They are going to get us into costume with make-up and will also be filming us. I haven't received any such invite so make a mental note to speak to Vanessa during the break. Daniel hasn't received it either, but Gaudi and Jon have. Although it sounds like it will be quite exciting, and I haven't missed a rehearsal yet so would prefer to keep it that way, I am in two minds about what I should do. I have plans on that Monday so would have to cancel those, and I also have some other volunteering to do for Macmillan, which I have committed to and couldn't justifiably pull out now. I am doing this with Misbah – an opportunity to spend the day together after so much time given to rehearsals, whilst giving time to a good cause. Although possible it will be rather difficult logistically as we are volunteering at Herstmonceux Castle in Sussex. I will have to return from that in the afternoon, pick up the kids from my mum's, drop them all off at home, and then go to the rehearsal.

I have no time to reflect on this further as Polly joins us, replacing Diane who is not here today. It's nice to see her again as she has been with her own county for much of the time and we usually stick to our own areas when on the FOP. I have still not been anywhere near the

Tor, which I would have liked to have seen up close, and maybe climbed up it, but it's not my role and therefore I have no reason to venture out that 'far'. I need to be fully focussed on what we are doing over here – that is part of everybody's role. All of us have specific parts to play and everything else has been taken care of.

Polly is here to talk us through the choreography and when to do it at the beginning. We are now going to do Levers/Pull and Chisel/Hammer after the seventh bang of the drums at the beginning, and then we will do Work Prep as we approach our structure, as before. There are also a few other minor changes, which do not quite register as I am still processing this thing about the seventh bang, but they will be cued, thankfully. Even as we stand here Polly is receiving new instructions in her ear piece, her IEM being tuned to a different channel to ours. In response to a question, she also mentions that Toby has been told to give us better cues. They have written him a script to read from!

They said we will be striking soon, but so often this has meant anything but. Tonight is no exception. We continue to wait. I notice two of the soldiers from Fife, Steve and Gary, are in full costume: khaki uniform, boots, puttees, webbing and make-up. Apparently they have been here for a while, arriving before everybody else to get into costume and made up. They have been working directly with Danny, Toby and the camera crew. There are no flags or emblems embroidered on their uniforms, since military representation of any specific nation is not allowed in the Olympics. However, the poppy moment is going to be a key part of our segment as it is there to commemorate the fallen soldiers from all wars, past and present, so some of the soldiers are guaranteed a close-up. They have been looking at how that will be executed, and of course working on their facial expressions by taking direction from Danny. Now that we are all here, in our normal clothes, they also want to see how well the soldiers' uniforms stand out in a crowd. They do look fantastic and I am just a tiny bit envious.

A few rehearsals ago some of the girls were wearing their costume skirts, just trying them out I imagine and getting used to working in them. I wonder when we are going to be rehearsing in full costume. Maybe we will have to wait right until the full dress rehearsals, which are not far off now.

Katie now comes over and asks the priority turf groups to gather round her. There have been some changes here too. Each group is going to move along one piece, so we are now striking the third piece from the top, which is smaller and therefore easier, although we still need all six of us. The reason for the change is unclear but I seem to hear something about the beam engine allocation possibly having changed. We all gather on our respective pieces and practise rolling them, working out the best method, and giving advice to those who are on our former piece as that required a fold first. With everyone more or less comfortable with what we are doing, the briefing is over.

It begins to rain lightly now. I pull my poncho out and open it up when the rain gets heavier. Within about 30 seconds it is pouring so Steve announces that we should all move into the voms and take shelter. Some of us run, some of us walk. By the time I get there and join the crowd that has formed it has become a total deluge and it is leaking into the vom. Most people move deeper inside but if I do that now, even with the cover above us I will undoubtedly get soaked, not quite having managed to get into my poncho as I ran to the vom. There is a spot literally about two feet square where the rain is not leaking in and the ground is actually dry. I stand there and put my poncho on, streams of rain water falling around me but not on me. It is quite surreal.

Almost as suddenly as it arrived the rainfall subsides and begins to clear. Steve wastes no time in getting the strike in, although we do a quick warm-up first with no music. Into our voms we go and line up. The turf is now soaked and will be heavy. The FOP will be slippery so safety has very quickly taken precedence over speed, so no haste and no striking of the ramps. Most of us keep our ponchos on. It may rain again whilst we are striking. Some of us have begun to take the occasional photo in the corridor as we wait. There is nobody to catch us here, and we do feel the need to document at least some of what we have experienced. Memories will fade so we need a visual record. I am sure there will be a lot of photo sharing after the Ceremony. I have been using my phone to take shots, mostly of our section of the corridor and the people within it. I imagine the people farther down are doing the same.

Tonight we hear a montage of songs and other familiar sound bites on our IEMs, just very short snippets. I don't know them all but I do recognise The Clash's London Calling, The Sex Pistols' God Save The Queen, Lily Allen's Smile, and the EastEnders theme in the melange of sounds. This is followed by some choir music which continues for a few minutes. I'm not sure how exactly this fits in or what it is supposed to symbolise, if anything, but it precedes Nimrod and The

Tempest speech, which is now playing in our ears. As we walk out of the corridor and into our bulge, with the tree being uprooted, I get the same feeling of wonder at the view of the audience directly in front of us. I'm still unsure about when to do the choreography but it's going to be cued so I just need to focus on the moment.

We hear Steve's "Standby strike. Strike... go." We move forward and there is no cue for the choreography, so hardly anybody does it. Not a good start. Work Prep is fine, however. We remove our fence, and do our priority turf, the new piece. It worked just fine and was much easier than usual, although there were no Warriors available so we had to take it and drop it onto the pile ourselves. These extra seconds make a difference but we are more than adept at a bit of improvisation now.

One thing that Josh, Gaudi and I discussed earlier was when to make our way to Vom 4 to pick up our shovels and wait in the smelting line. We decided that we should do it straight after our first piece of turf. This will mean we are not scattered during the poppy moment, and so will be more or less in a group when walking to the vom. Jon and Harry, being swings, could be anywhere so they will need to make their own arrangement, as will Daniel who is on a different piece of turf. The three of us walk together and this works much better. We pick up our shovels and form the line. Jon and Harry soon follow, although they stand in front of us, not behind us – a ploy to get closer to the ring I feel! Because we have only struck one piece of turf, it seems like we are here for a while, but that is also due to the strike going slower because of the wet conditions. Steve has already emphasised the need for safety and has told us that they are looping the music until the poppy moment to allow us to get to a certain stage of the strike without having to rush.

Eventually the music does slow down and the whistling begins. One minute later it's all go and we move off to the left and over to our ramp on the way to the trough. This time when we reach it I immediately notice that the trough is no longer hollow but filled, or covered, as if its lid has been replaced. When cued we begin to smelt. Everything then happens as it usually does. All of the chimneys have made it up successfully but as soon as we turn and move out to the perimeter they are brought down again and disappear back into the traps, the same with the beam engines and looms. The only large structure that stays is the waterwheel next to our ramp.

I have previously seen some of the smelters putting their shovels down and joining in with the choreography. This is a much better idea, rather than just moving on the beat, so on this strike I also turn my shovel, stand it up and fall into the combination. Once the music stops and we have turned to face the rings, all five again, a new part is added. After applauding the audience we gesture with one hand, turning back towards the FOP, as if to say to the audience "Look at what we've done", and then we turn to face them and take a half bow. We then move off the FOP, walking down the ramp or steps, whichever is the closest, and onto the M25 to exit the Stadium via the aisles. We are all allocated a particular block which will be our designated exit point, but this hasn't been confirmed for some of us yet. A member of the Mass Team notes this and says she will let us know. There then follows a 20 minute break. I head straight for the coffee counter which often gets busy and a long queue forms. The meal pack we have is exactly the same as ever, just different flavours and fillings.

Once I have eaten my meal I locate Vanessa and ask her about my accreditation, as I still haven't received the email. After Sunday I won't be able to enter the Olympic Park without it. She says that some people still haven't received the email but will definitely have it this week. I also ask her about the contingency rehearsal on Monday. She tells me that if I haven't had an email from her, I am not required as not everybody is. It was only a random selection of people who were asked. That suits me fine. It will cause me a lot less hassle.

After the break we are back in the voms to prepare for a dry run, although it doesn't happen immediately. Some of the guys often make up games to play. I also participate at times, but on this occasion I just chat to Jon for a while. We discover that we share the same middle name, although for both of us it is in fact stated as our first name on our birth certificates. We talk about this strange coincidence and Morocco, his country of origin. Misbah and I spent a week there a couple of years ago, with our only child at the time. Conversation always passes the time quite nicely until it is time to go through another strike.

The same montage of music that was played earlier recommences on our IEMs. I always keep one ear plug in, just in case of announcements, instructions, or the like. As soon as this starts to play out in our ears it is time to stop any games and stand up, if not already doing so, and get ready to go, all of us moving to our designated place in the line.

When leaving the vom this time it is much darker than when we came in, our entrance and exit either side of a sunset. The lights have been switched on and the Stadium is flooded in a subtle luminescence that can only enhance the effect this place has. Drums pound all around us and it sounds like the darkness that is forming the backdrop is being pierced with an explosion akin to the fireworks that will fill the empty air above us in less than three weeks. This time the cue is given and we do our choreography as planned. A good start leads to a good strike with few problems. It's only a dry run, so much easier, but it is still like any other strike in terms of timing and flow, and we do still need to play our parts with the same conviction that is expected of us every time now.

When the whistling begins some of the smelters are already lined up and waiting to move off. This is working much better, a long line of us with our shovels over our shoulders. From where I am standing I can clearly see the soldiers walking to the poppy field and stopping to pay their respects to the fallen. I wonder what effect this will have on the audience. I'm sure the same silence that surrounds the FOP now will be felt on show night. Seeing the soldiers standing there in their uniforms simply heightens the emotive tones of this interlude, this poignancy amidst the chaos that soon reconvenes, except this time the machinery and factories are in full flow.

This is demonstrated quite beautifully by our trough being illuminated in orange when we reach it this time, another development. We have something to smelt, although nothing is actually flowing of course. It seems that with every strike we do some more of the contextual void is being filled, drip-fed to us in a manner that belies our cynicism and serves to convince us that this is going to work. They knew this all along. We are beginning to believe it too. It is difficult to understate the sheer pride with which I am smelting and watching the Working Men and Women converge with their shovelling and pick axing, then walking in and stopping before turning around to form a ring like the one rising in the centre behind our backs. The choreography is sharp and nicely synced, each move taking on a significance that I haven't felt as keenly as I feel it now, symbols of the industry we have created.

When we are cued to stop and turn around, only four rings are visible; the centre one hasn't risen after all. Just a malfunction I suppose. Such an unfortunate one at that, marring what turned out to be a great strike. The outer rings still look impressive, four halos floating in the night. As we applaud the audience and show them what we have so cleverly done, Steve showers us with his usual accolades, before announcing the end of the rehearsal. It is quite late, so either because the team can no longer tolerate having to organise them, or because they finally feel they can trust us, we are told to take our bibs home, remembering to bring them to the next rehearsal. Steve also tells us that they are going to perform a test of the pyro shower, so we should stick around if we would like to see it. That is surely the reason why the middle ring didn't rise. It is late but I can't miss this. I hope there won't be a long wait.

Some people are clearly not staying, whilst others are patiently waiting on the outer portion of the black zone or in the seating area. Whilst they are preparing, Steve takes the opportunity to remind us that every strike we have done so far has been under different conditions: sun, rain, wind, wet, day, night, full run, dry run, strikes when we were learning new things as we went along, and ones when we kept stopping and starting. He tells us that we are the best cast group he has worked with. I wonder if he does really mean that. A few of us state the obvious, that he probably says this to everyone, yet some of his team who are close by are adamant that he has never said anything like that before.

After a while the ring illuminates, switches off once then lights up again, this time remaining that way. On the other side of the Stadium is the Tor with the tree atop. They are both almost sparkling in the Stadium lights, with the black sky above offering the perfect contrast. It is a picture of tranquillity, almost as hypnotic as a gushing waterfall set against the light of a full moon. The ring rises, fully loaded as it will be on show night, we are told. The music cuts in at the point where it usually is at this stage, our movements put into context by Steve. The ring is still rising as we are making our way to the perimeter. Small sparks fly off the side before it reaches its summit, and then a shower of sparks rains down onto the FOP, and keeps falling for about 20 seconds. It is indeed a spectacular sight. It will be five times this on show night. As I and several hundred others stand there transfixed, all I can do is imagine. We are watching from the black zone. We will be so much closer on the actual night. In a state of almost stunned silence I smile. The image before us disappears as the sparks slowly fade.

Steve graces the microphone once more to ask if some of us can stay just a little longer to allow Rick Smith to do some recording. There is no obligation, just as many as possible, as they have asked so much of us already and it is getting late. I do feel an obligation to stay and help out Rick Smith of Underworld. Will I ever be given this opportunity again? My internal debate is very quickly over.

Another spell of waiting follows, during which it begins to rain; another shower, but one that is the elemental antithesis of the one we have just witnessed. Still, there are hundreds of people left, all of us wanting to share in this experience, though we don't know what we will be called upon to do. When Rick Smith does walk onto the FOP with a few colleagues, and addresses us, his audience and collaborators, he takes us through a series of shouts and shrieks, as loud as we can, at different tones and durations, random and controlled, a single shout or a few in succession, all at varying intervals. He demonstrates and we mimic, although we don't give him what he wants at every turn, so we repeat until he has something he can use. Use for what? I have no idea and he doesn't think to tell us, or maybe just doesn't want to. We continue in this way for around ten minutes. By the end of it my throat is feeling somewhat hoarse. It is nice to have helped Rick Smith, although the cost is a very late night as it is going to take me a while to get home and I can't exactly climb straight into bed as soon as I lock the door behind me. There are always things to take care of before retiring.

The next rehearsal is on Saturday – the first compulsory one. I first looked at the original schedule all the way back in January. I noticed the compulsory rehearsals and thought nothing of them as they were so distant, the end portion of an extremely far-reaching arc. Yet here we are, sliding down the other side, almost at the bottom. It is fast approaching.

40

Accreditation And Skyscrapers

Wednesday 11 July 2012

I was by now growing rather concerned that I still didn't have my accreditation. Next Monday was when official Games time would begin, meaning no accreditation, no entry, so I emailed the cast team. I received a swift reply:

> Based on our records, you are showing as "Accredited", so you must have already picked up your LOCOG accreditation. There is only one card per person, even if you have multiple responsibilities for different groups during the Olympics.
> If you have picked up your accreditation, please check that it has the OOC code at the bottom. This is our code for the Opening Ceremony and is required to get you into the zone you need to be as a performer. If you have not picked up your accreditation, or it does not have OOC on it, please let us know.

So at least I knew that I didn't have to wait for an email for another card. Yet my card only had MPC and CDM on it, so I did indeed query this.

> We have added you to our list of performers that have this issue and require an "Upgrade Card". This will be a separate LOCOG card that you will place behind your accreditation and will have the required zone code on it for your Ceremony role. We are hoping to have these cards at this weekend's rehearsal. If not we will have someone outside the gate at the following rehearsal to distribute.

It did seem like they had the situation under control, and I didn't believe they would in any way jeopardize the entry of several volunteers, but I wouldn't be comfortable until I had my upgrade card in my hand.

Friday 13 July 2012

I responded to the costume team's email about spectacles today, just in case they were going to issue them as I preferred to be wearing something, even if I could get by without them. As they themselves mentioned, however, it would probably prove too expensive.

I also sent Vanessa a somewhat whimsical email – it was Friday, after all – asking if they could play Underworld tracks whilst we waited around. I had been listening to one of their songs a lot: 'Mmm… Skyscraper I Love You'. I suppose skyscrapers all owe their existence to the Industrial Revolution in a way. We were depicting the genesis of so much of modern life as we know it. The song is a mid-tempo dance tune that ambles along at a pleasant pace, slowly building but never accelerating unfittingly. In the final few minutes the beats are shed away and the listener is taken into a wholly different soundscape that evokes serenity, akin to floating on a secluded lake with nothing but the sky to look at. For some reason the end of this track reminded me of being in the Stadium, of spending long days there and milling around in between strikes, enjoying the sunshine when it made an appearance. Sometimes it is hard to explain why music conjures up certain images or sentiments. This was possibly one such occurrence of this. Whatever the reason, I would have loved to have been in the Stadium, on the FOP, lie back, close my eyes and listen to that song. Thirteen minutes of bliss. So I emailed Vanessa, not expecting a reply, but bless her that's exactly what she did. Rather than chide me for wasting her time she gave me a reason why they couldn't play Underworld's music in the Stadium. I had to content myself with another replay.

Later that evening I heard from Vanessa again, but this time one of her updates and not just to me.

> We look forward to seeing you all tomorrow. It's a big, big day as we move from individual segment rehearsals into transitions between them. Tomorrow is all about putting the show together.
> During this rehearsal you will do one or two full runs of your segment – but we will layer in your entrance onto, and

exit from, the FOP, and your interaction with the segments that come before and after you.

You will learn and rehearse part of your route from the cast holding to the voms. Be prepared for some extra walking. There will be a lot of waiting as every group gets set or reset into position, but it is an essential part of the show.

When your segment has finished you will be released, but if want to stay and watch the following segments rehearse, you may do so, provided you stay in your designated seating section and not wander around the Stadium. Tomorrow will be your only opportunity to do this.

41

Rehearsal 19

Saturday 14 July 2012
9.00am – 5.00pm
Olympic Stadium

Upon arrival at the Olympic Park entrance today we are greeted with much longer queues. I suppose there are a few groups rehearsing today, as per Vanessa's email, so it's going to be quite hectic. On the walk to the check-in area, past the as yet unopened concession stands, I hear official announcements being tested in English and in French, welcoming the audience to the Ceremony, and announcing the national anthem. After registering and collecting our morning snack we join a small queue leading to the costume area. They are handing out new gloves and claiming back the ones we already have, the yellow ones. I'm a bit disappointed about this as I want to keep them as a souvenir. They even have my bib number written on them in black marker pen, making them unique to me. Yet the guy distributing the brand new black ones is discarding the old gloves. When it comes to my turn he inexplicably asks me if I want to keep my yellow ones. I didn't say a word before he spoke, so I just say that I would and pocket them before he changes his mind. I take my new ones and continue to the steps outside, walking round and down as always, on the way to the Stadium, this time no bib collection tables present.

On the PA a rock band that I don't recognise has taken over from the Olympic officials, and is churning out one of their songs. The man serving tea and coffee says they will be playing on the actual night, but cannot reveal who they are, although they are well known. Not being au fait with today's bands means I have no hope of guessing who they are and nobody else present knows. It matters not to me, in any case.

We are upstairs again today. A steward directs us to a particular section of the seating that has been set aside for the Industrial Revolution. I find a place next to Josh and Alex. They are busy trying to identify the flags that are now hanging around the circumference of the Stadium. Josh claims to be bad with flags but I am a lot worse, only recognising a small handful. I can see Pakistan somewhere above the Tor. I'm not supposed to but I can't resist taking a photo on my phone to show Misbah. Doing this without being seen can prove to be difficult.

I soon give up on the flags and focus on the FOP. The GPL volunteers are present and performing various activities as required. Most seem to be simply standing around, although they have probably been directed to do that. Some of them are wearing their ponchos as it is raining lightly. The maypoles have coloured streamers around them, no doubt for use in some kind of village dance or custom. There is a shire horse in the tilled field that lies just below Fife and Essex. Only a couple of people are in there with it. We still haven't seen any animals, except for this horse and a couple before it, although those ones were pulling the carriages that will appear just before our segment begins. So far no animals have been mentioned since the second Dagenham rehearsal, and we have completed our segment now. I don't think they were ever going to be part of our act. A lot of people have expressed concerns about the well-being of the animals, that they will find the show distressing, but they will be long gone by the time it all kicks off and we obliterate their grazing grounds. From what I can gather, we won't even have the chance to see any of the animals.

Whilst the GPL people bear the rain and we sit and wait, the most striking visual element thus far has been the clouds that were promised in the press. There was just one at first but now I can count four large masses of white that look surprisingly impressive. It looks like they have been constructed using a series of helium balloons, all bundled together and covered in a coating, the exact nature of which I cannot discern from this distance, but the curves of the balloons have been arranged in such a way that they have formed a typically nebular object that will definitely earn some appreciation when viewed by an audience. In a word they are fantastic. They are being hoisted, and I suppose walked, around the M25 by volunteers, who will need to keep a firm grip to avoid them floating high above the Stadium. As this is happening, more music is being tested on the PA. Something choral is playing at the moment.

After sitting for a while, we are asked to leave the seating area and make our way down to the podium and back outside. In the case of Fife, we need to bear left and continue walking around the Stadium until we reach a crowd of people, other volunteers who have made it there before us. We are now beside the river and down a slope is a large entrance to the voms, except we are on the outside of the Stadium, not the inside. We are kept here for quite a while, in the rain, so most of us are in ponchos, although a few brave, or indeed crazy, souls refuse to be encumbered. I think some people haven't worn a poncho even once ever since we started to rehearse, all through the rain that we regularly fell victim to in Dagenham, and more recently here.

Eventually we do step inside the vom, although this is not Vom 5, so we enter the corridor on the right and walk round the Stadium again, this time backstage past various dressing rooms and cast areas, through a few corridors, until we are back in a familiar place, the white and grey of our little tunnel. Here we sit and wait for some time, the usual scenario, and then exit, although this isn't for a strike.

Outside we stand around for a little longer, still in the rain, just so we can get wetter than we already are. Diane addresses us whilst we wait. She emphasises how important it is, now more than ever, to stay focussed as we are fast approaching show night and we must get used to being, and remaining, in character for the whole time we are out there, during every single strike we do. This will ultimately help us appear more natural rather than having a contrived look, which is especially important since the cameras could be in our faces at any time. The audience in the Stadium will have an overall view of the show, but the viewers at home, all over the world, will be treated to regular close-ups.

As the rain takes a break, Danny Boyle speaks to us on our IEMs from the Tor. He tells us that a big meeting was held yesterday, during which they were told that the Ceremony has to be cut shorter to avoid it over-running. The committee asked Danny if any of the creative elements could be cut, but he flatly declined this proposal, since it is all about the volunteers as far as he is concerned. He expresses how difficult the meeting was, how their agenda was contrary to that of Danny and his team's agenda so they were at loggerheads for much of the session. The conclusion was a bit of a compromise: each segment has to be cut by two minutes each, so our section is down to 15 minutes, which was in fact the original timing they had envisaged. He believes we can still achieve everything we set out to do in this reduced time. I think we all do too. Our collective spirit is such that we know we can do this, whatever happens. We are all one enormous team and time and again we have somehow managed to get the job done. Two minutes is neither here nor there. It will be easy.

Toby now takes over to talk about the cues throughout the segment. As we walked into the seating area earlier we were handed a cue sheet.

Thank you for your patience during these last few rainy rehearsals.

We have been working to confirm cues for the Industrial Revolution choreography and have developed a clear script. Please find below a cue list and explanatory notes. It is important that you read all of the notes as there are extra details which may be new to you.

Weavers, Beam Engines and Ratchets: your notes are highlighted in bold. Please take extra care to find the notes that affect you.

From now on, you will always get a standby cue, and then a count of 4 in. For example, you will hear, "Standby Shovel/Pickaxe," then you will hear "1, 2, 3 and —" to start the choreography.

Please note that this document is a cue list for choreography only: it does not include individual entrances and exits.

CUE SCRIPT FOR INDUSTRIAL CHOREOGRAPHY

1. "STANDBY BULGE"
2. "BULGE GO" (please see note below)
3. "STANDBY STRIKE"
4. "STRIKE GO" (please see note below)
5. "STANDBY LEVERS-CHISEL"
6. "1, 2, 3 AND —" (please see note below)
7. "STANDBY SOLDIERS"
8. "SOLDIERS GO" (please see note below)
9. "40 SECONDS TO POPPIES"
10. "SLOWLY STOP WORK – SOLDIERS CONTINUE WALKING" (please see note below)
11. "STANDBY FOR WORK PREP AND YOUR CHOREOGRAPHY"
12. "1, 2, 3 AND —" (please see note below)
13. "STANDBY TO STOP CHOREOGRAPHY"
14. "1, 2, 3 STOP"

15. "STANDBY SHOVEL/PICKAXE AND CHOREOGRAPHY"
16. "1, 2, 3 AND —"
17. "STANDBY TO WALK IN"
18. "1, 2, 3 AND —"
19. "STANDBY TURN INTO COMBO"
20. "1, 2, 3 AND —"
21. "STANDBY STOP COMBO"
22. "1, 2, 3, STOP"
23. "TURN TO PYRO"

Explanatory Notes:

2. Move to bulge out of vom positions. Be STILL and keep your focus towards the Tor. There should be no talking and no fidgeting. Your performance starts now.
4. Stride on the beat. Focus forward to where you are going.
6. 1 x Levers/Pull, 1 x Chisel/Hammer ONLY. There is no Shut Boot.
8. "Soldiers go" is 1 minute 20 seconds to poppies.
10. This is a naturalistic stopping of work for a minute of silence.

Soldiers: we want to see you arrive at the poppy field, so leave the last bit of your journey for when the rest of the WMW are still.
Ratchets: If you are mid-ratchet please keep your hands on the ratchet for the duration of the minute's silence.

12. This is 1 x Work Prep then YOUR choreography. To clarify:

WMW: 1 x Work Prep + Combination of 1 x Shut Boot, 1 x Levers/Pull, 1 x Chisel/Hammer
Weavers: 1 x Work Prep + Loom choreography
Beam Engines: 1 x Work Prep + 2 x Dials, 2 x Levers/Pull
Ratchets: 1 x Work Prep but cut out counts 3 & 4 (the sleeve move) if your hands are on the ratchet handle!

If you are on top of or near your next strike piece go directly to it. You should fall into the combination on the move when you return to the FOP. Please ensure you fall in accurately, as everyone should be in sync across the FOP.

13. On this cue EVERY SINGLE PERSON on the FOP should STOP. This includes weavers and beam engine teams.
16. **WMW:** You should do Shovel/Pickaxe on the move towards the centre ring.
    Beam Engines: Resume 2 x Dials, 2 x Levers/Pull
    Weavers: Resume loom choreography
18: When you get the cue to "walk-in" this is the cue for WMW to stop Shovel/Pickaxe, beam engines to stop their choreography, and Weavers to stop their loom choreography, and walk in towards the ring. Every single person on the FOP should walk in, including Weavers.
20. Your turn to face the audience takes 4 counts then you go straight into combo on the move outwards. When you reach the edge of the FOP stop walking on the beat but continue the combo on the spot with feet firmly planted.
23. This turn is either to the left or the right. Choose your best side!

Miscellaneous Notes:

Remember to do 1 x Work Prep on your first strike ONLY. This is to your own cueing.

Ratchets: All four ratchets should come on together, and exit together once the chimney is up. Once the chimney is up, there is nothing to ratchet, so pick up your ratchet and go.

WMW: When you have completed your waves and your county is clear, you all need to anticipate your route for Shovel/Pickaxe and the walk into the ring. Therefore, do not obstruct yourselves by standing behind machinery when getting into position on the FOP. Give yourselves the clearest path possible.

You are always, always in focus and are highly likely to have a camera on you. Talking pulls focus and shouldn't be happening. If talking is absolutely necessary you should find the least distracting way to do so.

It's always beneficial to keep practising the choreography. Focus on finishing each move crisply.

This is all very insightful and it's great to see a summary of everything we have covered during the last few rehearsals. Toby covers some of it in his talk to us and also how we can achieve all of this in just 15 minutes, but the main message for the moment is to stay safe as the FOP is soaked once again. We probably can't do it in that time today, but Danny firmly believes we will do so eventually.

Talks are over and we all head back into our voms. We are held here for rather a long time. I suppose we are out of the rain, but it is so boring. Some people give up waiting and eventually try to get some sleep. Others just chat in their little groups. I decide to take a few photos on my phone, just as a couple of others are doing the same. This will be a memory like any other. We have so far spent many hours in this corridor and it is worth documenting.

The montage begins, followed by the singing, Nimrod, and The Tempest. Every time we strike the click track can be heard on our earphones and continues until the very end of our segment. It is so simple, just a constant clicking, each one a second apart, yet I enjoy hearing it on our IEMs. It has become one of the integral sounds of rehearsals for me. When the world is marvelling at what we are creating, and no doubt listening in wonder to the amazing and complex music to accompany us, we will also be listening to this completely stripped down track and syncing our footfalls with its constant and gentle beating.

We begin the strike, the GPL people gradually leaving as we walk on, brushing past them, and Toby is right about staying safe. The turf is difficult as it is wet and heavy, so we have to be careful when lifting it and ensure we don't slip as water drips down and coats the very surface we are walking on with a colourless patchwork of moisture. My earphones somehow disconnect as I am collecting my smelting shovel so for a while I am without cues, although I do know the routine now so I can guess what to do and when.

At the top of the ramp we run into some drummers, causing the two groups to get a little jumbled and our lines break a little. I fumble about with my IEM at the trough, my first opportunity to do so as I couldn't move during poppies. I finally regain a connection and wait for the cue to smelt, but it isn't given, so we don't actually do anything. Nobody takes the initiative and just starts, with the rest expected to follow.

The whole strike in all honesty is a bit of a shambles. Just when I thought we were making good progress we are hit with this. It's important not to feel too deflated, as it's only one strike of many more to come, but I sometimes wonder if we are ever going to actually perfect this. Almost every single time at least one thing doesn't happen as it should do, or we just run into some kind of trouble that takes too long to sort out so any sense of flow is lost. So much of our segment relies on the precise positioning and movement of so many people at any one time that it is impossible for it to be the same on every occasion, and therein lies one of our main problems: the need for improvisation and spontaneity practically every time. Katie has mentioned this more than once. Even on show night we will probably need to employ a bit of each, but sometimes it doesn't quite work out as we would like. With this in mind I leave the FOP for lunch.

During the break a member of the tech team gets his hand stuck in a trap or some kind of opening on the FOP – it's hard to see from a distance. He is clearly hurt as he cries out in pain rather loudly. For the next 20 minutes or so his colleagues help him, trying to free his hand whilst waiting for the medical team to come to his aid. Maybe his contribution to the Olympics will end now, so suddenly. He is wheeled off to applause from the volunteers.

About an hour later we are back in our curtain call position at the end of the segment. They direct us here and there, just attempting to smooth out the ring we have collectively created. I am still on our ramp to the left of the waterwheel, near the back with some space on my right for me to place my shovel before falling into choreography. We also get told that we will exit through the audience at aisle number 226, which means that once we are off the ramp we will have a short walk round to the left, past a few blocks, before walking up and out.

Instead of doing the expected reset, we are asked to go back inside the voms again and line up for what will clearly be a dry run. The rain has cleared now, although it is still cloudy and dull, so the poncho comes off and I fold it down. I've learnt that if you start off neatly it will fit into its pouch much easier. I have had more than enough practice at doing this.

The waiting ensues and just as last time we eventually make it out into our bulge position, listening to the tree being uprooted. Focus. Already in character. Listening to the clicking. Drummers drumming. "Standby strike. Strike…go." Another one begins. We get our cues this time, all of them. We smelt when we are told to. We go through the entire segment, all the way to going up the aisles. The strike goes okay, but not great. A tiny air of nonchalance is beginning to creep in. Even seeing the rings forming is becoming routine and therefore losing a very small iota of its original appeal, but they still look fantastic.

When we reach the podium level the smelters deposit their shovels on the side, opposite one of the refreshment tables. They are then taken back down and placed outside Vom 4. There is no rule for this. I suppose on show night, just like the turf and the other structures, we won't need to worry about them. We will just leave them and go.

Whilst we are standing on the podium level there is music playing on the PA, something classical. On the FOP the Warriors in their pink bibs are sweeping the stage, ridding it of all the left over debris like strands of straw, blades of grass from the real turf, mud and anything else that may have survived our final Hail Mary onslaught. Of course on this run they are only rehearsing as we have just completed a dry run so debris is minimal. They have been given a routine where they all form a line across the centre of the FOP, spanning it end to end. Armed with a wide broom, half go one way, and half go the other. Even this has been choreographed. As I watch them work I think how this will be their time on the FOP, their performance in front of the capacity crowd.

When they finish the entrance of the Queen is announced in both English and French – another rehearsal – followed by the National Anthem. Some people sing along, others stand up if sitting down. For the more patriotic amongst us, this must be quite a special moment.

After the PA falls silent and this unofficial break is over, we are called onto the FOP again, into our counties. We stand about for some time. Somebody reminds me that we are going to be allowed to stay after our rehearsal has ended to watch the NHS segment. That should be good to see. I'll stay for a little while at least, before heading home.

We are now told that a musical rehearsal will follow, mainly for the benefit of the drummers. We are cued to do our choreography as we walk to the perimeter, whilst the drummers rehearse cues for their own routines and movements, as previously established I imagine. We continue in this way for a while, before being asked to go back inside the vom and prepare for another dry run. If we do a reset now that is all we will do in the time available, so I suppose it makes more sense to get another full run in, which will be more beneficial. If nothing else, it certainly benefits our motivation and morale as it all goes much better, all the way to when we walk up the aisles and onto the podium. It's been a productive rehearsal and we have finished on a high note. Now it's time to enjoy the NHS.

Before doing so, I ask about my accreditation. I'm told to go to the registration area where it will be waiting for me. It's a quick process. My details are checked on the system and I am handed an Upgrade Card, which I have to wear behind my main accreditation at all times. I finally have the requisite OOC around my neck. As I leave to return to the seating bowl, an announcement has been made that there are Ceremonies t-shirts being distributed on the way out. A large queue has formed for these so it takes a while to reach the front but I eventually pick up a black one to add to the orange one I picked up in Dagenham during Jubilee weekend, which seems like such a long time ago now. We have come very far since those rain-soaked rehearsals.

Back in the seating area on the upper level, I am conscious of time, but we are kept waiting for quite a while before the music begins and the nurses and doctors pour out of the voms, maybe hundreds of them, pushing the beds that I've seen on several occasions. They are everywhere. It is hard to believe that so many full-size beds can be stored in the voms. Through a series of choreographed movements and skilful interaction, they manage to spell GOSH using the beds. Having witnessed this I can now recall seeing it on one of the Mass Team's plans that they carry with them everywhere they go – the letters were made up of a series of rectangular blocks. Now I know what they represented. Once again the nurses are pushing their beds left and right, this way and that, not one of them bumping into another. They are well rehearsed. The logo of the Great Ormond Street Hospital is now visible – the child's face. They have even made the tear falling from its eye. It's all very impressive.

Finally they manoeuvre their beds again to spell out NHS, which is what this segment is celebrating. The music throughout has given the segment a real fun element, in contrast to the dark, pulsating rhythms of our sequence which the audience will already have been through by this time. Quite abruptly the music is cut and the nurses and doctors have stopped for a regroup. There is no telling when they will resume, and I know it could be a long time, so I decide to leave for the day. I've seen some of it at least so I make my way out of a now much quieter Olympic Park.

42

A Day With The Family

Sunday 15 July 2012

Rehearsals had begun on 2 May, over two months ago. At first they had been easy on us, a few hours one week, a few hours the next, a break of a couple of weeks, followed by the same again. From 2 June, once they had weaned us, it had been relentless. I'd spent five days working and two days rehearsing, every single week. On two occasions I'd travelled straight from work to the Stadium. This had been my routine for 43 days, without a day off in between. Today, however, was my first completely free day in all that time. We had been looking forward to this, willing the date to come quicker so that we could at least spend one day during the summer as a family, and as such we took full advantage.

We didn't want a long journey there and back, as time was precious, so I'd searched the internet for something suitable. I happened across Knebworth Park: adventure playground, train ride, dinosaur trail, picturesque gardens, and a tour of the stately home. There was something for both us parents and our two daughters. On paper it sounded like a great day out. In practice, however, it didn't fare as well as we'd hoped, or indeed expected, but we still had a nice time exploring the gardens, letting the children run around, and me taking photos to show that the summer had not been purely about my Olympic experience.

Our eldest, Sabirah, only three years old, was in her element as she witnessed 'in the flesh' the dinosaurs that had been the latest object of her fascination, or dinofones as she so affectionately called them, not quite able to master the lexical puzzle presented to her on TV. This was one of the main reasons for coming here, and it was great to see her so happy.

Rehearsals had become such a large part of my spare time. We had spent entire days in the Stadium. During the week I would muse over the session we had had the previous weekend or would look forward to the one that was imminent, and wonder what new developments we would be faced with, or how much progress we would make. Today, however, I managed to leave everything related to rehearsals firmly where it belonged and forgot about turf rolling, removing fences, strikes, voms, bulges, rings, smelting, drummers, tors... just forgot about rehearsing. I was glad to be with my family and my focus was on them.

Over a late lunch we did, however, discuss how show day was fast approaching. Soon the tables would be turned, where days out would once again be commonplace and rehearsing a thing of the past.

Later that evening, with the kids tucked in bed after a thoroughly enjoyable day, I received the final confirmed times for all of the dress rehearsals. The ever-decreasing schedule now looked like this:

DATE	TIME	VENUE DETAILS/NOTES
Wed 18 July	12:00 to EOS	Stadium COMPULSORY
Fri 20 July	12:30 to EOS	Stadium COMPULSORY
Sat 21 July	14:00 to EOS	Stadium Dress Rehearsal COMPULSORY
Mon 23 July	14:00 to EOS	Stadium Dress Rehearsal COMPULSORY
Wed 25 July	14:00 to EOS	Stadium Dress Rehearsal COMPULSORY
Fri 27 July	14:00 to EOS	Stadium SHOW DAY

They mentioned that any cast arriving after 5:00pm on dress rehearsal nights would not be allowed on site. I wasn't quite sure about that, but it was best to arrive in good time, so I duly noted the timings.

Tuesday 17 July 2012

Vanessa wrote to us again today to inform us of a significant change to the way in which rehearsals were going to be conducted.

YOUR HOLDING AREA HAS CHANGED. Your cast group will be held at Eton Manor from tomorrow, NOT the seating bowl.

Eton Manor is a purpose built Paralympics venue so it is available for Ceremonies during the Olympics. It is a good 27 minute walk from Stratford Gate. You are welcome to enter the Park here, but you can also enter via Eton Manor Gate, which is a 20 minute walk from Leyton tube.

REMINDER – No photographs, no video, no tweeting. We are so close – please don't spoil the surprise.

Your segment precedes the Athletes Parade. By the time you return to your holding area and get changed the Ceremony will be ending. Experience shows it is best to leave the Park before the audience and athletes in order to get onto public transport in good time. We strongly encourage you to use Eton Manor Gate for your exit and go to the Leyton tube.

43

Rehearsal 20

Wednesday 18 July 2012
12.00pm – EOS
Olympic Stadium

On Monday I finally received my technical rehearsal ticket that I won in the Games Maker ballot. I've already decided to hold a raffle at work for this, my third ticket, in order to raise money for Macmillan. With such an exclusive prize, I am sure I can persuade people to part with their money and benefit from such a rare opportunity, albeit on their own. I just have to create a poster and pin it up around the office, and then employ my powers of persuasion, which are in fact rather under-developed, but the prize on offer should work to my advantage. I can then add this money to the funds I raised for my 10K run which I did before one of the rehearsals. It's a good plan, I feel. However, I have no time to implement this today.

Originally I had taken the day off work, the same for Friday, but with the schedule now finalised, I can work for a couple of hours and then leave for the rehearsal. I've decided that I would prefer to walk to Eton Manor from Stratford, through the Park, as it is much more scenic, despite it being a longer walk. I am aiming to arrive at the Park at around 12pm. There is no sense in reaching Eton Manor at that time as I am well aware of what that will entail. I leave work at 11.15 and begin the journey to Stratford.

We are in official Games time now; it actually began on Monday. I checked more than once that I had all of my accreditation cards before leaving for work this morning. I now have to wear the enormous laminated card around my neck, my upgrade card positioned behind it, and my Ceremonies ID.

I arrive at 12pm and get through security quite quickly. The walk to Eton Manor is indeed long and the 25 minutes or so mentioned in the email is by no means an exaggeration. On the way there it begins to rain lightly. We are almost in the tail end of July and it just isn't letting up. As I walk through the Park, I see the venues and structures that I saw during my venue training a couple of weeks ago, except that now there are no barriers blocking our way along the main path. Seeing the Velodrome up close is a highlight. I would love to see inside, get on a bike and swirl my way around its track.

Onwards I go and over a bridge giving easy access across a very busy road, I'm not sure which. Looking back I see the Stadium in the distance and realise just how far I have walked. Eton Manor is just ahead and there is a queue to enter the site. Our passes are checked, the security personnel verifying that we have the necessary OOC on our accreditation. Once through we walk to another queue leading to the registration area. Next stop is meal collection. They have set up a couple of tents for this. I wonder if the move to the new holding area will mean a change in the contents of our meal packs. I expectantly open the brown paper bag to reveal none other than the sandwich that I had chosen, a granola bar, some Pringles, and a Braeburn apple.

A text message this morning instructed us to go to the Sports Ops area, which is where I am being directed now. Down a sloped path, with a grassy area on the right, there is a board with various signs and messages on it. Taking a left here I go past various holding rooms and cabins. There are lots of people milling around, walking in and out of the rooms, which are very large and full of white chairs arranged in rows. The holding area for Group 44B is at the end of this path, first cabin on the right. My ID is checked before I am allowed in. I'm told to just take a seat. The same white chairs fill most of the room. I notice that they all have numbers on them, our bib numbers, so I find 461 and place my bag on the plastic seat.

Along one side of the cabin there are tables with the usual tea and coffee making facilities and the recycling bins alongside them. In the front corner, next to the entrance to the cabin, and on the far side towards the back, there are clothes rails upon which our costumes are hanging, covered in plastic sleeves to protect them, idly waiting to be filled with our working bodies. Looking around, I notice that there are only men here. I suppose then that we have been segregated, meaning we will get changed in here too. I get into my coveralls, take a seat and begin eating my lunch.

We are kept waiting here for a long time. We are used to this but this seems to be a much longer wait than usual. Nobody has mentioned anything about getting into our costumes, but some people have taken it upon themselves to do so, maybe just to try them on. I prefer to wait until we are told. I decide to go and find my one, which doesn't take me long as they are all in numerical order, as would be expected. It is hanging on the rail against the front wall. I take a look at it and it's more or less as I remember it. I'm looking forward to wearing it and seeing if it makes me feel any different. We've been playing the role of the Working Men and Women for a long time now but I think wearing the costume will complete the picture mentally as well as physically.

Minutes have become hours, and for the last hour or so it's been rather dull. I've been chatting to Josh, Chris, Gaudi, and the others from my section of the lines, drinking coffee, and just taking advantage of this slow start by resting my eyes, never actually sleeping, although there is only so much resting I can bear. I've been outside a couple of times, watched as the entire area has filled with people. It's not just the Working Men and Women here today, but the NHS, the Green and Pleasant Land volunteers, and the drummers too. There are thousands of people present, all in separate holding areas. Chris has been distributing the Fife badges to those of us who ordered them. I put one away and pin the other to my coveralls. They do look fantastic; every detail of his design has been reproduced perfectly. To add to the hats and t-shirts of other counties, we now have these badges in the Kingdom of Fife. I personally think we have the best of the bunch, and it's nice to also have an object to represent us, even if it is less conspicuous than those of other counties.

When we do eventually walk to the Stadium, progress is very slow. We set off in different groups, according to the segment and the vom we are in. There are so many of us that we can only shuffle along at a slow pace, stopping often and for too long. Going past the hockey arena, which I didn't look at on the way to Eton Manor, we stop and are stood here for a very long time indeed, or so it seems. The flags of the nations competing against each other in hockey are arranged in a long row, Pakistan amongst them. Maybe this is the year when they will reclaim their gold medal of old, although I believe the last time was many years ago.

On the move again, the Stadium is very slowly getting closer, and after some time we are back where we were the other day, outside the vom. We are held here for a while until there is room for us to move inside. We go round to our familiar corridor, just like we did previously, except this time there is a much bigger buzz about the place. We walk past children, Suffragettes, and various other volunteer groups. It feels much more like a show environment, not that I have any past experience of this, but it's what I imagine it would be like. Once we are in our area, we can only sit and wait, trying somehow to pass the time yet again.

When we are called out bodies rise, legs are stretched, mobile phones fall back into pockets, gloves are pulled on and we prepare for work. We only do a brief mimed strike to cover the transition from GPL to the Industrial Revolution. Poor cues are given for the choreography, but it doesn't matter a great deal as the strike is cut very quickly and we are back in our buddy lines on the M25.

The waiting continues but with no roof above. Light rain begins to shower down upon us. It is around 4.30pm and we have done very little. People have left work needlessly, some of them incurring a small loss of earnings that won't be reimbursed. Frustration kicks in if it hasn't already. Silent resentment needs no words. An exchange of smiles is enough to acknowledge this. I remain focussed, although on what exactly I'm not quite sure. Less than zero, it just can't be helped. Wait. Wait. Wait.

Back in the vom, we are about to strike. It doesn't begin well. The choreography is passable and there are new ropes on our fences, which is unexpected, so we have to untie them before moving them, wasting precious time. We then go to the wrong piece of turf. This is a knock-on effect from there being just one person to a rail, rather than two, as they are lighter now. It's a bit confusing but we manage to work it out. The rest of the strike is reasonably good, even if the end is patchy. The cues could have been better and the rain could have helped us by moving to the outside of the Stadium, or simply stopping. Striking in a poncho is never ideal.

We break for dinner now, although it takes them around ten minutes to actually announce this. I collect my meal pack to the sound of the James Bond theme tune on the PA. The Warriors have already swept the FOP. I consider what I am going to do as I've left my insulin in Eton Manor. I should have known we would be given a meal. With another sandwich, granola bar, crisps and apple being broken down in my system, my blood sugar will go through the roof.

My contemplation is interrupted by the sound of one of the drummers announcing very loudly that there is a cupcake for each and every one of her fellow performers, but drummers only allowed. That means 1,000 cupcakes. Now I can bake a bit, indeed I am quite good at it, but to make and decorate a thousand little cakes is very impressive

255

indeed, a monumental effort. I have no idea how she managed to
bypass the rules and get so many boxes of cakes into the Stadium in
the first place, but well done to her.

Back to my dilemma. I have no choice but to walk back and
retrieve my injection. It's a long walk. It's best to just get on with it
rather than pondering aimlessly on how frustrating this is. I inform
Vanessa that I'll be back soon, and begin a fast walk to our holding area,
eating my dinner on the way. By the time I get there I'll be finished
and can take my insulin.

I keep my earphones in and my IEM switched on. In this way I
can hear what is happening in the Stadium. The NHS segment is being
rehearsed. It would have been an ideal opportunity to see all of it, but
I can only hear the music plus the sound of rain hitting my poncho.
Hopefully I will get another chance. I hear something about Marys
standing by, but I have no idea what that means.

When I reach Eton Manor, the bottom of my jeans soaked and
feeling uncomfortable, the place is empty except for a security guard
and a cleaning lady. I ask her where she is from, just making
conversation. Hungary. She tells me that she has worked in the
Stadium and has seen our segment. Her choice of word to describe it
is, curiously, 'amazing'. I am actually taken aback by this, but there is
no hint of humour on her face or in her tone. I thank her kindly,
although I still feel that this can't be right. It's surely just a mess and a
picture of chaos and disorder. I acknowledge that we always manage
to clear the FOP and the machinery and chimneys rise, the ring gets
forged and then they all converge, but it simply feels like it couldn't
possibly look good. If this lady is indeed being serious then some of
Steve Boyd's enthusiasm after our strikes begins to make more sense
now, as he and the team do have an elevated view. This one comment
has lifted my spirits immeasurably. All we need now is for her
sentiment to be multiplied by 80,000 on show night and we may just
be able to call our piece a total success.

I decide to gather up my things and take them with me on the way
back. At least I can avoid having to return here after the rehearsal. For
the fourth time today, I begin the walk that lies between Eton Manor
and the Stadium. By the time I get there the break will be over. On
the IEMs Steve announces that all three segments will be repeated after
the break so a reset is required. I'm about half way back at this point
and beginning to perspire. Before heading into the Stadium I remove
my coveralls and let the light rain cool me down. The reset is under

way. I see Elia on the podium having an extended break it seems, so I chat to her whilst arranging my things near the seats at the very top, taking note of the block we are in so I can easily find my bag at the end. There is still a bit left to do so I return to the FOP and lend a hand with some turf that is still to be positioned properly. Josh tells me that the NHS segment looked really impressive. There were Mary Poppins coming down from the 'sky' and landing on the FOP. So they were the Marys I heard on my IEM. It sounds great and I'm just a little annoyed that I missed it all. Josh says that their segment makes up for everything that is lacking in ours, so I tell him about the Hungarian lady's opinion of our segment, which may help change his mind. I would love to see what we look like but I can only wait until it has been broadcast on TV.

After the reset we meet with Katie to try and resolve the confusion we experienced with the priority turf. By the end of it I'm still a little unsure about who is doing what so I think the best thing for me and Gaudi is to just go wherever Elia, Josh, Chris and Nancy are when we reach the turf.

Whilst Katie moves on to another group, we walk back to the M25 and are soon summoned to go to Vom 4, just the smelters. A costume guy shows us the protective head gear we are going to be wearing for the remaining rehearsals, complete with goggles. These will be kept on each shovel, ready to be worn before we form our lines. He mentions that we may also be given a balaclava to keep in our pockets, although I can't see what purpose that will serve. It's good to have an extra piece of equipment to get into though, as close to a costume change that I'm going to get. After another pep talk care of Katie we all move back into the voms to prepare for the strike. The Green and Pleasant Land performers take their positions on the FOP. Whilst they go through their routine, leading up to when we essentially oust them and take over, we occupy ourselves in any way we can.

Earlier on, when we were here waiting for the strike, Josh and Chris devised a game involving an empty water bottle and its bottle cap, a finger flick and a strike of a different type. This is what boredom has achieved and driven some of us towards. I participated too. Now they are continuing, just as a lady on our IEMs tells us that at the end of the rehearsal we will be given our two dress rehearsal tickets. They are going to be distributed in the cast holding area at Eton Manor. A frustrated smile splits my pursed lips as my brain registers yet another run of that long walk. My head falls limp in front of me as I first consider missing it, but then deciding that I don't want any issues with receiving the tickets so I best pick them up tonight rather than waiting.

With my eyes closed I listen to the montage sequence that has now begun. We are on very soon. I do like these small snippets of Britishness, mashed together with such skill that a smooth flow is maintained throughout despite the abruptness of the cuts. Choir singing is followed by Nimrod with "Be not afeared..." over it. Time to stand and form our lines for another run, never the same as any we've done before. The line snakes through the doors and quickly branches out into the bulge, all of us huddled together and looking towards the Tor.

Around 15 minutes later we are looking up at the Olympic rings again. The strike was much better than the first one. Everything went well: structures, turf, smelting and choreography. A successful run ends the rehearsal. Now it's time to go and claim my tickets. Run number five, although in the company of hundreds of others it doesn't seem quite so long. A queue has formed when I arrive at Eton Manor. Everybody is handed an envelope containing two tickets. They have a bar code system in place to confirm that we have indeed received them. No extras, no replacements. Seat allocation is random; we take what we are given. Once secured I begin what will definitely be my final run today as I make my way back to Stratford station through the Park again. Six times I will have done this, each one taking around 20 minutes. I think back to my run for Macmillan in June. Two members of my team walked the distance at a leisurely pace in around two hours. With a few simple calculations I ascertain that I have covered over ten kilometres today from my walks back and forth between the Stadium and Eton Manor. That's a good bit of exercise and my legs do feel like they need a rest now.

On the final stretch before the bridge that leads away from the Stadium, past the Aquatics Centre, I can see a few people gathered on the edge of the path, looking intently at something. When I reach them, what I now see is probably the most amazing thing I have seen in the Park so far. Underneath the bridge, just ahead, is a water feature where columns of droplets are falling intermittently, forming a temporary curtain of water, a bit like a row of harp strings. At first I don't quite see it, but looking closer I can just about distinguish a word, visible only for about a second. The drops are forming the word as they fall. With every cycle a new word can be seen for about a second. Each word is different every single time. At first I stare in disbelief.

This very quickly turns into awe. The effect is heightened by the now fading natural light and the increasing illumination around the droplets. Behind me in the Stadium they are conducting sound tests, the same music that is used in the NHS segment. I've now been looking at this superb feature of the Park for a few minutes and still I haven't seen the same word twice. I'm not even going to begin to work out how this is achieved. My brain just isn't built for that, instead preferring to be taken in completely by the wonder of this trick of light or brilliant design. Every few seconds a new word falls. I attempt a few photos but my phone isn't quick enough, so I make a brief video. It's rather hypnotic and it is only the promise that I will more than likely be able to see this again that tears me away from this spectacle. It would be rather appropriate if the last words I see are HOME, followed by NOW. No such luck, but what an incredible display. I suspect I won't be the last person to be amazed by what I've just seen.

44

Rehearsal 21

Friday 20 July 2012
12.30pm – EOS
Olympic Stadium

Since being issued with our dress rehearsal tickets, there has been a lot of activity on the Facebook page with people swapping tickets for ones that will give their family and friends a better view of the county they are in. Somebody has even set up a separate page just for this. People have worked out which blocks are close to Fife, for example, and exchanges are being offered and taken, with the deals planned for today's rehearsal. From reading some of the posts I believe my tickets are on the Tor side but I decide to just leave my allocation as it is. Wherever my brother and his friend sit, they will surely enjoy the experience, and there will be little chance of them spotting me in the mêlée that is our strike. Besides I need to concentrate on my work. I leave a little later than today, having completed some tasks to at least avoid an enormous backlog next week when I will be off for most of it.

On the train to the Stadium I send a text message that has become an annual occurrence for me – wishing my friend Sonia a happy birthday. I never remember anybody else's special day, indeed I never attempt to. However, exactly 22 years ago today, whilst Sonia was celebrating her fifteenth birthday, I was on a train to another stadium in Wembley, to attend my first ever concert. For that reason this date carries some significance and Sonia is forever associated with it, even though it would be four years before we would actually meet.

Madonna's Blond Ambition show that evening was an incredible spectacle, the best thing I'd seen in my 15 or so years of life thus far. Fast forward 22 years, almost to the hour, and I am on the way to rehearse for the biggest event I will probably ever be involved in, in terms of sheer magnitude and splendour, a concert being akin to a primary school play in comparison. A tenuous link I think not.

Despite my late departure I still arrive at around 12.30pm. It is quiet at the entrance to the Olympic Park so I reach the front of the PSA very quickly but I get a full bag search today. The culprit is my cycling multi-tool, spanner, tyre levers, and various other accoutrements that I always keep in my bag. They haven't noticed these before. It's all a bit random.

Once through security I begin the long walk to Eton Manor. Other volunteers and Park staff are dotted about, walking around, barely filling the vastness all around. In a matter of days my views will be blocked by the enormous crowds of people surging through the Park, going to events, enjoying the open spaces that haven't been opened yet. There are railings blocking the paths that veer off into the greener areas. No queues have formed in front of the food stalls. The world's largest McDonald's has yet to serve its first burger. The Park Live screen is still waiting to be switched on. Soon the place will be teeming with the world's general public and the Park will never look like this again. I make a mental note to bring my camera one day and capture the Park with nobody in it. I have been granted this opportunity through my volunteering, access before the mass influx, a chance that I will regret if I miss it.

When I finally walk past the Velodrome and approach Eton Manor, the queue to collect our IEMs and get into the cast area extends all the way onto the bridge, over the dual carriageway. As we wait it begins to rain lightly. I don't mind this as long as it doesn't begin to pour, even if we are more than used to striking in such conditions by now. As I move closer to the front I see volunteers arriving from Eton Manor Gate, which I haven't used yet. I manage to reach the holding area relatively dry, having collected my meal packs. I notice that some people are wearing their costumes. Soon I confirm that we are all going to be in full costume today so we need to get changed at some point. I have my lunch first. There is plenty of time and I can't wait to tuck into yet another tub of Pringles, a granola bar, an apple and a sandwich. I have eaten enough of the latter now to have decided that I do not much like them. Too much bread and flavourless filling, but I still eat them with thanks as there is no other choice, and it is offered to us free of charge, courtesy of Olympic Ceremonies, as stated on the label. They didn't have to give us anything, I believe.

As I eat I get interviewed by Brian. He is working with some of the drummers to reproduce the experience of rehearsals into a soundscape, interspersed with spoken word made up of responses to questions that he has set. I was more than happy to volunteer for this, and now answer his questions with pre-prepared responses. I basically just say what I wrote, having no idea how my answers will be used.

With the brief interview over and lunch finished I get changed. It takes me a while to arrange my things, working out what I can take with me. I only have two pockets now, although they are quite deep at least. My dark grey corduroy trousers are loose-fitting, which I am thankful for as they will be more comfortable in the hotter weather. Some people have waistcoats, others even have jackets. I just have a beige shirt and braces. I've never had to put braces on before. The buttons they attach to seem to be quite loose but they do hold. A member of the costume team shows me how to adjust them to relieve the tension a little. Some people have belts instead. Josh and I also have a pair of very large pale orange gloves, like gauntlets, which are issued to the smelters. They are brand new, completely spotless, which won't do at all. He offers to cover them in a bit of make-up that is kept in the back of the room, to give them a dirtier and more worn look, as he is going to do the same to his ones. He returns with two pairs of much more appropriate looking gloves, now peach and black. I put away my standard issue gloves and finish getting changed.

All around me the room is full of people who are getting into their costumes, others making tea and coffee, or just sitting and chatting, the costume team offering help where it's needed, finding replacements if possible. It's a nice atmosphere to be in. A while later they give out hats. I'm not sure if the smelters will need one but I take one anyway. I would prefer to wear it until I have to get into my smelting cap and goggles.

The waiting continues. On the way to the toilet at one point I see people in their costumes. There are all manner of outfits. Some people are clearly dancers, dressed in an incredible array of colourful costumes. There are nurses, doctors, rural folk, costumes that I can't quite identify. It is an awful lot to take in and everyone looks fantastic. I can't believe the enormity of it all. Thousands of costumes have been created. To even design such a diverse mix of clothing is beyond me. Looking at everyone around me, I am overwhelmed. There are costumes I would prefer to wear, ones that make me wish I was in a different segment, although this thought is only brief. I wouldn't want to be anywhere other than the Industrial Revolution, more specifically in the county of Fife. That is where I belong now.

We eventually make our way to the vom, just like we did on Wednesday, stopping and starting. This time the sun is beating down and I am really very relieved that I am only wearing a thin shirt. The people wearing jackets must be feeling rather uncomfortable in this heat. Just as we did earlier in the week, we walk according to our segment and our vom, thus each county is more or less together, but all of us are walking in a sort of chain. With a thousand of us we are an enormous mass of Working Men and Women, all the more so because we are in costume today. There are many shades of brown, beige, black, and grey, stretching into the distance in a long line. Some people are taking photos of this influx, standing on benches to capture as many of us as possible. It is a truly amazing sight to see us all like this, dressed to do what we have been rehearsing for so long. I am slowly beginning to feel different, feelings that I didn't have back in Eton Manor. It's almost as if this long walk is us travelling to work, all as one, off to another shift in those dark and sweaty mills.

Talking to Steve, he mentions how they have spoon-fed us slowly, not just the logistics of our segment but our performance too, the characterisation behind it. Ever since we have moved to the Stadium we have added new things, from moving into the voms, to completing the segment, seeing the rings, taking bows, and exiting up the stands. We have been asked to focus on our characters, being in the moment, and we have done so. We have moved to Eton Manor to get used to being in our final holding area and walking to the Stadium. The first time we were in our own clothes, today we are in costume. Slowly but surely they have been edging us towards the final night, just a few rehearsals away now, almost conditioning us into believing in what we are doing and in the logistical aspects completely, as well as being the part, not just playing it. The transition is almost complete. By show night I have no doubt that mentally we will be exactly where they want us to be.

When we are on the final stretch to the Stadium, walking past the BBC studio, there are a couple of film crews filming us as we walk down. Vanessa takes note of their details, probably just confirming that they are permitted to be there. I thought this was supposed to be top secret, yet it looks like the public will at least know what we look like in costume before next Friday. I find this a bit odd, but they know best, and also know what is and isn't standard practice.

Once we are inside the vom we walk through and go to our corridor. On the way there I see lots of performers in their costumes from the History Parade. There are Sergeant Peppers in yellow, pink, blue and red costumes, seemingly reproduced exactly as they appear on the album cover. I am sure they are as accurate as they can be. They look absolutely stunning and I feel a genuine hint of envy as I walk past them. Elsewhere there are performers in red military costumes, others wearing some kind of regal attire, but I can't identify them. There are also girls in frocks with faces on them. Apparently they are the ones who will walk with the athletes when they enter the Stadium and carry the name of the country. Paul's girlfriend is one of them. I do love their outfits. I'll have to get a photo at some point. Some people are dressed in completely black outfits. Even their faces are black all over. I've no idea who they are, but I am told they are dementors from Harry Potter, so I presume they are in the NHS segment.

We sit and wait for quite some time with no update on when we are expected to perform. What we are told is that we should wear our ponchos today as there is no laundry service, so if our costumes get wet they will smell, and stay like that until show night. Maybe that will make them more authentic, but the general consensus is that ponchos will be best.

Although water is in plentiful supply, with pallets of bottles in our holding area and the podium level, there is nothing inside the vom. However, somebody has discovered that there is a fridge in the cast area through some doors, so I go to get a bottle. Inside this room there are Caribbean migrants, also from the History Parade, in their suits and dresses, some of them with old style suitcases by their side. I can't help but stare – they all look amazing together. I get my water and return to our own area in the corridor.

Eventually we go out for a full strike. We are back now into our usual routine, the only difference being our costumes. As the tree is uprooted and the Warriors, who are also wearing the same style of costume as we are, start pouring out of the Tor, I notice this time that some of the GPL people are carrying the maypole that is in Fife. They are doing their own strike just as we are about to do ours. It all starts well. Gaudi and I have our Work Prep timed perfectly now and the fence strike goes smoothly. The turf is slightly confusing. Last time when some of us were going through our priority turf routine, somebody suggested rolling the saw tooth lengthways, although I didn't think this had been set in stone. In the strike we did later we rolled our turf in the same way we had always done. Tonight, however, one of us has had to go to another piece, so our new person starts to roll differently, which throws us a little. But as always, we get there.

This is exactly what we are expected to do: cope with the small changes as they happen, and improvise if needed.

Having deposited our turf and made our way to Vom 4, we have to put our smelting caps and goggles on when we pick up our shovels. My hat goes into my pocket and with a bit of help I put my cap on. The goggles are over our caps. The costume guy tells us to put them on when we are at the trough. There is still some confusion when we are there, whether or not we are supposed to be moving on the beat, and when we start smelting. There is no cue specifically for the smelters, but surely we should be smelting before the forgers have something to forge, rather than at the same time. The goggles also won't go over my glasses. Other people are having the same problem. I just leave them as they are and concentrate on smelting. Over to the left of my line of sight I can see the beam engine operators doing the Dials routine. That is one thing I won't get to do, that and Shovel/Pickaxe. Everybody has their own part to play, and not a single one of us can do a bit of everything.

As the segment nears its completion, when we are in the outer ring doing our choreography, I can see some performers in very colourful carnival-style outfits, more of the History Parade. It's hard not to take a peek at them, but I will have to be more focussed on show night, only looking straight ahead. Any focus I did have at the beginning has been lost with the onset of minor issues and breaks in routine. Being in costume can only have so much effect. If things go wrong the cracks very quickly appear. There is still a lot of work to do before we can say we are absolutely ready, with only a week to go.

After the strike, whilst the Warriors are sweeping the stage, we are told we can go – no more run-throughs until tomorrow. I decide to watch the NHS segment, as others are doing the same and nobody has said that we need to leave. Maybe this time I will get to see it all. It takes a while for it to begin as one of our chimneys is stuck. This has happened on a few occasions. They can't get it down so the tech team are being kept busy, as well as under pressure to sort this out, I imagine. When they do get it to move it goes wrong and bends over at an impossible angle without toppling over, the illusion of solidity destroyed. It takes quite a long time to get it to straighten up and disappear inside the trap, so the NHS segment starts much later than planned. Whilst this has been going on, a lot of the members of the History Parade have been walking into the seating bowl armed with meal packs. I hear that they are being handed out to anybody who wants them. They have been walking in with boxes of them and distributing them to their fellow performers from their groups. I am tempted to go and get one but I don't want to miss the NHS so I stay where I am.

When they finally begin they soon have to stop due to another technical issue. There is just a week to go and problems are still rife, which is very worrying. I still haven't seen anything that I haven't seen already and it's getting late. I need to go to Waterloo after this so will have to leave soon. They resume after several minutes and then it is full steam ahead. There is a lot of dancing involved, children bouncing and somersaulting on the beds, followed by a section where the dementors I saw earlier storm the stage. There is a lot going on. Captain Hook and Voldemort are towering high, instilling fear into all of the children. When the Mary Poppins come down it looks superb. I barely notice them from being so focussed on the FOP. She comes and banishes all of the villains. It's rather chaotic, a bit like our segment, so there is a lot of coordination and choreography. Apparently with the lighting it looks incredible. I have yet to see this but it's something to look forward to, even if the first chance I get is on the TV after the actual event.

With this segment over I leave and walk all the way back to Eton Manor. Lots of people choose to stay but I need to get going. It's a nice walk back. The sun is shining, it is warm, and there isn't a rain cloud in sight. There are not many people around when I reach the holding area. They are handing out meal packs here too. As the sandwiches are perishable they have to throw them out if they are not eaten today. There are boxes and boxes of meal packs, six in each one, waiting to be claimed or wasted. They are encouraging anybody left to take a meal pack, even a box if we want it. I hate to see such waste but what am I going to do with six meals. I deliberate for a minute. Even if I have to get rid of the sandwiches, I could keep the rest at least. The catering staff try to persuade me to just take a box. I finally agree, deciding that there will be homeless people in Waterloo so I'll just give somebody a free meal. Why can't they just do that?

With a box to carry in addition to my own baggage, and in this heat, I walk to Leyton tube station. On the way there I see one guy with three boxes of meal packs, 18 in all, piled on top of each other. He is wisely taking the bus. Maybe I should have taken more boxes. I convince myself that it would have been impractical, especially on the tube, which may be crowded. With my one box and heavy bag over my shoulder, I am already sweating, my t-shirt almost soaked through. When I finally get on the train the sweat is pouring down my face. It takes me a long time to cool down. I tuck into one of the meal packs in an effort to get my energy levels up again after all the walking I've done since leaving the Stadium. The heat has taken its toll.

When I reach Waterloo I approach the first homeless person I see, a man who clearly doesn't look as well as he probably should. He looks up at me as I ask him if he'd like something to eat. He is barely audible as he gives a very slight and expectant nod so I hand him a meal pack, which he gratefully accepts. I give him another one and leave, not needing the thanks that he offers me more than once. I don't have time now to find anybody else, but later on I see somebody occupying the same spot, a lady this time. She is more vocal, and is not going to be refusing any food that is offered to her. I pull out a meal pack and tell her it's courtesy of the Olympic Ceremonies. I don't think she cares. The way in which she asks me what's inside, her face lighting up at the prospect of something decent to eat, the expectation in her eyes, makes my heart sink into my ever full stomach. I tell her what she can expect and then give her all three of the remaining meal packs as it's getting late and I need to get home. The sandwiches will keep for longer than deemed by the use by date, and the other items for much longer. She now has a very small stock of food to last a day or so. I wish I had taken more boxes. I bitterly regret not doing so. All I can think of on the way home is the amount of food wasted and what I could have done with it. I could easily have handled a few boxes. Any discomfort would have been short lived and I could have just gone to my comfortable home and taken a shower. I acknowledge that I have done a good thing but the opportunity to do more has been missed, and for no good reason. The look on her face returns to me again and again.

45

Rehearsal 22

Saturday 21 July 2012
2.00pm – EOS
Olympic Stadium

Today is the first day of Ramadan. Last night, after arriving home and managing a few short hours of sleep, I woke up to have breakfast when it was still dark outside. My diabetes consultants say I should probably not fast, which technically makes me exempt, but I prefer to at least try, seeing it as an acceptance of defeat if I just go with their advice. I can be very stubborn at times. Besides I usually manage to fast most days without my blood sugar levels hitting either end of the scale. It's all about control and I usually manage it.

With my sleep disrupted even more than usual, it is with some fatigue that I make my way to Stratford today for our first dress rehearsal. I received a text this morning to say there will be no watching after our segment. We are in full show mode so we must go straight back to Eton Manor after we have finished.

I decide to head for Eton Manor Gate as it is a shorter walk from Leyton tube. I can't consume a single drop or crumb until sunset and I need to preserve my energy to keep sugar levels up. Every year I stop cycling to work for a month when I am fasting as doing so will almost definitely give me hypoglycaemia.

When I arrive there are maybe two people waiting to get through security. Some members of the Mass Team are enjoying the sun just beyond the PSA. The weather is perfect and there is a bit of a festival atmosphere today. Lots of volunteers are on the grassy areas, just sat about chatting, sunbathing, reading, and relaxing. The only difference of course is that we are not waiting to spectate but to perform. I can't believe how nonchalant I have become about this.

After registering I move into the meal queue where a few members of staff are handing out green stickers to be stuck onto our accreditation cards. These will be required to enter the cast holding area on Monday.

Everywhere we go security is stepping up. Last night, when leaving the Park, they were checking our accreditation, presumably to make sure that we were allowed inside in the first place. I never lose sight of the fact that we are in such an exclusive position; I am rather enjoying these special privileges.

When I enter our holding area I immediately notice that lots of people have been made up or rather, muddied up. So it's full make-up today then. There are soot marks on people's faces, on their hands too. Some people have even stained their costumes for added effect.

David walks in and sets his things down in our row of seats. In one of his bags he is carrying none other than one of the official Olympic torches. On Thursday he had the honour of being a torchbearer. Like all of the people who were fortunate enough to do this, he was nominated by members of his community and then chosen to carry the torch. Anybody who has managed to make it to the exclusive list of 8,000 torchbearers has done so because they have done something amazing, or they are a pillar of their community, respected and appreciated by their neighbours. David is one of them and as a result Fife can boast a torchbearer within the county.

He briefly shows it to those of us with him, not wanting to reveal it completely for fear of causing a rush for photos and a glimpse. As he pulls the cover over the top, the gold sheen glimmers in the light from above. It is a thing of beauty. I'm not sure if I truly feel this, or I've just been taken in by the prevailing Olympic spirit that I have been directly exposed to for longer than I could ever have imagined before I began this journey. I do, however, feel proud to have seen and briefly touched one of the official torches before the Games have begun.

I find my seat and notice a couple of boxes next to the tea and coffee facilities. They contain granola bars, tubs of Pringles and apples, presumably the ones left over from yesterday. Instead of binning them they have created a free for all, something they couldn't legally do with the sandwiches. I put my things down, including my two fresh meal packs, and dive in for a few extras. If I can last until sunset, by which time we will probably be inside the vom, I'll just have to break my fast with a couple of granola bars and then eat properly after our segment.

I get changed and test my sugar. It's at 6.4. This changes things a little. With all the walking we will have to do, not to mention the actual strike, there is no way I will last another six hours or so. I can't risk having a hypo whilst I'm in the vom as the only available food will be my granola bars, which provide a relatively slow sugar release. There is no sense in being unrealistic here. I have to break my fast. I did also promise myself I wouldn't risk low blood sugar whilst performing, which is why I haven't told them about my condition as it only causes unnecessary complications. I therefore have a sandwich whilst I am in the queue for make-up. I can attempt to fast again tomorrow.

The queue is moving quite slowly as there are only two make-up girls to help us get ready. They were saying earlier that we can apply it ourselves but I prefer to have it done properly, so would rather just wait. It takes a while to get to the front though. She applies it a bit lightly because I tell her to go easy on my eyes because of my corneal grafts. I think this has made her too cautious as I can barely see anything on my face so I come back after a while and have a go myself. They have tables set up on the side with make-up and mirrors. It's very easy to apply too much so you have to use wet wipes to tone it down, although it is equally easy to wipe it all off. It takes a bit of practice to blend it in nicely. One guy has completely covered his face – his natural flesh tone is not even visible. He looks very amusing. It takes him a while to get it all off and start again.

Once I am happy with the way I look, my face dirty and blackened, I go to work on my arms, just in case I decide to roll up my sleeves. I then stain my shirt. There is no point in trying to keep it looking clean; it's not supposed to be that way. The make-up area is full of people dirtying their faces and any exposed skin. Some of the guys who will be operating the beam engines have their tops off. They mentioned this a few rehearsals ago, asking for volunteers who won't mind taking their shirts off. They have to apply make-up to their whole upper body, including their backs. On the walls there are images of workers from the period and tips for us to recreate the most appropriate look, including styling our hair correctly, although in my case I'll be wearing a cap so I don't worry about this. My hair is too short anyway. Looking in the mirror at myself, I do look like I've spent a long time in a foundry. I look dirty and I look rough. My beard has been growing quite nicely over the last couple of weeks. The make-up gives it an added depth, the gaps effectively filled in. I'm definitely happy with my appearance. I've no idea what Misbah will think though. I'll take some photos of myself before today's rehearsal is over and show her.

There is still plenty of time left until our segment begins. As it's a full dress rehearsal we won't be on until around 9pm tonight. I take a short walk outside, just looking at everyone in their costumes, soaking up the atmosphere in the cast area. I am fully aware that soon this will all be over. On the way back Danny Boyle turns up. We haven't seen much of him of late, although he's still been around at every rehearsal. He gets lots of cheers as he walks down the slope to our holding areas. He soon makes it into our area but is only there very briefly before he moves on. He isn't signing anything now, and isn't posing for photos. I can't imagine what he must be feeling, now that his own, much longer, journey is drawing to a close. Of course he is an internationally renowned director, an Oscar winner. He is used to the big stage, but even for him this is a massive undertaking and all critical eyes will be on him next Friday. We just have to do the best we can and hope we play our part in his success.

With nothing much to do, I keep looking at myself, adjusting my make-up, toning it down, adding some here and there. I am more or less happy with it but a little undecided. Looking at other people makes me think twice. There will be three more opportunities before it's all over though. This is just the first time. One of the team comes round and hands me a long strip of cloth, just a rag really. It's to be tied around our necks.

Having nothing more to do inside I go outside again. Seb Coe was here just now, talking to people, although I only see the back of him as he goes back into the building opposite our holding areas. I think he came over to meet some performers, probably had some photos taken, maybe even signed autographs. I go and sit down on the grass where Chris, Josh, Gaudi, Harry and Jon are sat in a circle, which makes a nice photo.

Looking around, I still find the diversity of the costumes amazing. Every time I look I see people dressed in outfits I've not seen before. The dancers are mainly dressed in very colourful costumes, or ones that indicate a style of music, like punk, glam rock, or disco. Some people are dressed up to look like David Bowie, I believe. It's difficult to fully appreciate the time and effort that has gone into putting this all together. The costume department's efforts are almost beyond comprehension. I think about how I will never be involved in anything like this again, and how it is indeed almost over.

Despite Vanessa's warnings, people are freely taking photos and posing with each other. So many people want to have their picture taken with performers from different segments, in different costumes, mimicking each other's moves. As people pose along the path that leads to the holding areas, several people come and try to get a photo before the group breaks up. The nurses seem to be very popular. There is a real buzz and camaraderie coming from every cast group.

At 7.10pm we get a half hour call. At least we now have a time. Katie has appeared and is milling around amongst her county. She suggests getting a group photo of Fife on the grass so we begin to gather people together. It takes a while but we manage to get a large group of Fife in the same place at the same time, have a couple of photos done and then we are told to move away. We attempt the same on the path that leads to our holding areas, next to the crates of water. It isn't as good a setting but we now have more people from Fife so the photos we take are all the more complete. No doubt these photos will be on Facebook by tomorrow and we will all have a valuable memory to treasure. Photos like this are usually a one-time only prospect so it is nice to have secured it now.

Finally, after the promised half hour plus an added bonus that nobody really wanted, we walk to the Stadium. It's been such a long wait today, but now onwards. Everyone looks great. One thing that I have noticed is that all of the costumes appear to be different. I keep comparing one with the next, and with mine too, yet as hard as I try I cannot see two that are exactly the same. Lots of people have a shirt like mine, but they all have a different pair of trousers, or they have a belt rather than braces. Where trousers are the same, boots differ. Some wear hats, some are without. The more I look, the more confident I become that we are all different. Across all of the Working Men and Women, the drummers, the Warriors and the technical team who wear costumes, more than 2,000 of us, we are all wearing the same style of clothing, yet neither one of us looks exactly alike. That is indeed an impressive feat and I would congratulate whoever has managed this.

As the Stadium draws closer, I try to imagine what it will be like on the actual night. It's not really possible. Words fail me when I try to express what this all means. We are closer than yesterday and with each passing day emotions drift into unknown avenues. A few photographers and cameramen greet us as we walk. Pictures of us appeared on the ITV and Channel 4 websites last night. Suzanne had a great shot, right in the camera. They are up to the same again tonight. Some of us, including me, unashamedly adjust our position on the path in order to walk right past a camera. I suppose it would be good to get in a shot, just once, giving us a visual record of what we have been doing this summer, something to show people and the kids, as we probably won't get a chance like this again.

I love the view of the Stadium as we walk into the vom, down the slope. We can see one of the rings that will converge with four others within the next hour or so. At the moment, it is just sitting above the Stadium's edge, hanging on cables. Walking through the corridor, there are not so many people tonight, but we get plenty of looks of approval as they see us in our costumes.

Once in our corridor, the usual waiting begins, although tonight we know we will go on around 9pm as this is just like show night. They are going to be timing us, making sure that we stay within our allocated slot of 15 minutes. I hope to see the pyro shower tonight. Surely they will be testing it. At the very least I hope the chimneys behave and go up and down as planned. I feel a bit nervous, but don't know why. We have done it so many times. We will be fine. It's the same routine. And we can deal with problems.

As the hymns and Nimrod play I fumble with my earplugs, making sure they won't fall out. I can't push them any farther into my ear without doing some damage, but I keep trying to do so. I have to relax. My hands are as deep into my gloves as they can be but I keep pulling on them. I'm being like this yet there isn't even an audience tonight. In fact there are around 1,000 people watching us, but that is no different to what we have done during rehearsals, other groups sometimes watching, just as we would watch the NHS segment. Gaudi asks me to confirm some of the choreography. His own nerves are doing their work. He knows it as well as I do.

Eventually we make it out. Yet again. We have done this countless times before. It's no different. Breathe. I have decided to take my glasses off tonight, just to see how it goes. This is a part of my dress rehearsal to see if the lights will affect my vision. Very quickly I ascertain that they do but I'm sure my eyes will adjust. I can still see everything.

The strike begins and the choreography is cued in. I somehow lose myself and it goes astray. Very frustrating, but onwards we go. Work Prep and the fence strike are fine. We find a clear path back to the ramp. My eyes have more or less adjusted and I can focus ahead without being dazzled. I join the end of our turf and help roll it. There are some different people here. It doesn't matter, just roll. When we lift it somebody is facing me, ready to walk in the wrong direction. This is not the way we should be doing it. We walk on the right. Confusion sets in but I stand firm. I have no idea why this has happened but I foresee a chain reaction if we continue like this. Eventually we sort it out and walk down the ramp just as we have always rehearsed. One guy gets knocked by my end of the turf as he reaches the top of the ramp, loses his footing, but continues.

There are no Warriors to take our turf so we have to walk all the
way to where it gets deposited. This delays my arrival at the smelting
shovels. There was a lot of traffic on the walk and it wasn't as smooth
as usual. I kept getting caught amongst the small crowds of workers. I
still manage to put my cap and goggles on and get in line in time for
poppies.

This one minute is not only very emotive, but it is also a chance
for us to gather our thoughts and prepare for what is about to follow.
My goggles begin to steam up but there is no moving during the
whistling. When we are cued in for Work Prep, I give them a wipe
with my glove before moving off. It just does the trick and I can see
again.

The walk to the trough goes a bit wrong. There is a lot of traffic
and somehow I get caught up with some forgers so I end up at the ring.
It takes me a second or two to work out where I am in relation to
where I should be, but then I see that my position is to the right. I get
there in the end. Most people are not moving on the beat but I keep
my feet going, remembering Diane's instruction. Some smelters begin
as the trough lights up, before the cue is given. That does make more
sense I suppose. Good improvisation. From here everything goes fine
from all sides as far as I can tell.

We move out and as I reach the outer ring I fall into my
choreography, which goes well. The music continues. Behind us the
rings are converging. Around a minute later the music stops and we
turn around. It is with some degree of disappointment that I look up.
There is no pyro shower tonight. Only the middle ring is fully lit, two
are partially lit and the other two not at all. I'm not sure if this is a
technical glitch or they are simply saving the shower for Monday, but
I would have liked to have seen it. At least the strike and our segment
are complete though. We applaud and bow to a non-existent audience
for the very last time. We then file out very quickly. "Go, go, go" is the
message on our IEMs. There is no feedback, just get out quick. Of
course, our part is over but the show is far from complete. Just as our
experience ends, somebody else's is just beginning.

We leave our props on the side and I start the walk back with Josh,
followed by Alex. As we are walking round the outside of the Stadium,
the James Bond theme is played. Tonight, much to our surprise, we
see a helicopter up above. Lots of people are looking to see why it is
there. This soon becomes apparent when two people parachute down,
landing just outside the Stadium. James Bond and one of his aides I

WAVE FIVE: THE STADIUM

suppose – very cool indeed. Even during dress rehearsals we are seeing new aspects of the show.

Some of the Thanks Tim performers, from the dance segment, are waiting outside, ready to go on, even though they are not due to perform for at least another half an hour. Further along there is a thick line of them, formed just beyond where we walk down the slope into the vom. They applaud and cheer us as we pass. It does feel good, but I am also somewhat embarrassed by it, so I just walk past without saying anything. I could have wished them good luck at least, but my usual timidity overrules any other ideas I may have.

On the walk back Josh and I compare notes. The turf was the main problem, we feel. His IEM disconnected quite early in the strike so he couldn't hear the prompts. Both of our goggles steamed up. Things were a little messy at the trough but otherwise it went okay. We both agree that despite these minor issues it was a successful dress rehearsal.

Whilst it is happening there isn't really any time to think about how it all feels or to process any frustration at things not going to plan. We need to remain fully focussed on what we are doing as there is so much to do and possibly react to, not to mention having to stay in character the whole time. It didn't actually feel enormously different to yesterday's run, but like then we didn't have much of an audience. I think the overriding sentiment is that it is over so quickly, almost like a flash. Maybe these dress rehearsals are supposed to prepare us for that, as much as anything else. Three more times we are going to have to walk away almost as quickly as we have begun. Once we leave the Stadium there is no turning back and our time is over. Tonight we know we will be back, but on Friday we are going to have to let go. I have no idea how that will feel.

Listening to my IEM on the way to Eton Manor, which is still transmitting perfectly despite the increasing distance, the NHS music begins on time, so I suppose that means our chimneys went down with no problems. The tech team must be proud and a little relieved too. Thinking about it I didn't actually see the chimneys rise. I've considered this before, and now make a note to be more aware of this during the next dress rehearsal.

Once we get back to our holding area, I get changed and spend a while removing the make-up. It only comes off with wet wipes, and although provided, they are not in large supply.

When I leave I see Elia returning. She stayed back and managed to watch the NHS segment, despite our strict instructions to the contrary. Gaudi stayed too, but then they were asked to leave.

I walk back to Stratford with Chris. For him it went really well, apart from our priority turf. We speak about how unfortunate it will be if we don't make it onto TV. After all the anticipation and the promises made by Danny Boyle that they are going to get everybody's faces on camera, I think everybody is at least quietly hoping they will appear in front of the global audience for at least a couple of seconds. For the vast majority there will never be a chance like this again. Before that, however, Monday is looming. It is undoubtedly going to be incredible. The Stadium will be half full we are told, and that means performing in front of 40,000 people. I honestly cannot wait.

46

Messages From Everyone

Sunday 22 July 2012

Brilliant job yesterday! We have a big week ahead.

Monday 23 July: Full Dress Rehearsal with an audience (our LOCOG friends and non-Ceremonies Games Makers!).

No jewellery (wedding bands/religious items are okay). Wear contacts if you have them, or glasses if you need them for safety. Ear plugs should be skin shade or tan – no white and no colours. Remember, you're in period costume so approved additions should fit in or not call attention to themselves.

New later arrival time (applies to all future days): 3:30pm at Security (as you have seen, lines are getting longer). 4:00pm check-in at Eton Manor. Gates open to audience at 5:00pm – you do not want to be stuck in line with them.

As well as both ID cards, everyone must also have Monday's GREEN dress rehearsal sticker. On Monday you will get a second sticker for Wednesday. On Wednesday, you'll get a third sticker for Friday. This is standard Olympic protocol due to the Ceremonies being such popular events. You will also get a hand stamp at check-in each day.

Bibs: No need to bring this. It's yours to cherish forever and ever.

Photos: Please refrain from posing and taking photographs.

Respect: Please be respectful of staff and other volunteers doing their jobs. If someone is asking you to do something, please listen, and help us out by following instructions.

Sitting in the seating bowl after your performance is not permitted. We have an audience now. It is imperative to return to Eton Manor, change and get on transport before it shuts down.

Have a great time. We love your energy and performance.

Monday 23 July 2012

We are now four days away from the Opening Ceremony – can you believe it! This afternoon we are welcoming hundreds of you to our security team for your first shift on the Common Domain.

If you have watched a television or picked up a newspaper in the past week you will have heard stories about G4S and Olympic security. We just want to assure you that security has been strengthened by the addition of greater numbers of military than originally planned. They are a brilliant team and we think you will really enjoy working by their side.

Once you've checked in you will be grouped with at least eight others and you will all be introduced to your team leader. This will be a different person every single day, as will the members of your team. This is a great way to meet people from all walks of life!

The meal voucher for those on early shifts will entitle you to a free lunch. If your shift starts early, make sure you have a wholesome breakfast before you set out! If you have an afternoon shift, eat lunch first because the meal you are served is dinner.

Don't forget your accreditation and don't forget to wear your uniform! Also, bring your camera to capture all the memories of the Games!

And that's it! We are REALLY grateful that you are giving your time to the Games and can't wait for you to join our team.

Dear Volunteers

Good luck tonight and on Wednesday and remember, amongst the many surprises, the single biggest surprise will be how professional you are. A couple of thoughts to help you achieve this:

Look after your costumes! They are your passport to Friday night. Hang them up in the holding area. Care for them and you will look even more fabulous than they do.

Don't look at the cameras and they will look at you. Look at the cameras and the editor will avoid you. Obviously this doesn't apply to the curtain call when you can finally gaze back into a billion adoring eyes!

In Green and Pleasant, Pandemonium and Second Star on the Right (Swing Out Sisters!) please don't wear anything anachronistic: jewellery, visible piercings, spectacles etc. and try to disguise your IEMs as much as possible please.

Finally, remember these are dress rehearsals for us all to discover what it is like to perform in front of an audience, to improve our show as well as to entertain, and begin to introduce the public to what we have created together.

Oh, and wouldn't you know it, it's going to be hot so drink lots of water and look out for each other.

Thank you
Danny

47

Rehearsal 23

Monday 23 July 2012
3.30pm – EOS
Olympic Stadium

With that bit of wisdom from our Director in tow, I begin the day at work as usual. We have been told to arrive at 3.30pm today. After the frustration of waiting for hours on Saturday they have had a change of heart and it is most welcome. It means I can get some more work done before leaving and saving half a day's annual leave at the same time.

When I arrive in Stratford there is a real hustle and bustle about the place. It's very warm so a lovely day for it. There are Games Makers everywhere as there will be spectators today so their services are required. I suppose for them it must be quite exciting to be on a shift today. Some very lucky ones will be inside the Stadium.

On the train here I decided to create a visual record of the walk to Eton Manor. After today the Park will not be the same, especially with 80,000 spectators walking around, so today is probably my last chance to do this. I begin snapping as soon as I alight from the train, taking a photo every 20 metres or so, or whenever the scene changes significantly. The exit from the station has changed, not the usual walk through the tunnel with the large photos of Games Makers on the walls, but I suppose it's a record of today.

All Stadium staff and volunteers are being directed through a barrier they have set up, manned by Games Makers and security personnel. The main purpose is to keep spectators out until after 5.00pm. I show my accreditation and walk through, camera at the ready. I don't photograph the security area but over the next 20 minutes or so I manage to capture most of the route to Eton Manor, except for our check-in area. I don't think it wise to get my camera out there. In most of the photos there are very few people, just an empty Park, and that is exactly how I want them. This walk in itself has become a significant aspect of rehearsals, so much so that they have had to provide mobility vehicles for those amongst us who find the distance a challenge.

In the queue for our meal packs we receive a blue sticker on our accreditation for entry into the cast area on Wednesday. We also have our wrist stamped with a dove. It's two meal packs again, the only difference being the choice of sandwich, which is better than usual today. Armed with my tuna and falafel meal packs I walk down the path into our holding area, taking a bottle of water on the way. Lots of people are out on the grass again, although things are a little subdued today. I'm sure lots of people won't turn up until later after waiting around for so long on Saturday.

As I enter our specific area I am told that we need to be changed and made up by 6.30pm. There is plenty of time left. I sit down to eat one of my meals. Although I managed to complete my fast yesterday, I have decided, after Saturday, that it's best if I don't fast on performance days. I need to ensure my energy levels remain in a comfortable zone. Whilst I eat an announcement on the Tannoy asks us to text any of our friends, meaning fellow performers, if they haven't yet arrived, and tell them "to get their arses here now". They clearly want to make sure all cast is in the holding area long before the spectators begin to file in, and if the sound of the person's voice didn't betray any nerves, her use of language almost has done. I'm sure with an audience of so many people, all of the tech and operations teams are just a little bit on edge. Everything must go right tonight, or at the very least major problems be avoided. If they know the entire cast is at least present, I suppose that is one small step closer to success.

After a little while it starts to get busy in the changing area. The lady on the Tannoy announces that spectators are being allowed inside the Park. The gates are open. I'm not sure if I feel excited or apprehensive. I just do like many others and start to prepare myself for the night's performance. Costume first, then get made up. We have been given a strap for our IEMs, to hold them firmly in place, so this I tie first around my waist. I do all of the make-up myself tonight, taking care not to apply too much. As soon as we get outside it's possibly going to start dripping, owing to the heat. I stain my shirt a little more, rubbing it into the collar and the sleeves. My neck comes next. Surely this would also succumb to the dirt and grit. It's hard to know when to stop, especially since some people look like they have been rubbing their faces in a chimney sweep's brush. I leave the area, knowing that I can simply return if I feel the need to apply some more dirt to my face. It's strangely therapeutic.

I just wait around now, drink a coffee, spend some time chatting with people, walk about, and play mindless games if somebody thinks to begin one. Some people take the opportunity to read. There is one guy from Fife who I see every rehearsal, keeps himself to himself, his face always buried in a book. Each to their own. I prefer to just sit and soak up the good vibes, observing, and trying to form at least some indelible memories, for I know most mental images fade with time, yet this guy sees this break in activity as a golden opportunity to keep his pages turning. Other people have taken to getting members of their county to sign plain t-shirts, transforming them into an irreplaceable souvenir of three months of their life.

Katie arrives in the holding area so Wasif gathers people together to give her some presents for which he has been running a collection over the last week or so. He has done the same for Diane and Pete too. She is very pleased with what Wasif has bought for her. One of the presents is a day in a spa, if I've heard correctly. She will certainly need some time to wind down after this is all over. She makes the inevitable speech, just a short one. She says our segment looks absolutely amazing on the video. I've heard that some of the nurses have also said it looks superb. Maybe it is the very chaos that is so appealing. It's always nice to hear what other people think, especially if it's positive.

Katie has her own t-shirt for people to sign so we set to work on it. Presentations and activities like this are an indication that things are beginning to reach their designated end. People are securing their mementos and taking photos. In just a few days the entire experience will be a thing of the past, only to be looked back upon. Annotated pieces of cloth and frozen moments in time will induce smiles and set our minds racing with thoughts of strikes, hakas, turf, drummers, rings, and a plethora of proverbial pieces that, when joined together, will be culminating in 15 minutes of unimaginable wonder on Friday. It's very nearly time.

Before that, however, we have to practise. We get called outside a while later, just to get us ready to leave, although this is just another form of waiting. I take some photos, and soon we are walking to the vom, following Vanessa who is holding aloft a sign with our vom number on it. We walk over the bridge, already having stopped and started a couple of times. A group of Working Men and Women wave to the motorists whizzing past below us. What must they be thinking?

Once past the Velodrome I can see the Stadium in the distance. I wonder if we will hear the crowd as we approach. The fact that we are walking to the Stadium means they are more or less all inside so they won't see us coming. I hope we will see the pyro shower tonight. Surely they will include that. Sometimes I still can't believe I am part of this, on the way to perform in front of 40,000 people. I haven't even fully contemplated Wednesday, when it will be twice as many. My mind is a mixture of emotion and expectation, thoughts racing around as chaotically as the Working Men and Women do in our turf strike. There is no point in trying to anticipate what I will feel tonight. I have nothing to compare this to. I can only let the minutes tick away until the moment is upon us.

Before we walk down the slope and into the vom, there are security personnel checking that we have a dove on our wrist. Of course, we have no accreditation tonight, same as Saturday, but security has been heightened because of the occasion, so our doves serve two purposes. We walk into a large mass of people and are held there until there is room for us to enter. We have a view of the auditorium so we can see some of our audience as we walk past. Just thousands of people stacked high. They have no idea what is about to take place. The Green and Pleasant Land performers are out there, enjoying their time in the limelight, soon to be taken over by us.

In the corner of this vom, just before the doors where we enter the corridor, one of the looms is waiting to be wheeled on when required. Looking at it up close it is an amazing prop, a behemoth of our segment. It is enormous and I'm sure it takes some exertion to effortlessly push them up the ramps.

As I stand beside it, feeling smaller in its presence, Danny Boyle can now be heard on our IEMs. He is addressing the audience before the show begins. He mentions to them about keeping the secret and how they are helping us prepare for the actual night. It would be a great service if they help us save the surprise, and not be tempted to use twitter, Facebook, You Tube and the like to spoil what we have worked so hard to preserve until Friday. He goes on to speak about the technical issues that may occur. Some will be deliberate, some will be cock-ups, but they won't be told which is which. He then speaks about us, the volunteers. We are an amazing group of people; we have given up so much time, in much worse conditions than tonight. It's our Ceremony. This country is ours. He mentions that the people in the audience, the mums and dads, our friends and family, have done something right, as the volunteers represent the best of us. It's a very flattering thing to say, although I'm not quite sure how much of these accolades we deserve. Of course that is simply opinion that will differ from one person to the next. He finishes by saying that they are the first people ever to see this show. The audience is very much a part of it so tonight is the first time it has been put on in earnest.

From our corridor, we wait for a while. At least it feels like a long time. As we walked through I managed another glimpse of the audience, a wider view this time and it just looked amazing, a sea of people. Of course I have been in this sort of environment on countless occasions, but to be backstage waiting to go on makes it four times more special.

Before we go out I hear that Diane has been given her present. I managed to miss the presentation, but I'm sure she was very pleased.

Eventually we hear Nimrod, and the lines from The Tempest. Sometimes I play out my role, reminding myself of where I need to go, usually whilst we are listening to this. Tonight is no exception. I go over my choreography very loosely, stretching my arms only half way, a very casual rendition of the moves, no emphasis at all. A stretch here and a stretch there, an adjustment of my ear phones, moving my IEM belt underneath my shirt an inch to the left, as if it makes an ounce of difference, making sure everything in my pockets is safely stowed, checking my laces and my braces, lifting my hat a little, pulling it back down, running my finger in between my neck and my collar. I wouldn't call these rituals, more like final preparations before we go out yet again, just to shake off any tension. I need to get out there now so I can end this ever so mild display of insanity. I am ready to do this.

We walk out of the vom and into our bulge formation. I don't really notice the audience so much now, as I am just concentrating on my performance, looking ahead, at the tree, and then just focussing ahead and on what is about to happen. Mentally I am anticipating our cue for choreography and concentrating on extending my right arm first. If I do that, the remaining moves will follow naturally. It's been instilled in us. The first beats of the drums followed by the shout are enough to make me really hear the sound of the audience. The excitement in the air feels heavy, and as the full force of the drummers hits the speakers it truly is like an explosion of the senses.

As we go into our choreography, if I had feelings of belonging before, those same feelings have reached a new level of intensity now. I am a part of this group, all of us as important as each other, all harbouring a common purpose. I am a working man of the Industrial Revolution. I am focussed and I am determined. I am that attitude that Toby has schooled us in. Whether or not I can keep this going for the next 15 minutes remains to be seen, but right now every pore is playing the part. These feelings have been slowly creeping in and now is the time to translate them into my performance. The combination of the incredible sound of the drums and the attitude we have to adopt gives rise to a tremendous feeling of empowerment for what we are doing here.

It is going well tonight. No confusion on the turf. The walk to Vom 4 offers no obstacles. Our shovels, caps and goggles are inside the vom, lined up against the wall on the right. I have a bit of trouble with my goggles but the costume guy puts them right. I think it's just nerves as the poppy moment is mere seconds away. I make it to the smelting line, and there are loud cheers from the crowd as the music slows down for the memorial. It's a chance for them to catch their breath, I suppose, after the assault on their peripheral vision, with so much to keep track of.

The whistling always sounds amazing. The view that we get from the edge of the M25 as we wait in line is sometimes overwhelming. I can see almost the whole auditorium, although only by looking askance rather than turning my head. No movement allowed. The current state of the FOP is a mixture of crimson light, the green Tor, dark grey chimneys, people scattered everywhere, machinery visible, the sky gaining darkness with every minute that passes. It is a sight to behold, a summation of where we have got to thus far, and the best is yet to come. I acknowledge that I definitely didn't see any of those chimneys rise. This is testament to being in character at all times and not letting my eyes drift, only doing so now because my eye movements are disguised.

Once again my goggles begin to steam up, but I can still see. The walk to the trough is much smoother tonight. The music is so loud that the voices on our IEMs are barely audible. I don't really hear the cue to smelt but I just follow the others. The trough lighting up is also as good a cue as any.

The rest of our segment goes fine. There is a bit of confusion over when to move off after turning, but we just improvise. By now I can barely see properly because of my goggles but I still manage to find my place on the ramp. The choreography goes well but I can't see the thousands of people who are right in front of me. All I can see are lights dazzling me, which is a shame, but the people are certainly there.

When the cue to stop is given one poor guy at the front misses it and keeps going for a few more moves, although it's better for that to happen now than on Friday. We stand as we are for a good few seconds and then we turn. We are not deprived tonight. All five rings are lit up, sparks are falling from all of them, although only a bit at first, and then we are finally treated to a full pyro shower. It looks incredible. To echo Steve Boyd's words during one of the rehearsals, we are the luckiest people to be so close to it. He now adds, quite simply, "You guys are *so* good." I think every single person on the FOP is stunned, transfixed by the sight before us, coupled with the music that is the same melody as the whistling, only now it is sung by a chorus of children, I believe. I've always felt that these final few bars are ethereal and climactic, and as they slowly fade out so does our segment, giving a mixture of melancholy and joy. I can't believe it is over.

The crowd has erupted. As the cheering and applause continue, we turn around and face our audience. We haven't quite finished yet. We are still in the performance. I lift my goggles up to see, before we applaud them, show them what we have done, and then take a bow. It's a strange feeling now because it doesn't feel as amazing as I thought it might. Maybe it is all so routine now and it happened so quickly. With the same haste as last time, we leave the FOP. The crowd does seem a little subdued when we walk up the aisles. I can't quite decide, but I thought performing in front of so many would be enormously different, but it hasn't been the case. It's almost an anticlimax to what I was expecting, but even so it has been quite an experience, and I am already looking forward to more of the same.

When we get to the top we put our shovels down and shake each other's hands – me, Chris, Josh, Gaudi and Daniel. It is a nice moment. We have pulled it off under full show conditions. The significance of this, after all of the doubts and supposed inability to ever get it completely right, is not lost. It is a major accomplishment, for us, for the Mass Team, the dance captains, and the tech team, for Danny Boyle, Toby Sedgwick and Steve Boyd. We have achieved what so many said would not be possible. It feels great.

With the show continuing behind us, we start walking back, past some of the audience members who are getting drinks. On the FOP the Warriors have finished sweeping and the James Bond theme is playing. Looking up at the sky, we can see the helicopter again, but no parachutists this time.

We walk past some dancers who are waiting to go in. They applaud and congratulate us. Their fervour is still fresh as they wait for their own moment to experience the half-filled auditorium. I do hope their performance goes as well as ours did.

A little further down there are more dancers, and with this comes more applause and words of kindness. A girl, presumably from the costume team, is handing out wipes at that point, so we can start cleaning ourselves on the long walk back, if we so wish.

Back at Eton Manor it's the same routine with getting changed, cleaned, and ready to leave. I think it will be different on the actual night. There will surely be more of a buzz. An announcement is made that the Central Line has been part suspended so I make my way through the Olympic Park for the Jubilee Line rather than trying Leyton. I quickly realise that this is a big mistake as I walk into a crowd of spectators, who have by now begun to leave the Stadium. It takes a while just to leave the Park. I try to hear people's thoughts on what they have just seen, but the constant din is just too overpowering, so I cannot discern anything of any value. There does, however, seem to be a general feeling of surprise and wonder. People are happy and most have definitely enjoyed the show.

When I reach the main street going through Westfield, the crowd is halted for a very long time. This has not been one of my best ideas, thinking that I may beat the crowd and escape. I don't think the delay was severe even, as Transport for London would describe it. Vanessa and her team did warn us against doing this, and alas she was absolutely right. From experience, they do know best.

With nothing to do but stand and wait, I get chatting to a fellow performer, talking about how it went. We both agree that it was incredible whilst it was happening, but the crowd afterwards could have been better. Still we wait; almost an hour has passed. I suppose this dress rehearsal was for Transport for London too, and I feel they have shown themselves to be unprepared, with only half the crowd that will be present in four days' time. Hopefully they will learn from this because they can't have a crowd like this waiting here for so long on subsequent nights.

Finally we make it to Stratford, over the bridge, down the steps, and into the station. The journey home is much longer than it should have been, but I get there eventually. I will definitely be leaving by the Eton Manor Gate and on to Leyton on Wednesday. I suppose going home with the audience was a bit of an experience, but not one that I wish to repeat.

A day's break with lost sleep, and we will be doing it all again on Wednesday. This time there will be an audience of 80,000 people, and my brother Zak will be watching too. It keeps getting better and indeed closer to the end.

48

Rehearsal 24

Wednesday 25 July 2012
3.30pm – EOS
Olympic Stadium

Today is the final dress rehearsal. Even though it's so hot and a longer walk, I go to Stratford Gate as I won't get a chance to do this again after Friday. It's much nicer than walking the streets of Leyton.

Before I enter the Park I go to the Games Maker check-in area, Cherry Park, as I feel it is at least worth a try to change my shift on Saturday. I really am dreading somehow managing to begin at 06.30am after show night. I still can't see how that will be possible. There are lots of Games Makers here, all waiting to be allocated a team for the afternoon shift in security. I walk over to the check-in desk and explain my problem. Even now I feel a little apprehensive openly saying that I am going to be in the Ceremony tomorrow, just in case they have second thoughts about my being a Games Maker too, just out of principle.

It transpires that changing my shift is easy. They have a shortage of volunteers for the early shift on 9 August, so I swap for that date. I will still have to get up at the crack of dawn, but it is a great relief to know that I won't have been performing in any ceremonies the night before. The lady shows me a white board that lists shifts where there is a shortage of staff. If I wish to sign up to extra shifts I am welcome to do so. I politely decline the offer and leave.

As I walk past the Stadium I hear our segment's music being tested. Just a few weeks ago this would have touched a nerve or two. Now there is neither a tingle nor a single hair raised on my neck. How incredibly indifferent so many rehearsals have made me, although in truth I couldn't be less so about what I am going to do within a few hours. And tonight I have a personal audience.

Soon my brother, his friend and 80,000 other people will begin entering the Park. I held my raffle yesterday for my third ticket. I created my poster some days ago and advertised the prize. The response wasn't quite what I would have liked, but I sold a few. I think some people were put off by there only being one ticket, whilst others probably decided they wanted to enter but work conspired against them and they never managed to find me. In the end, whatever the prize, even one as exclusive as this, you have to go to your customers and flash the tickets in their faces, use your charm to get them to part with their cash. I neither had the time to do this, constantly trying to keep on top of things before my absences this week, nor would have been any good at it. Besides I imagine there would have been too many questions about Friday night, with me having to repeat myself over and over, even having to talk about myself and what I'd been up to, something I find difficult most of the time. Whatever the case, my age-old introversion far outweighed my desire to expose my secret with such outward intent. Even when questioned in front of my own team when I drew the lucky name out of the hat, I was dragged far from my comfort zone. So it was, with only a handful of names competing against each other, that Jack was pulled out and awarded the privilege of seeing the Ceremony, truncated maybe, but live.

Over at Eton Manor, there are more barriers up now and more ID checks. One sticker is seen and another one is stuck, this time purple. My wrist is stamped with a drum. I am allowed through. I look inside my meal packs, seeing if by any chance there will be something different, just because it's the final dress rehearsal. We don't even get a different fruit – two Braeburn apples. Thank you all the same.

It's now the usual routine of sitting in the holding area, eating lunch, getting dressed and made up, then wandering, loitering, and whiling away the hours. There is an announcement on the Tannoy that provides a combination of amusement and disbelief: one of the Warriors was spotted talking on his phone during Monday's dress rehearsal. We are told to do what should be so completely obvious to everybody involved.

At around 7pm we are given a one hour call. I receive a text from my brother. He is feeling the buzz and atmosphere around Stratford as he arrives with his friend. It will be interesting to hear what he thinks about it afterwards, although I'm not nervous about his approval or lack of it even. I am confident that the doubters will be silenced and left stunned at the sheer spectacle, and will then applaud us as eagerly as those who have never lost faith in Danny Boyle's vision and his ability to showcase our island in the best possible way.

Earlier on I sent an email to my friends, most of whom have had no idea about what I've been up to over the last few months. Without revealing anything, I told them to look out for me on TV on Friday, and added that I believe wholeheartedly in what we are trying to achieve and convey. For me personally, it's not a problem if people don't like what we have produced, but more a case of them not understanding, so the meaning will be lost. Like Danny told us, this is indeed a spectacle that will culminate in the forging of the rings and an amazing pyro shower, but there is also drama and it is this that may not quite make it through to the other side in one piece.

Looking around the casting area, people are just chatting and enjoying the final couple of days of the experience. Everybody is relaxed and confident about what lies ahead. Even with a full audience tonight we are unaffected by the occasion, or at least it isn't apparent. We have definitely been well prepared and rehearsed.

A couple of months ago the mere thought of performing in front of a packed audience made me fearful. Now, even though there will inevitably be nerves just before we are on, I am looking forward to getting out there and showing all those people what we have been working so hard to achieve and show to the world.

For now, though, I get busy with a game of snooker with Josh on his Blackberry. We have to pass the time somehow. Katie turns up and says hello to people. She always puts in an appearance, ready to be with us on the FOP and helping where she can, directing us if required.

As the time to leave approaches we are called outside again and gather in our groups, and eventually we begin our walk to the biggest performance so far. Earlier in the day there was a discussion in the Facebook group about some of our cues, the choreography at the very end, and some other suggestions that some cast members have had. Liz has volunteered to send a message to Vanessa to raise these issues with her, in the hope that we will hear from the Casting and Mass teams to see if they can approve what we propose. As we are always in Eton Manor now, and we only go to the Stadium for our performance, we don't have the same access to the people calling the shots. On the walk I remind her of some concerns regarding smelting, so she can include those too.

When we approach the Riverbank Arena, there is a large digital clock visible. It reads 20.12 just as we pass. On Friday this is when the pre-show will begin in the Stadium, with the Green and Pleasant Land performers having a game of cricket or football, enjoying a picnic, tilling the field with the shire horse, and other such activities of which I am unaware, just as we will be walking to the Stadium.

After checking that we have a drum on our wrists, we once again enter the vom and hear Danny making his speech to the audience, only this time we can't hear him on our IEMs, only in the background. He is probably saying the same things as he did on Monday.

Walking to our corridor always involves a bee line to use the facilities, which in itself includes a final look in the mirror, not that we can do anything about our make-up now. Other performers are always scattered about, all in their allocated areas, waiting for their cues to go on. In one of these spaces Diane is addressing members of Fife. She was so pleased with her presents, and very flattered that she received so many words of thanks in her card. She very kindly offers that we were the ones actually doing the choreography that her and the other dance captains taught us, at the same time as learning how to shift so much turf and all of the other structures and terrain. Yet we always showed so much enthusiasm when it mattered most. She feels rather humbled that we would thank her. It is such an emotional and heartfelt speech, that I think she very nearly sheds a tear. She wants to try to stay in touch so will join the Facebook group when she can. She very rightly compliments Wasif on being a fantastic self-appointed social secretary. This moment is yet another indication that our time is almost up, but I feel that it will not be the end by any means.

With just 15 minutes to go now, I begin to feel nervous as we wait. I don't know why. It's probably just nervous energy as I'm not worried about what we have to do. I know it well.

Around half an hour later it is all over. The strike was really good tonight; in fact the entire segment was great. Being in front of a full house was actually another anti-climax. It was just another strike and I didn't really see the crowd until the very end. It's amazing how focussed I have become, and that is testament to the skill and experience of the team behind all of this. To think that we were no more than a disorganised rabble in the early days.

The choreography at the outer ring was excellent and really tight. As I walked to the edge and found my place, I took my cue to fall in from Chris, the one who created our badges, and within a couple of moves we were both perfectly synchronised, him standing just in front of me, his bare upper body blackened and mine clothed in my soot-stained shirt. There was something special about being in that small group on the ramp tonight. We were all in sync and moving as one.

Behind and above us the rings were converging slowly. The lady on our IEMs said it looked fierce; she repeated that more than once. As the music continued to play we shut, slid, pulled, chiselled, and hammered, over and over. We just kept it going, as instructed, until we were cued to stop and turn. The pyro shower looked much better tonight with all of the rings illuminated really well, just glowing deep amber above us. Once again it was such a privilege to be stood in that outer ring formed by us and looking up at another five interlocked two below three. Such a wonderful sight and the noise made by the audience was almost palpable on our backs. And still, this was just a rehearsal.

Walking up the aisle, the crowd is much more responsive than the previous one, people shouting "Well done, guys", children high-fiving us, applause aplenty. At the top the ushers, Games Makers and security staff are reacting in the same way. This is really very special.

After depositing my smelting cap, goggles and shovel, I decide to try and hang back tonight. I know I should be walking back to Eton Manor, as that is still part of the dress rehearsal, but this is the last chance I will ever get to watch the show live. Friday will be nigh on impossible so I really make an effort to stay behind. It is not easy. I get told several times to leave by the security staff and Games Makers, but I just keep walking around the podium level, trying to hide amongst people. I am one of many attempting to do this. Together we are far too conspicuous in our costumes and keep getting told to move on. They are literally on patrol and I'm sure they have been briefed specifically to look out for performers who haven't left.

I leave the podium area and just re-enter further along. At one point I even manage to take a photo of the crowd. Here, a Games Maker mercifully allows me to stay for a few minutes, after much persuasion, although she is reluctant to do so. Soon she asks me apologetically to leave as she is likely to get into trouble if caught allowing me to stand within two paces of her. I say thank you and cause her no more bother.

Still I persist, finding more places to stand out of sight. I see Elia and Liz. They are not even making any effort to hide and they are still there enjoying the show. I stand with them for a couple of minutes. By doing this, constantly trying to evade capture, I manage to see the NHS segment, which looks stunning with all of the lighting. This is followed by the Chariots of Fire theme tune being played. As the instantly recognisable piano line kicks in, Liz expresses quite clearly

WAVE FIVE: THE STADIUM

what she thinks: "This is such an amazing piece of music." As we stand here, in the Olympic Stadium, two nights before the thirtieth Olympiad officially begins, she has a good point. In the context the power of this piece is hard to downplay. It is very special indeed to hear it in this place.

We are soon asked to move on. We separate to make it easier to avoid being seen. The Thanks Tim segment is beginning with what look like illuminated ropes. I haven't seen any of this section until now. Once again I am asked to leave. I walk away, then find a quiet area which is just a little secluded. Standing on one side of a pillar I manage to stay there for a couple of minutes, but I am no longer relaxed. Instead I am just waiting for that hand on the shoulder.

Finally Vanessa finds me and tells me "You have to leave", spoken rather firmly with a none too happy look on her face. This is fine; she is only doing what she has to. As I move away she literally steers me to the exit, making sure I go out. I think it is time to really leave now. No more coming back in. I've broken the rules long enough. Eton Manor it is then. I see a few Working Men and Women on the walk back. Elia says that she saw one girl take her costume off to reveal her normal clothes underneath, but even she is now walking back so she was also caught out. They are being so strict and vigilant, but I can understand why, and I won't be trying this on Friday. Tonight was an exception. After stepping off the aisles, walking back to our holding area is part of our performance and we must abide. We have been drilled in this and the vast majority of us no longer question why we have to do so. It is our duty as performers to act professionally and we have accepted it.

Back at Eton Manor, I get changed, and whilst I am removing my make-up some guys are still returning. It is quite late and the show is over. They managed to stay until the end. Very lucky they were. Gaudi is amongst them. He actually found a seat to sit in and had no trouble at all throughout the entire show! It's all very random and just down to luck I suppose.

On the walk to the station, definitely Leyton this time, I reflect on the show. It really was great tonight. I have no idea what Friday will be like, even after experiencing a capacity crowd, but it will be the last time we will ever perform our segment. That is a certainty, and it's going to be emotional. And what's more, the world will be watching. Maybe I won't get a sense of that. I'll have to wait and see.

My first Games Maker shift is tomorrow. I have to forget about the Ceremony for a day and concentrate on that. It's going to be nice being in the Olympic Park for something other than rehearsals; a novelty indeed. It will also be good to hear what other Games Makers thought of the dress rehearsal – some of the audience tonight was made up of them. At the very least I have something to occupy myself with between now and show night.

49

Games Maker Shift 1

Thursday 26 July 2012
1.00pm – 10.00pm
Main Press Centre

After arriving home late last night, I got up within a few hours of going
to bed, to eat my breakfast, for I am fasting today. Unlike rehearsals, I
don't expect I will be doing anything particularly energetic so I will at
least attempt to get through the day with no food or drink.

My time to wear the Games Maker uniform has finally come and
it is with some pride that I get dressed and ready for my shift, having
caught up on sleep a little. I thought I would feel self-conscious
walking the streets in my uniform, but everybody knows who we are
by now and there are plenty of others doing the same, even though
the Games haven't begun yet, so any reservations have been put to bed.

It's quite warm so I don't wear my jacket, storing it in my bag
instead. They are rather small, I discover, and my jacket takes up most
of the space inside. I check that I have everything, including my
accreditation, and I leave.

The journey is trouble-free and I arrive on time. I heard Boris
Johnson's message several times on the way about 'getting ahead of
the Games'. They have set up a website dedicated to providing
information and travel tips during the Olympics. With only a day to
go it is unclear how London's transport network will cope with the
influx of visitors.

At Cherry Park I register and receive a meal voucher, which is
specifically for today, and a pin badge as a gift for volunteering. During
the course of our shifts we are going to receive small gifts like this.
This one is bronze and exclusively for Games Makers, not available
anywhere else. I assume a silver and gold one will follow. I am told to
go to a seating area at the back and wait to be called by a team leader.
Gradually Games Makers gather around the tables, all waiting, and
after some time we are called, the team leader, who I recognise as April,

confirming that we are all in the Main Press Centre today. We are going to be taking a shuttle bus to our venue as it is quicker and more convenient. After going through security, we make our way through some workforce only areas and onto a road where we catch the bus.

As I thought, it is nice to be in the Park for something other than rehearsals, and now I am beginning to see parts that I haven't seen before, and which the general public won't be allowed access to either. On the short journey to the Press Centre I can see guest-only entrances, manned by security, and roads that are dedicated to Olympic traffic. We pass the Athletes' Village. Some of the windows have flags covering them, representing the nations of the occupants. I can only wonder at the atmosphere within those walls as the athletes prepare to realise their dreams over the coming days and weeks.

As we alight we have now entered the press area and we have to show our accreditation, the security staff checking that we have the requisite MPC on our passes. We walk down the side of the International Broadcast Centre, which I recognise from my venue training a few weeks ago. To the left is an area which contains all sorts of cabling, satellite dishes and other communications equipment, of which I have no comprehension, all fenced off and secure. Walking past the Main Press Centre building and on towards the PSA where we will be working, we have left the public area of the Olympic Park far behind. The only people who will ever be where we are now are journalists, broadcasters, the military, security personnel, and a small proportion of Games Makers. I don't have access to any of the competitive venues but at least I have this, which is something.

Once we are inside the PSA we are divided into two teams, a team leader for each. We are further divided up into pairs, two people to a lane, and then we are plunged into what we briefly covered during our venue training. One person scans passes, making sure the accreditation is valid, indicated on the screen by a green bar, and the other helps load the trays with whatever needs to be put through the scanner. Everything else is covered by the military personnel – the actual checking of trays as they are scanned, any body checks that are required if the alarm sounds as the people walk through, and bag checks that are required.

Interaction with the journalists is minimal. Most of them are in a hurry to get through security and be on their way. Some are friendly, offering smiles and small talk, whilst others are clearly in no mood to be removing their belts, their keys, their coins, and their laptops from their cases. Some of them have more than one, and by their heavy sighs and tired expressions it is quite clear that they have been in and out several times already today, on each occasion having to go through this unwanted routine. Still, I am polite and courteous, as expected, and try to get them through as quickly as possible. One man is quite vocal in his description: "the worst Games ever". They haven't even begun yet. It does make me wonder about what security has been like at past Olympics, and if London is going to set a new standard. I have to say security is very tight, and maybe some of these people, who obviously travel from one event to the next, have not had it so bad before.

I am with a girl named Connie, who is a student. The Games Makers are made up of a very broad spectrum of people, but many of them are students who have opted to do something very worthwhile during their long summer break. Over the next few hours we take turns scanning and loading trays, and that is more or less as much as we are required to do. The PSA is by no means busy so we spend long periods just chatting with each other and the members of the armed forces. They make no secret of the fact that they do not want to be there, yet they are friendly and helpful when a problem occurs. Still, a lot of them would much rather be somewhere else, doing what they have signed up to do – being soldiers in the traditional sense. They are getting paid for this, of course, and find it hard to understand why anybody would want to actually volunteer to do it, for nothing.

The soldiers in my lane are definitely more interested in Connie, this young student, than in the hirsute man that is me. I haven't shaved or cut my hair for several weeks. They ask her personal questions, they flirt with her, they take every opportunity to clown around when there is nothing else to do, one of them almost knocking over a very large stack of trays. They are certainly bored and tired of doing what they were never supposed to be doing.

Some of the equipment we have to pass through the scanners is very impressive. I have never seen such large lenses before. There are enormous tripods, very heavy cameras, and all manner of accessories and attachments. I take great care when handling them, although they are quite happy to just trust me, not once asking me to be careful with the very expensive tools of their trade.

I lose count of the different nationalities that pass through, but I do know that almost every continent has been represented during my shift so far. One celebrity goes through my lane: Gabby Logan, who only has a belt to pass through. Some people approach with everything that would set off the scanner already in their hands, ready to place in the trays. These are the sorts of people the security staff like.

So my shift goes until it is time for my break. We are sent relief and Connie and I, with a couple of others, make our way to the staff canteen, which is in the same complex for MPC volunteers. My fasting is going fine so I'm just going to sit and take a break. I've already spoken to my team leader who says it is okay for me to go and break my fast at around 9.00pm. The canteen will still be serving hot food.

I ask Connie what she thought of the dress rehearsal, after she reveals she was lucky enough to be given a ticket. She enjoyed the Thanks Tim segment the most. Of all the people who have given me feedback, she is the first to not mention the Industrial Revolution as their favourite part. Speaking to a few people on the way to the press centre in the afternoon, they had nothing but praise for our segment, and thought it was amazing that I was actually in it. Listening to Connie now, I'm somewhat surprised to hear very little about our segment from her, but at the same time it's nice that she appreciated the dancers as much as she did.

When asking my brother for his reaction yesterday after the rehearsal, he thought it was all superb. He loved it when the Mary Poppins flew down. I got the impression that he didn't quite get what we were doing in our segment, seeing it simply as an elaborate set change. This has been mentioned on our Facebook page, with the friends and family of some people not really understanding the dramatic element, so a few amongst us feel that an explanation of some sort is needed. It remains to be seen what the reaction will be like two days from now. Jack didn't hold anything back in his praise, describing our segment as "…by far the best. It was absolutely stunning. The most spectacular thing I have ever seen. I felt so privileged". That was of course great to hear.

After our break we return to the PSA and continue in much the same way as before. I leave to break my fast just before sunset, and by the time I return the shift is more or less over. As it is very quiet now, we can go a little early. We have a quick debrief and then make our way back to Stratford Gate via the shuttle bus. It is dark now and the Olympic Park has taken on a different appearance to when we were travelling through earlier in the day. The next time I am here on a Games Maker shift the place will be teeming with many thousands of people. Tomorrow there will be 80,000 spectators and many others filling the current void. This is the final night that the Park will be practically empty so it's nice to have been here. On the journey home my thoughts are filled with just one thing.

WAVE SIX

THE
CEREMONY

50

Show Day

Friday 27 July 2012
3.30pm – EOS
Olympic Stadium

It's been over six months, or 192 days to be precise, since I received an email informing me that I had been chosen to perform in the Opening Ceremony tonight. With that email came a long list of rehearsal dates, which included entire days that needed to be set aside to practise whatever was in store for us. All of that is now in the past, except for today. When I first saw Show Day at the end of that list, I felt nervous, long before I even knew what I was going to be doing. We have been sent updated schedules a few times over the months, the list slowly getting smaller with Show Day approaching. Finally it is here, and I am on a high even as I sit at work. Some people have taken the day off but I need to complete some tasks before I leave for the Park. I feel no nerves and have no qualms about what I will be doing tonight. I am ready and I am excited. Any thoughts I may have had about tonight being no different to Wednesday have been proven absolutely wrong because today is different. I feel it in myself and in other people too. I can hear small bits of conversations about tonight's show, speculation about what it will be like, and where people will be watching it. There hasn't been much talk around the office in the days leading up, but of course today is the day and excitement is now brewing.

We've been told that the Olympic torch will be on board the Gloriana and travelling down the Thames past our offices at around 11.30 this morning. From the fourteenth floor of my building we have a fantastic view of Vauxhall Bridge on one side and Westminster on the other, a perfect vantage point for a quick glimpse of the torch. We'll be able to see it approaching and then continuing on its journey down the river. I have my camera at the ready.

In the meantime I have work to do and I've also received a final

303

email from the Ceremonies team, which was actually sent late last night. This just heightens the anticipation ahead of tonight.

It's SHOW TIME!
Here is some information for tomorrow night.

EXITING OLYMPIC PARK
Tomorrow there are three big changes to the show: Athletes, fireworks and the audience staying to the end.

Our journey back from the Stadium may require us to cross the path of the waiting athletes. Please use the managed crossways to avoid the wrath of security.

There are fireworks at the end of the Athletes Parade and at the end of the show. There is a Pyro Exclusion Zone that comes into effect at around 11.15pm (depending on the Parade). This means you should be clear of Eton Manor by 10.45pm if you are exiting via Stratford Gate. If you are late, you will be held in position for up to one hour – not something you want to happen.

WARDROBE
There are a number of costume pieces that were hired for the show which cannot be kept. For the most part (other than soldiers) you may keep your costume.

GIFTS
As a token of appreciation for all of your hard work, there will be both a certificate and official Opening Ceremony programme for you tomorrow.

Not long before the Gloriana is due lots of people leave the building and line up across Vauxhall Bridge and along the river. Some of us prefer to take a position in the large meeting room on our floor which gives a view of the whole of the riverside. It is perfect for taking photos. When the torch is on the approach I am still at my desk so I have to rush to the meeting room, camera in hand. The boat is not going to hang around and is travelling quite quickly. I do manage to get some good shots and some close-ups too. It's nice to have seen the actual torch, albeit from afar and through a window.

A couple of hours later I have left work behind and now I can just get on and enjoy the day as it unfolds. I am on the way to St. Pancras where the special Javelin shuttle train takes passengers to Stratford in just seven minutes. If you show your accreditation you can ride it for free. I probably won't get a chance to use the service again so I want to take advantage today. On my Games Maker shifts it won't make sense to travel to St. Pancras from Croydon just to take the Javelin. I was on the Facebook group earlier and a few people would like to do the same – Elia, Andrew, Fiona, Jay, and a few others – so we have arranged to meet up.

When I arrive I wait for people by the platform. St. Pancras is an amazing station and there is a lot to look at. I was here a few months ago and I had a chance to look around before catching my train. There is an enormous sculpture at one end of a couple embracing, with other bronze carvings around the podium upon which they are standing. I remember seeing the Olympic rings that are hanging above this sculpture and looking forward to the time when the Games will be in full flow and London will be packed with people from all over the world. Back then Olympic fever was very much in its early days. Throughout the day so far I have been reflecting on the lead up to this as well as tonight's performance. I am sure LOCOG could articulate a lot better than me the journey they have been on to reach this day – the planning, the funding, the pitfalls, the shortfalls, and the emotion that goes into such a gigantic undertaking. All of tonight's performers and technical team have been on a long journey too. It is the culmination of so many hours put in, so many changes, more strikes and run-throughs than I can remember, all those dreaded resets, a summer of Pringles and granola bars, rolling turf and moving fences, and of course, waiting.

My thoughts are interrupted by Jay who is wearing his orange Ceremonies t-shirt. Russell soon follows, with Elia close behind. Naturally we are all feeling excited about tonight. We need to meet Fiona downstairs so we make our way to the lower level where we bump into a large group of people from Fife: Brian, Paul, Liz, Nancy, Marge, Lucy, Yading, Dia and Andrew amongst others. They have marked the significance of today by travelling on the Emirates Air Line and even somehow visiting 10 Downing Street.

We split into two groups, some preferring to grab a quick sandwich and head to the Park, whilst some of us head for a buffet lunch at a local restaurant called Kitchin, suggested by Marge. We pick up Fiona on the way there. I haven't interacted socially with most of the people around the table, but better late than never. Elia has called David who also joins us so we are a group of about ten.

After lunch we need to get going as it's now mid-afternoon and the spectators will be allowed in soon. With the Javelin we quickly reach Stratford International and from that point onwards everything is about tonight's Ceremony. Everybody around us is excited and expectant. The whole of Westfield and the vicinity is alive with people who are either going to be inside the Stadium tonight, or who at least want to be nearby. There are spectators, Games Makers, marshals, and more accredited people than I have seen so far. All of the shops have been closed for the last hour or so. Underground staff are in the middle of the assault on their service, and the worst is yet to come.

It is now almost 4.00pm and already it is becoming difficult to walk through the crowd. We are all aware that we need to get into the Park quickly so we waste no time soaking up the atmosphere. At Stratford Gate the line is thick. It almost looks like we will have to queue with the spectators but somebody spots an opening where they are letting those with the correct accreditation through the gates. We need to push through the crowd but we manage to get in, which comes as a relief.

Leaving behind part of our audience, we get through security quickly and then walk through the Park to Eton Manor. This in itself is an experience. It is a far cry from how I left it last night, as expected. This is not the same crowd and atmosphere as the dress rehearsals. The air is thick with the sort of buzz that I have never experienced before. The world's eyes are going to be fixed on this place tonight. So many countries will be broadcasting this event and countless televisions, computers, screens, notebooks, and phones will be tuned in to the show that I am going to be taking part in.

All around me there are performers as well as spectators who have beaten the queues and are now enjoying the atmosphere. On the short walk so far I've seen people dressed in magnificent outfits, members of the military, police officers, broadcasters, journalists, photographers, and Games Makers performing all sorts of tasks and duties, including welcoming and entertaining the crowd with the use of loudspeakers. I would never have been assigned such a role, since a very outgoing personality is clearly a requirement. There are Park staff members selling programmes and merchandise. Most people are of course here for the first time and are having their photos taken with the Stadium as the backdrop. Jay offers to take my photo in a similar pose. Since this morning I've been taking photos and documenting the day, but this will be the first one with me in it. I would never have thought to ask for this, but I am indeed thankful as the photo is great, and is in fact the only one I have of myself and the Stadium.

Our progress through the Park is quite slow as we pause frequently to take in the scenes before us and feel the atmosphere. On the coloured carpet and beyond there are several groups of school children. I'm not sure what they are doing here, but they will have some kind of role to play, even if they are here simply to watch the Ceremony, although I suspect they have some other purpose.

As we walk past the BBC studio, I once again see Gabby Logan on the balcony they have set up. Their studio building is quite unique in that it is made up of shipping containers. I reckon this will become a bit of a talking point in the press. After taking a few more photos I try to make swift progress through the Park, made easier since the main crowds are now far behind. On the way I catch up with Chris, Josh, and the other Chris so I walk with them. We are all in high spirits.

When we reach Eton Manor the queue is quite long. When collecting our IEMs we are given our final stamp – a bell. It takes a while to reach the registration area. I scan my Ceremonies ID one final time and in return I am handed a copy of the programme and a certificate which is printed with Danny Boyle's signature. It is a nice souvenir of the time we have given to make tonight possible. The programme contains every volunteer's name and there is a section that has lots of our faces too. There are hundreds in there, but very small, so it will take a while to look through them all to see if I'm in there. This is a task for later.

Having collected our final two meal packs, containing not a single surprise, we enter the holding area. As we do so there is an announcement being made about the cut-off time to return here after the show, after which everything, including personal items, will be disposed of, so we have to come back in good time. I doubt that this will be enforced, but I don't plan to find out personally. Our IEMs must be returned for use in the three remaining Ceremonies, and as already confirmed, we may keep our costumes.

Looking through the programme I see that our segment is actually named Pandemonium. This is news to me and I think it is quite fitting. I've always liked that word and it does reflect with some accuracy what our performance will look and feel like tonight. It almost sums up the last couple of months. Pandemonium indeed.

As soon as I have had a coffee I get changed and made up. It is more fun today. There is an added significance to what we are doing. The mirrors provided are constantly filled with the reflections of working men transforming their flesh tones into varying hues of the same black. Some are going all out for the final night, whilst others still settle for no more than a few smudges. I usually go for something in between, but I put plenty on tonight as this is the final one. I don't do my arms though as I prefer not to roll my sleeves up – something I established during the dress rehearsals.

I now spend quite some time chatting with people, walking around inside, and taking photos. I have an idea to get portrait shots of as many people in Fife as I can. On the Facebook group a few days ago I saw some photos that had been uploaded by Andrew. These had clearly been taken using a very good camera, and by somebody who knows a bit about photography. There were some amazing shots, and one in particular caught my eye of an extreme close up of somebody's face, all made up. It was a fantastic image. This gave me the idea I have now. Rather than full body shots, group photos, posed photos, and the like, I just want a facial shot, dead pan, no expression, close up. I can't quite do what Andrew did with my compact camera, but I will do my best and then crop and play with the colour balance later. This is the last time we are all going to be in the same place in costume and in full make-up. So I wait for people to get into costume and made up and ask for a photo, making sure they don't smile for the camera. I ask Josh to take mine.

After a while I go outside and see Elia. I get her photo and then we take a walk around the cast area. Everybody seems to be up for tonight and ready to go. Groups are posing for photos everywhere, forming all sorts of combinations. Every time I see somebody who I recognise from the Kingdom of Fife, I ask for a photo. In this way I am accumulating a nice collection of pictures of us, but I am relying on my own skills of recognition. Even after around three months with these guys, I don't know everybody. If I was less reserved I would do as most people would and simply shout at the top of my voice, asking anybody from Fife to come over and pose for a photo. But I wouldn't even do that for money so I have to settle for my own flawed method.

One of the dancers from the Thanks Tim segment has asked some of the Working Men and Women to do a demo of our choreography so she can film it on her camcorder. Somebody then gathers several of us so we can walk and do the combo for her, which we do up the slope as she records. She absolutely loves it, as do other people who are watching us. I think it's hard to fully appreciate what we have been taught and are about to perform as we have lived it for so long now. It has become a part of our day-to-day lives.

During one evening at the beginning of May we learned forty movements, with another eight the following week. We can now perform them with our eyes closed. On top of that we have learnt how to shift the enormous set that is on display right now in the Stadium. That set is incredible. We can't quite remove it with our eyes closed, but when we get our hands on it, nothing remains that shouldn't be there by the end of Hail Mary. And we can do it over and over and over again, without fail, and make it look good. We really have come a long way together. It's no wonder people are impressed.

For a while I do much the same, wandering, waiting, taking more photos. Even Vanessa has her camera today, doing more or less the same as me, taking lots of facial shots. Katie arrives and people gather around her, just chatting and listening for any new bits of information. She is in full costume tonight, which I haven't seen before. She is of course out there with us so has to be dressed up, just like all of the Warriors, Pete, Diane, and the rest of the dance captains and Mass Team. Looking through the programme earlier, there is a group photo of the Mass Team. Katie is in the middle, looking like she owns the shoot, total attitude in her expression. I tell her as much and she quite agrees!

Eventually we are called outside in the usual way. Making sure I have everything I need, including my camera tonight, I wait with the others. It's quite a while before we head off, beginning our final walk to the Stadium. Progress is slow. On the bridge some people go through the usual routine of waving to the cars passing underneath, except tonight people beep their horns at us. We are held here for some time, so I continue to take photos of people.

On our IEMs there is an announcement that the Red Arrows are en route to fly over the Park. I explain to Gaudi what they are as we are given a countdown. I believe this is in time with the start of the pre-show at 20.12pm. After a few seconds somebody spots them in the distance. Unsurprisingly I can't see them, but as they approach and get closer it is of course difficult to miss them. There are nine or ten of them in formation, leaving trails of red, white and blue smoke in their paths. It lingers above us as they head for the Stadium. It's a fantastic start to the evening and heightens our collective spirit as we continue our walk to the vom.

As we approach the Riverbank Arena, the sun is beginning to set. Lots of us stop to take photos, standing on the benches as hundreds of Working Men and Women march on behind us. As I turn and rejoin the group I find that I am surrounded by strangers, having fallen behind from my own county. For some reason this unsettles me just a little. I hurry on and see Jon and Harry who have also been separated from everybody else. Once we are back with Fife my mind settles back down as everybody around me is familiar again. These are the people I know and who I have come to feel most comfortable with. Familiarity is what we are relying on tonight, and this tiny episode has proven that.

On the final stretch there are officials and Games Makers asking us to keep to the left, but also wishing us luck and applauding us as we walk past. Once again there are members of the press waiting for us. The excitement is growing as the vom gets closer and show time approaches. We get a bit of light rain when we walk past the BBC studio, but it doesn't develop into anything more. Even so, some people decide not to risk it and pull on a poncho.

At the very last checkpoint we show our bells to the security personnel and then walk down the slope and into the vom. Some spectators above us take photos as we pass below them, before disappearing out of sight.

Inside the vom it is very busy. The looms always look so impressive as we walk past them and into the corridor. Danny Boyle is addressing the audience again. There is no need to mention anything about saving the surprise tonight. The guys from the Windrush part of the History Parade high-five us, and performers wish each other luck. I tell myself that this is just like the other nights. Even the wait before going on has been skilfully included in the dress rehearsals. There is no need to feel nervous. Once we leave our corridor we will be in character, and then it will be a case of just doing what we have done so many times before, for one final run, never to be repeated. Three months of rehearsals, one final performance, and then it will all be over. It's going to be my final 15 minutes in this wonderful Stadium, and I do believe I will feel rather sad afterwards. I don't have any event tickets, so this really is it.

On our IEMs we can hear the occasional cue or instruction being given to the Green and Pleasant Land performers, something that we have been listening to for the last few rehearsals. We have never had the opportunity to see them properly as we are always stuck in this corridor preparing for our own performance, so most of the direction means very little. I still haven't seen any of the animals, except for the Shire horse once. It was never meant to be I suppose.

I take a few final photos in the vom. All in all I have just over 60 shots so that is more than half of Fife, which I am satisfied with, although I could easily have taken more. It's too late now as the music in our ears has begun. As the familiar montage of snippets of The Clash, The Sex Pistols, EastEnders, Lily Allen, Pink Floyd and various other sounds is playing, the lady who will give us our cues asks the maypole children to keep wrapping, presumably meaning the ribbons around them. There was one rehearsal when the ribbons around the Fife maypole were so entangled that several of our group spent a very long time putting it right, taking an inordinately large amount of team work and coordination. I'm not sure why Working Men and Women were tasked with doing it. I quickly check my phone and there are messages from Misbah, my brother, and a couple of friends, wishing me luck.

Towards the end of the montage a countdown begins from ten down to one. This is new. We must be on air by now, or maybe once we have counted ten. In the vom we join in and there are cheers as we reach zero. It is very nearly time. In our ears we can hear the balloon children being asked to go. I haven't seen any balloons before, so something else that is new. There seems to be a problem as they are asked several times to leave. Maybe they are caught up in the moment and have forgotten their cue, but they get there in the end. It must be incredible for them, being in front of such a large audience.

The choral singing begins and it is very soothing. It sounds very special tonight. I think it's the knowledge that this is now live around the world. This is the very final take and it is all real, as opposed to pre-recorded footage being used. Some people are singing along. I don't know what people can see on their TV screens but they must be wondering what is going to follow. Whilst the world watches, we hear the very familiar voice of Steve Boyd on our IEMs. It's nice to hear from him. After he briefs us on a couple of minor changes just for tonight, he asks us to reflect on how far we have come, how many long rehearsals we have been through in the wind and rain in Dagenham and the Stadium. He then adds something very touching, asking us rhetorically if we are all Olympic friends for life. I would like to think that this won't be the absolute end. I take a few deep breaths, as Steve advises, and do a final check of everything. Toby comes on and wishes us good luck. "Have a ball", he adds.

Nimrod begins and Kenneth Branagh enters into his "Be not

afeared..." speech from The Tempest. As with the singing, it sounds great tonight. He is out there right now, on the Tor, reciting the very words in our ears. This is his time to shine, the world watching. We are mere seconds away from leaving our corridor. I see Joseph and a few others hug each other. By the time we end our segment we will have dispersed, ending up in different parts of the Stadium. Some of our paths will most likely not cross again as we become part of a much larger crowd on the way back. I've spent around three months with these people, yet I don't know them all, and they not me. It is still sad that this is the very last time we will all be in the same place at the same time, in our buddy lines.

Just seconds to go and I can't see Gaudi. He sometimes does this, but I'd feel more comfortable if he was in line with me. I know he will fall in at the right time, but his disappearance adds to my nerves. They have shown their face now. I am about to go out and perform in front of a global audience of a billion people. Maybe they will never actually see me, but that makes no difference to me, here in this corridor. Simultaneously I am feeling the adrenaline. I want to get out there. I want to begin. Fence, turf, walk to Vom 4. Easy. Everybody else knows their part. Unless something goes horribly wrong, we just perform as we have rehearsed, just like on Wednesday. This is no different.

I give my choreography one final run-through, and adjust my ear plugs. They can't fall out, not tonight. I know we are going to be called out very, very soon. I clap my hands together. I am ready. Please can we begin. The legs in front of me begin to move towards the exit so I follow. Here's Gaudi, right on time. Chris and Josh behind us shake hands, wish each other luck. I am focussed ahead. I feel Josh's hands on my shoulders. I turn around and I shake his hand, followed by Chris's, and then Gaudi's on my right. Now let's do it. My adrenaline is going through the roof and I need to get out there. Click, click, click, click, click, click, click, click. Thank you. Let's go. The maypole children are still being cued. We wave to Diane, and to everybody else who isn't due to leave just yet. Out through the door, round to the left, looking up. I love this view. It somehow looks different tonight.

I am in character now. Our performance has begun. A cloud hits my eye line, one of our fake ones. As we move into our bulge the audience members in the stands immediately either side of us notice us and look. I ignore them as I focus on the tree as it begins to be uprooted. Those who are going to carry guard rails are lined up on the side, ready to lift and move off. The Green and Pleasant Land performers are all in their positions, waiting, watching. I just look towards the tree, thousands of spectators in my peripheral vision, unknowingly willing me to break my spell, but I remain focussed. There are cameras everywhere. They could be on me at any time.

The drum crash sounds monstrous. Steve cues us to strike as the drums are rumbling. The people at the front will be moving off now and our bulge slowly opens out as the full thundering of the drums surrounds the Stadium. As my section of the bulge walks towards the ramp, the people on the front fences are already doing their Work Prep. I feel like this is different. A second later I can see that this absolutely is different. The atmosphere is indescribable. We are live on air around the world. I cast this thought aside as we stand by for our combination. I must remain focussed since this is several levels above Wednesday and I can't let the occasion affect my concentration. Choreography is counted in. On cue we do two rounds of Levers/Pull and Chisel/Hammer. Apart from having to turn to face my fence whilst still in the combination, it goes well. The first significant task is complete. Gaudi and I step forward once the last of the upper fences has passed us, and we do our Work Prep. As we walk down the ramp, following Josh and Chris, I feel more relaxed. I have my spot that I am focussing on and my eyes are fixed on that. I don't even see the audience. The lighting, which seems brighter, is helping me with that.

We place our fence, not quite as smoothly as we would have liked, then head back for our turf. There is a lot of traffic and it's hard getting out. This is our fault, though, as we are supposed to go round the back of the dollies, not through two of them. Just nerves I suppose, but still a very silly move.

Walking up the ramp the lights are causing me to squint, but I should be okay. I look for Josh, Chris, Elia and Nancy, my fellow turf rollers. It's best to just follow Gaudi, who is right in front of me. I have to walk over some turf that is being rolled in my path, then take my usual place on the end, the dartboard side, crouch down and prepare to start rolling. I usually fold the end over, the point of the triangle, to make the rolled piece a little shorter. As I turn left to do so, I see a camera right by my hands. There are a couple of cameramen there. Respecting my space, they take step back, but keep the camera fixed on me. It seems rather low, as if it's only on my hands. It matters not. Within a second I look away, recalling what Danny Boyle told us: if you look at the camera the Editor will cut you out. I wonder if I have blown my chance to be on TV, although I don't care as I concentrate on looking ahead, excited that a camera is even on me. There were cameras during the dress rehearsals, but this is the first time I've been close to one. This could be my moment.

We stop rolling whilst the far end sorts out a problem. I look over to the right, waiting to see when it is okay to continue, and then it is a smooth roll to the end. On Chris's count we lift. It is dry and feels relatively light on our shoulders. There is no confusion about which way to go as we follow Josh's lead. Another group waits for us to walk down the right, before they follow behind with another roll of turf. At the bottom Pete signals for us to stop and wait for the way to clear. We are held for a few seconds as people carrying parts of our jigsaw move with haste past us.

Behind me across the FOP more turf is being rolled. The Isle of Wight has a lot of this to deal with. Berkshire will be busy removing the cricket pitch. Elsewhere hedges and corn are being wheeled off, the first chimneys and beam engines will be rising out of the traps, all of the guard rails in place. Ratchets are being taken on and placed around more chimney traps. The Brunels and Suffragettes will be in full flow of their own performances. Everywhere Working Men and Women are taking this set apart for the very last time, never to be reset again.

When we offload our turf onto the Warriors, I turn immediately and walk back the way I came, dodging people with sections of corn, although I get a little stuck. The traffic is not flowing as well as it might. I see Alex from Gloucestershire take a bit of a knock from a roll of turf, but she appears to be okay. Elia, Nancy and Chris are walking back up the ramp to join the rest of Fife on the dartboard, whilst Josh is ahead of Gaudi and I on the walk to Vom 4. I am careful not to lose my focus as I am completely in the open now and it would be easy to sneak a look around the Stadium. I don't see a single member of the audience as I approach the entrance to the vom, a high camera panning over me.

Some of the smelters are already lined up outside. I walk inside, still on the beat, and as soon as I am clear of the stands on either side I fall into a normal walk, quickly remove my hat and put it inside my right pocket. I choose the first shovel I see, being reminded to put the goggles on before the hat. On my IEM I hear a 40 second cue for the poppy moment. I want to at least be in line when the music stops, otherwise I will have to wait inside the vom during the whistling. My goggles go on easily, but I fumble with the cap, before I manage to get it on. As I do so my left ear plug falls out. I must have about 20 seconds

left. There's no time to remove my thick-fingered smelting glove, so
I struggle with my ear plug but manage to insert it, pushing it right in
for good measure. The costume guy adjusts my cap for me, and then
I'm ready. As I turn my shovel and set it onto my shoulder, I step back
into the beat to exit, the click track guiding my steps. We are told to
slow down and stop just as I reach the back of the line, precisely where
I wanted to be.

An enormous cheer from the audience signals their appreciation
of our performance thus far. They always enjoy this part, probably
seeing it as the end of the first phase of the segment. It's a very
powerful moment. Everybody is still, no movement at all. As with
everything else so far tonight, the whistling is so much more emotive
than usual. Some people have opted to take their hats off at this point.
There is a silence in the audience that isn't quite absolute, but enough
to convey the profound effect this moment is having.

Looking up I can now see the chimneys on the FOP for the first
time. Dusk has almost passed and given way to darkness. The full
aspect before me is incredible, Working Men and Women dotted about
everywhere, some of them half way up a set of steps, others on the
M25. The Tor seems to be glimmering in the lights, just as my goggles
begin to develop a thin veil of fog. Not again. I should be able to put
this right with a quick swipe of my glove once we are allowed to move
again. About half way into the silence Steve quickly asks those who
can to help out the central counties with turf before going into
choreography. Somebody comes up behind me and pulls the back of
my smelting cap taut. I don't move but am thankful for the adjustment.

The drums begin to pound once again and the audience is
reawakened from its momentary trance. We get a count of eight and
then it's into Work Prep, which we can't do fully as we are holding our
shovels. People who placed their turf down pick it back up and
continue what they were doing before the pause. In a few moments
the head of our line moves off and we all follow one by one. The best
is yet to come. Soon the History Parade will start to emerge from the
voms and they will have priority over the M25.

We reach our ramp in good time and pass a group of Brunels at
the top. The Fife chimney towers above us on the right as we walk past
it and bear left, making our way to the trough. We walk over the very
last pieces of turf. The looms that have been brought onto the FOP
by the tech team are now being operated by the weavers. They have
their own choreography to convey weaving and finishing. Around the

beam engines workers are performing Dials and Chisel/Hammer alternately.

Steve announces that Jersey still has a lot of goods that need removing; at this point anybody can help wherever it is needed. It's all about just getting it off and out now. We need to move on to the final act – the one that is going to hit the world in a way they would never have imagined.

We make it to the trough and take our positions. I make a mental note that I am two behind Gaudi or two to the right as we turn. This will be my marker for spotting myself on TV later. Aside from the occasional lapse in concentration to process such thoughts, I do not lose focus on what we are doing here. I am on auto pilot. Cameras could be on us at any point. They will surely want to focus on what is happening at the trough. I'm still moving on the beat, waiting for our cue to begin smelting. The trough sparks up, the molten metal having been released from the crucible. The orange glow snakes its way past us and round to the left, all the way along to the ring in the centre. The smelters begin panning it along, ahead of cue, but it makes more sense this way. I follow suit and as I do the cue is given, although it is directed more at the forgers who are now swinging and striking the ring. I can hear the clanging of their mallets behind me, although they are not actually hitting the ring itself. We all know what is concealed inside and it is not something that should be struck with any kind of force. It must still look amazing from the audience's point of view.

They have surely by now realised what is happening. We are forging the ring, slowly leading up to the astonishing finale. What must this look like on the world's TV screens? When that molten metal flowed past it really hit me that I am down here in the epicentre and we are producing something that will almost certainly be one of the defining moments of this entire Ceremony. We have taken the Green and Pleasant Land and created this industrial city of chimneys, beam engines, and looms, right before the audience's very eyes and we are now crafting a very simple ring but it is a thing of beauty on this particular stage.

The heat created along the trough with the sparks has steamed up my goggles even more now. I can see but not properly by any means, and my thoughts now focus on how this is going to affect my performance. I can't just stop smelting as it will ruin the look. Besides it looks like they are foggy on the inside. Attempting to reach into my goggles when they are strapped underneath my cap, with a shovel in

WAVE SIX: THE CEREMONY

one hand, will be an operation far too cumbersome. This is annoying but I have to deal with it. We are live here. I can only continue as I am. The cue is given for everybody to stop their combination. Every single person stands still for a few seconds, before being instructed to fall into Shovel/Pickaxe, gradually moving closer to the centre where the forgers and smelters are busy working together to forge the middle ring of the five. The weavers continue as they were. It's tempting to take a look around and watch everybody performing their choreography, but I concentrate on keeping my head down, looking at the trough at all times as I repeatedly pull my shovel back, lift it over and then back again, until the Working Men and Women have been told to walk into the centre. Shovel/Pickaxe stops and everyone forms a perimeter around us. The looms are being taken off. The smelters are told to stop and turn around to face the centre, whilst the forgers continue. Now I can see the ring glowing, just a few metres in front of me. It's a joy to be so close to it, even if I can't see it as clearly as I might and it's only for a few seconds. We are cued to turn and walk. All of the Working Men and Women step back into their combination as they walk to the edge of the FOP and form a ring. The smelters move off, our shovels on our shoulders, and we disperse in whichever direction we have chosen previously.

I can't see well and wiping my goggles does nothing. It's dark, and although I know where I am going, I'm not completely comfortable here. Somebody walks directly across my path and I avoid a collision. I move slower than usual as there are still hazards. I'm trying to find our ramp. The occasion and my situation have definitely taken their toll on me. I mustn't panic; I have to get a grip as I strain my eyes to see. I think I have it in my sights. That's definitely the waterwheel. I now walk forward with less caution and take my position in the outer ring to the left of the wheel. Placing my shovel down I am faced with another problem as I try to see where we are in the combination. I really cannot tell, even when this close to everybody on the ramp. That extended right arm could be part of Levers/Pull or Chisel/Hammer. I just fall into a move; it's better than keeping still, and besides I think I can see where we are. Actually, maybe not. Am I in sync here? The guy I am following seems to be unsure himself.

My vision is now very hazy and I have lost it completely. This can't be happening, tonight of all nights. I wonder how I must look in front of this entire section of audience, making everybody else look bad. Can they actually see me at the back? This is the last time I will ever perform on this stage, and I am messing it up. Reason has been lost and I am now in a mental mess as I grow more frustrated. I pause for a second to try to get in sync. The hand claps of Chisel/Hammer, or Shut Boot/Sliding Doors will be obvious. Where are they? Why is it taking so long? Just start a move, whatever seems best. But I can't see, it's pointless. I am becoming more and more agitated. If this is on TV I will look rubbish and I will make everybody around me look rubbish too. I do truly believe this as I stand here in disbelief that this is actually happening. It went so well on Wednesday, and it was acknowledged on our IEMs. There is no word about our performance tonight. Maybe it isn't going well all round. Certainly not for me anyway. On my IEM I hear "Working Men and Women, stop." Those few words could not have been more welcome. That is probably my worst performance. On show night. I am horrified as I turn around.

Whatever just took place is rendered irrelevant as I look up in absolute awe at the pyro shower and the rings. Even my foggy goggles can't hide this from view. The audience is going crazy with what is probably a mixture of joy, wonder, disbelief, and pride. It is just a magnificent sight, more so than on any other night, and I just stare at it, as I am sure a billion others are doing, except that I am right down here, with around 1,000 others, closer than anybody else on the planet. Except for the forgers. They are in fire retardant clothing and are right beneath the shower, sparks raining down on them.

The shower fades, as does our music, but the glowing rings remain, just hanging against the darkness of the night sky, amber on black. Toby tells us that "it's been a pleasure working with you, Working Men and Women." There is complete sincerity and appreciation in his voice and it means a lot that Toby Sedgwick is saying this to us. Soon the rings also fade as the final pyrotechnics contained within are exhausted. It is all over, but for our curtain call. Steve tells us to just feel the applause and love on our backs, and then to slowly turn and face the audience. I now lift my goggles onto my forehead and applaud those who are applauding us. The noise around the Stadium is incredible, all of these people cheering for what we have just created. We turn and extend our arms towards the FOP to show them what we have done. I see Jay just behind me. We turn back and once again applaud the audience, which isn't what we usually do, and then we take a bow. I feel completely elated at the fact that I am here right now. In a way I still can't quite believe that the world is watching us as we stand here. We may not be in shot right now, but we are a part of what they are seeing. I will always be able to say that I was there.

Steve is on our IEMs now and has to get us out of here quickly. Anybody who needs to return to the FOP and remove guard rails and troughs must do so now, and the rest of us need to go through our usual routine of getting off the FOP and up the aisles. There is urgency in his voice and he emphasises more than once that we must be quick. As I walk down our ramp, Steve takes a few seconds to congratulate us and acknowledges that we "are now part of the cultural record of London, forever and ever". It seems like more people than usual are walking up the press aisle. Steve reminds us politely, ever the professional, that we don't have to choose that aisle. I see Josh as I walk round to the left and towards our allocated exit. I haven't fully processed what Steve has just told us, but I do feel an enormous sense of privilege that I am here. I can't shake this feeling. It is more than I could have imagined.

Toby now has a few more words to say: "Well done, Working Men and Women. Thank you very much. You're all truly stars. Thank you very much indeed. That was beautiful. Thank you. I think you've had an effect over the entire Stadium." He is on fire now. Whatever he may have lacked at the beginning, with the brevity that he is known for at times, he has more than made up for with these very kind words for us. He is genuinely grateful and his voice is a clear indication of that.

My enormous disappointment finally comes back and I tell Josh about my nightmare with the goggles and choreography, not that he can do anything. Amidst my elation there is outright dejection. As we walk up the aisles, Steve still telling us to quicken the pace, the spectators either side are cheering and clapping, the ushers are high-fiving, the other officials congratulate us too. I smile and am thankful for the attention, but my disappointment is lingering. My emotions are going from one extreme to the other within a couple of heartbeats. After all the rehearsals and practice, I just wanted to put in a solid performance, even if nobody actually saw me. Yet it is all over now, and one certainty is that there will not be another chance to put it right. I'm going to have to accept this.

We put our shovels on the side, as usual. Josh and I take our caps and goggles as souvenirs and walk out, not even looking back towards the auditorium, so drilled we are. We know we have to leave and tonight is not the night to cause any sort of disruption. Outside a few people have gathered, waiting for others to arrive. We start to move off and all around there is a lot to take in. People are congratulating each other, words of celebration are being exchanged, praise is being given and received, handshakes and smiles are in abundance. I see Gaudi and Daniel and move towards them. Josh is still with us. We start to walk off when I feel a tap on my shoulder. It's Daniel. He wants a photo of him in his smelting cap and goggles. He has even brought his shovel back out. I can't say I'm in the mood for this, and don't wish to get separated from the others, but this is the last chance he will have to get this shot, so why shouldn't I oblige him. Be nice, I tell myself. My mild trauma is not his fault. Still, I just want to take the photo and go. He haphazardly tries to replace his goggles and cap, whilst keeping his shovel at hand. I think he can sense my urgency. He poses, his goggles are wonky, I take the photo, and go. I immediately chide myself for being anything but nice. I turn around and he has gone. I make a note to apologise if I see him again. It just wasn't the best time.

The others have gone ahead, but I see Alex. She says it went well for her, despite that knock that she took. Josh returns. He was trying to buy a drink but was refused. Apparently the bar staff have been instructed not to serve any performers tonight. Our job is to go back to Eton Manor, just as we have rehearsed. Behind us in the Stadium the show is continuing. The next performers are waiting in the voms for their final moments, preparing for their own time in the limelight.

Up ahead some of the Thanks Tim dancers are waiting. They are naturally excited. The show is in full flow now and they must be able to feel the energy of the audience, which is surely energising them and pushing their adrenaline levels higher.

I get separated from the others in the crowd so check my messages as I walk. I don't have many. Sonia was certainly impressed, calling it "the greatest show on Earth". My brother, Saleem, thinks he saw me rolling some turf. I immediately think about the camera that was on me. It's far too much of a coincidence. I reply to confirm that I was indeed rolling some turf when there was a camera on me. It must have been me. Well that certainly makes up for my disaster at the end. I was on TV around the world. They did say that they would try to get us all on camera. I can't wait to watch the footage and spot more of Fife.

Further ahead the mass of people is thickening. The athletes are leaving the village to make their way to the Stadium. We are stopped in our tracks to let them pass. I wonder how long they are going to hold us here. Not long, I discover, as they let us through within a few seconds. They want us away as quickly as possible. I am now on Britannia Row and it is full of people, mainly performers and personnel. There is constant cheering as the athletes pass. The children

I saw earlier in the day are lining the Parade. So this is their role. They get to see all of the athletes, get close to them, shake their hands, and maybe even have a brief chat. Inspire a generation indeed.

I see David watching, just like I am doing. I learned a few rehearsals ago that he is friends with somebody I used to work with who is also Canadian. It just came up in small talk. The Parade is up to C, and he spots Canada. He gets excited as they pass. It's a nice moment for him, but he doesn't have a camera so I take a couple for him. I'll upload to our Facebook page at some point and he can download them. The Parade is extending back quite some way, turning towards the Athletes' Village, which is perpendicular to my path. Any ideas I have had about attempting to see the Pakistani athletes or Team GB are rendered futile. I will be here for hours if I do that.

So I continue on to Eton Manor. With the path relatively clear now, I make good progress. There are Working Men and Women all around me. I still feel disappointed about my performance but the feeling is no longer as intense. On the bridge that leads to the Basketball Arena and Velodrome, I see Paul, Saw and a few other guys from Fife. They can't believe it is all over. From here, looking down the river, we get a great view of the Stadium, illuminated and filled with spectators and performers. We can hear the music that is playing inside. We no longer have any right to be in there. Just minutes ago we were all inside performing in front of a global audience. That's in the past now, and it is a bit of a body blow. It was over so quickly. This is the one thing the Ceremonies team couldn't fully prepare us for. I know that I will be back in the Park as a Games Maker, so I'll at least be able to see the Stadium from the outside, but for some people, if they don't have event tickets, it's the end of the road. After all the time we have spent in there, letting go will be difficult.

Back at Eton Manor, Chris and Josh have returned. Chris has a live feed of the Ceremony on his iPhone. The Thanks Tim segment has begun. It looks great. Any footage we have ever seen of the Ceremony has largely been a wide view from the podium level and upper stands. Here there are close ups and shots from the FOP itself, the cameras right amongst the performers. It gives a completely new perspective and looks superb.

I'm in two minds about what I should do now. I really should go home, leaving any revelry behind, and get on with following Ramadan as I should be doing. Yet this night will never repeat itself again. I'm undecided as I get changed. Josh and Chris say goodbye, hopefully not for the very last time. They are still in costume and are headed for the Podium Bar. Entry is by ticket only. I never did purchase one as I had the idea of going home more or less straight away. It didn't quite seem right to go out and have a good time when, in a few hours, I would have to get up and begin my fast as part of the holiest month in the Islamic calendar. Josh offered me a spare ticket earlier in the day but I declined. A friend of Chris was looking for a ticket so he wanted it, but Josh very kindly gave me preference. Even if I was to go, the ticket would be wasted as I wouldn't stay for very long. It was much more appropriate to let Chris have it.

I see Gaudi and speak to him just as he is about to leave. He had a good time and feels that it went well. We say our goodbyes and he is gone. Jon and Harry are still there. They are going to go to Stratford to see what is happening and see if they can get into a bar. Like me they haven't been very organised with post-show celebration. As a county, we have managed to hire out the Lighthouse pub which is nearby in Hackney, but that is for later in the night and I definitely have no plans to go there. I would love to celebrate with everyone but it just isn't appropriate for me tonight. Still, I decide to join Jon and Harry, for a while at least. We spend some time getting cleaned up and then leave the holding area for the very last time.

We leave by Eton Manor Gate. A left turn takes us out of the Olympic Park. The bubble is very slowly bursting. There are lots of people on the way to Leyton and presumably on to Stratford. We meet a girl who was responsible for making our costumes. She is a student and has worked for free – a volunteer just like the rest of us. We all congratulate her and her team on such a remarkable achievement. She confirms what I have always firmly believed, that every single costume is different in some way. They put a lot of time and effort into this and she appreciates the fact that it didn't go unnoticed. We also meet some of the nurses, still dressed up. They had a great time and their performance was for them the best one they had done. I suppose you can't ask for much more than that. It does, however, make me think yet again about my own disappointment.

We reach Stratford fairly quickly. Although the spectators will be in the Stadium for a couple of hours yet, it is still very busy. There are barriers and security personnel at every turn. Only people with full accreditation are allowed into the Westfield area. This is indeed a privilege since lots of people in the crowds will not get any further than the barriers in place. They are here simply to soak up the atmosphere and see whatever they can manage, including the fireworks. But we are granted exclusive access to the Park vicinity, and I can't help but take advantage on this one night of endlessly exclusive entitlements.

The whole area is extremely vibrant and full of noise. There are performers and press milling about amongst film crews who are eager to talk to people who have just taken part in the Ceremony. On the way to the Podium (we are going to at least try to join whoever is in there from Fife), we bump into Mikele, still in full costume. He has been interviewed by an international TV channel and is very pleased about it. He is visibly on a high. I think everybody is. My earlier disappointment is finally beginning to fade. The world's press is here, trying to get a piece of us for an account of the experience, one that I was a central part of. What's to feel upset about? In talking to Jon, I am reminded that the editors will have cut anything that didn't look great, and of course there was an enormous amount of footage to choose from. It is their job to pick the best shots and make us, as a group, look well rehearsed, professional and as good as they possibly can. The audience would hardly have noticed any mistakes, especially with the amount of people and everything that was happening. When we were in the outer ring the real rings would have been converging, and that would have been the focus of their attention, not the odd performer having trouble with the choreography. I have nothing to feel down about. I should be proud that I was a part of it. I am proud. I begin to really appreciate what we have all achieved. What is more, I appeared on global TV. I have received at least one more text to say that I was seen very close to the camera. That more or less confirms my suspicions. I have always thought that I would never be interested in appearing on TV, that I would never be bothered by it if it ever happened. I can categorically say that if I was going to hold that view after tonight, then I would be a complete liar. I love the fact that my face appeared all over the world for at least a couple of seconds, especially in this context. I feel extremely fortunate that I have something to show to my daughters when they are older. I will take great pleasure in explaining to them what we were doing, why we were doing it, and indeed why they are so lucky as a result of the real Industrial Revolution that we were depicting. They will see me and hopefully feel proud that their dad was there.

Over at the Podium there is no way of getting in. No wristband, no entry. We see David stood outside. Somebody has bought him a drink from inside. It's an open bar so we can see the screen they have set up, but not as clearly as we would like. We decide to try The Cow instead, but before we do so a reporter, from South Korea I believe, asks Mikele for a quick interview. He gladly agrees, saying that he will try his best as his English isn't great. She asks him about the cast experience, the segment he was in, and what it was about. His response is very fluent and well formulated, despite his doubts about his language skills. He talks about how we did it for Danny Boyle and wanted to make it look good for him. It was great working for him. David also contributes to explain that we were workers in the Industrial Revolution segment and we were taking the land apart to make way for industry and factories.

Once at The Cow we somehow persuade the doorman to let us in, then even manage to find a table. Jon, Harry and I sit with the screen behind us, waiting for the fireworks, the part of the Ceremony we will be able to see as long as we are near the Park. We watch bits of the show and chat about our own experiences tonight. We all agree that one of the aspects of our segment that we are most proud about is that we had the Olympic rings. And in such breathtaking fashion too. Behind us the Athletes' Parade has been under way for quite some time, and nearing the end. There is a large group of Brunels and other Working Men and Women filling the bar. Lots of people are still wearing their costumes. I wish I'd left mine on. I did think it a shame to be getting changed back in our holding area. I'll never wear it again and I did enjoy being in it, feeling the part. After a few short moments of deliberation I decide to just get back into it. The trousers are very baggy, worn with braces, so they will easily go over my jeans. I'm only wearing a small top so the shirt will fit quite comfortably over it. It's nice to be in costume again and it does make me feel like it isn't quite over yet, just a minuscule thread to hang on to. Going home may be a bit strange, although this is indeed London, a place where people don't give a second look to the most outlandish and peculiar wardrobe choices.

Before the torch reaches the Stadium, The Cow closes and we are asked to leave. Our only choice is to head back to the Podium to try and get a glimpse of the action on their screen. The view isn't great as a fairly large crowd has formed and it is difficult to see over people's heads. The screen is elevated but not high enough for comfort. On the side some of the Thanks Tim dancers are having their own little party, going through their dance routines on the pavement, for the benefit of onlookers and themselves too I suppose.

We spend most of our time standing on tiptoes, trying to see who the torch bearer will be. There has been a lot of speculation but nobody knows for certain. Finally we see David Beckham on a speedboat doing exactly that along the Thames. He is rushing to the Stadium, to the place right behind us. I saw that same torch this morning travelling down the same river. I have no idea where it has been in between, but it is finally on the last leg. Once inside, none other than Sir Steve Redgrave, five-time Olympic gold medallist, takes charge. Arguably a natural choice. Earlier in the evening Bradley Wiggins got to ring the giant bell to kick off the Ceremony. One of Great Britain's finest and most prolific Olympians now gets to end the proceedings.

The music playing as the backdrop to this is based on the same choral chant that was juxtaposed with our pyro shower. I excitedly mention this to whoever wants to hear, feeling quite honoured, in fact, that our music is loosely accompanying this historical moment, but nobody is actually listening to me. This is fine. What is happening on the screen is far more important than my ramblings. It seems strange that what we are watching is happening not too far away, in the place where we played such a large part less than a few hours ago. I momentarily think back to the day over seven years ago when I was sitting at work, just down the road from Trafalgar Square, watching on TV the moment when all of this began, when we knew this time would come in our city.

Sir Steve now does something that I don't think anybody was expecting. He lights torches held by seven young athletes, representing the future generation. So they are the ones who will light the cauldron. I wonder if anything like this has been done before. What an incredible honour for them. Inspire a generation. How brilliantly visionary of Danny Boyle and whoever else had the idea to do this, an act that so perfectly embodies one of the key slogans of our Olympic Games. After tonight Danny Boyle will surely be offered the knighthood that has been the subject of speculation since long before tonight. The fact that he has confided to us his lack of interest in accepting it is immaterial. The offer made is in itself an honour bestowed upon him.

One thing that my brother Zak mentioned after witnessing the technical rehearsal was that it made him proud to be British. Danny Boyle has undoubtedly made Britain very proud tonight. Not only because of his unique vision, but also because of what he has given to the Olympic community and the country. I think he has inspired more than one generation, and not just nationally.

When we see the cauldron come together, the petals that have been given to each country joining to form a whole, I for one am completely lost in the moment, the beauty of the sight before us, coupled with the hypnotic music, rendering me almost numb. Attempting to contemplate and comprehend the symbolism behind this cauldron is just not possible right now. I am glad I am seeing this just a stone's throw away from where it is actually happening.

So begin the fireworks. From where we are, so close to the Stadium and Olympic Park, it just looks mesmerising. The sky has simply erupted into an explosion of bangs, popping, crackling, screeching and magnificent colour. I've never seen a display quite like it. It is relatively short, but very intense. On that note the Ceremony is over and many thousands of spectators will begin to file out of the Park after an unforgettable night's entertainment.

For me it is time to go home. The night must end. Some people will go to the Lighthouse to continue the celebrations as a county, but it is not for me tonight. We make haste now as we try to beat the fall out. After just a few paces I feel somebody grab my rucksack. It is Elia with David, a different one. There are several of his namesake in our county. The crowd is thick but she noticed my costume amongst everyone. She managed to stay and watch the entire Ceremony after our segment ended. She did explain to me how she was going to achieve this when we were in St. Pancras. It was a very well thought out plan and it worked for her. Apparently quite a few people stayed behind and successfully evaded capture. Well done to them – how very fortunate.

As we walk to Stratford, down the main street and over the bridge, we talk about the Ceremony and reaffirm that it went well for us all. Jon and Harry disappear in the crowd and I don't see them again. Elia is going to the Lighthouse to join some of the others from Fife, and Dave is heading home too. We say our goodbyes and agree to meet up again at some unknown point in the future. Everybody went their separate ways after our segment ended, but it would be nice to have a mini reunion some time. It doesn't seem right for it to all end so completely, not just yet. We shall see.

With that thought lingering I leave. A few people on the underground notice me in my costume and comment on what I've been doing between themselves, but nobody talks to me. By now I am well beyond the Olympic zone and feeling self-conscious and relieved that I'm being largely ignored. I spend the train journey looking down at my boots. I should have changed out of my costume for the journey home, but it's a bit impractical now. Walking through London Bridge is fine, however, since each passing face changes instantly. On the platform I find a pillar to stand against and avoid at least one compass point's attention. Nevertheless, within a few minutes a girl approaches me, asking "Working Men and Women?" Of course I acknowledge what she already knows. Only a performer would say something that so accurately describes what I am dressed up as.

There is a bit of a wait for our trains so we get talking about tonight and the overall experience. She was part of Lancashire, so was amongst the counties who, earlier on today, were asked to go to the Stadium, rather than Eton Manor, for a briefing and some notes about tonight. All of those performers were allowed to take photos of anything they wished. They had the Stadium to themselves. She took photos of everything she could and nobody said a word. The technical staff were taking photos of the volunteers. I can't help but feel very envious, although in some ways it may not be such a bad thing that I wasn't given the opportunity as I may have exhausted my battery taking endless photos of the set, close ups of every corner of Fife, the view from here and there, this angle, that angle, killing my battery in the process. It would have meant no portraits of the Working Men and Women of Fife. I can't wait to put those shots together, crop them, and run the colour down, taking the life out of our flesh tones. I just wish I had taken more.

The girl, whose name I haven't even asked, then goes on to relate a somewhat worrying story about how she and some friends managed to get into the Athletes' Village. They got through security by telling them they had lost their way and were trying to find a way out. Instead of telling them to go back the way they'd come, security sent them onwards, to go through the village to leave the Park. I can't quite make sense of that but why would she lie? With such a golden opportunity so easily presented they didn't exactly rush through. Unbelievable. In a few days I am going to reconvene my role in the Security functional area as a Games Maker. I hope the operation is much tighter when the Games are in full flow.

Around an hour later, walking home from the station, the streets practically empty, I can only think that it really is over. I am on the very last stretch of my journey home. No more rehearsals, and no more strikes. Already I want to go through our segment again. I can't wait

327

to watch it, but that will have to be tomorrow. Tonight, or this morning by rights, I need to relieve myself of my costume, cast it aside to be packed away, and get back to my wife and family, even though I have nine Games Maker shifts to go, some of which will require my absence from home for the majority of the day. Life isn't quite going back to normal just yet, but a very large part of what has made it so special for me over the past few months, and so stressful for my amazing wife, has finally come to an end.

51

In The Press And On TV

Saturday 28 July 2012

When I had got in the night before, the flat was silent. Any remnants of the high that I had been experiencing had ended as quickly as the reason for my euphoria. There had been nobody to congratulate me and nobody to greet me. I'd felt a little empty for maybe two minutes before accepting that it had been me who had kept my wife waiting too long. She must have been exhausted after yet another full day looking after the kids with no help from me. Having changed and caught up on my prayers, I had retired and slowly drifted back down from my cloud. Within a few hours I had to get up, have breakfast, and begin my fast. I hadn't even been tempted to watch footage of the show. My brain had been urging me to let it rest and I had complied quite willingly.

A few hours later, my wife declared over a very early breakfast that she had enjoyed watching our segment and had been very impressed with the spectacle. She had felt proud to see me amongst everyone and thought the Industrial Revolution was by far the highlight. I had received a few messages confirming much the same. It was nice to finally see some feedback from friends and family, and great to hear that they had loved the show, not just our segment but all of it.

In the morning I went to the nearest newsagent and bought one copy of every national newspaper. For some reason I felt like I needed to explain to the lady behind the counter, so I simply said that I had been in the show last night. Her monosyllabic response told me that I needn't have bothered; she was probably just glad to shift more stock then she would have expected from this single customer.

For the next couple of hours I perused my purchases. Lots of newspapers chose to lead with the image of the pyro shower. One title issued a cover poster with some fantastic shots of the Green and Pleasant Land, including some great close ups of a few lucky volunteers. There were plenty of shots from the Industrial Revolution, but no close ups of members of Fife, or indeed our county. One overhead shot did show us at the end as a group, at the time when I was busy messing up my choreography. I could just about make out where I was standing, near the waterwheel, but could barely see myself. It was nice to be able to say that I was somewhere in that photo, however. The NHS segment was given reasonable coverage in pictures, but the Thanks Tim dancers were mercilessly ignored on the whole, which I found a real shame as there was some wonderful imagery in their section.

In terms of journalism, Danny Boyle and his team had won over practically the entire national press. The Ceremony was branded a triumph, lauded at every opportunity. Some were bold enough to insist that it had surpassed even Beijing's superlative effort. The fact that it was already being called the greatest Opening Ceremony in the history of the Games, regardless of difference in opinion, made me feel extremely proud. The critics had been left stunned, finding it impossible to remain silent, and the nation felt immense pride, not only at the way in which our country had been represented to the world, but also because it had been a reminder of what our country has contributed to humanity. Danny Boyle so brilliantly encapsulated industrialisation, free healthcare for all, iconic music, classic literature, the internet, incredible musicianship, revered comedy, celebrated cinema, political movements, and a host of other typically British imagery and history. I spent most of the day thinking about this, and it made me feel proud to have been born on this small isle of wonder.

When I finally sat down to watch the Ceremony with Misbah on the laptop, I had already read comments about it in the Facebook group. Whatever had happened inside that Stadium, this was what the world had seen. All of the snippets at the beginning were put into the context of pre-recorded footage that somehow became a live broadcast. The balloon children now made sense as the countdown was shown. It seemed strange to be looking from the outside in, seeing us file out of the voms and hit the FOP.

For months we had seen the Brunels doing their own thing, but not quite knowing how it would be used and where, since we were concerned with doing our own thing too. Now I understood what their specific choreography conveyed. There was one shot of a few of them going into Levers/Pull twice, double time, and it looked so impressive, not a single glance sideways and all of them in sync.

Seeing myself was surreal but very special. I was a bit disappointed that the lighting had caused all of my make-up to be lost. My face looked far too clean and that isn't how I had wanted to be seen. I wished I'd applied much more make-up. Strangely my beard also remained invisible to the camera. All that aside, I was the most prominently placed in the shot, but it was great that all of us on that piece of turf were visible. Katie also appeared in the background. James, Liz and Dia were very clearly shown on the ratchets. So many people were given close-ups, yet hundreds of the Working Men and Women would have tried in vain to see themselves. In the end there was only so much that the film crew and editors could do.

As the segment unfolded I could see that they had featured more or less every aspect of our show at least once. Shots of the drummers entering, of us leaving the voms, fences being taken, turf rolled, the Brunels and Suffragettes, chimneys rising, ratchets aiding this, choreography interspersed with structures and terrain being removed, soldiers during the poppy moment, and then into the final act when the beam engines and looms were being operated, the forgers and smelters forging the ring, the History Parade featuring the Beatles, the Windrush, an Old London paper boy, which I hadn't seen at all during rehearsals, Shovel/Pickaxe followed by the combination, then choreography all round as the rings converged above, culminating in the pyro shower. It was all there, just maybe not quite in the ideal ratios. I felt that the Brunels were too heavily featured, and our toil was maybe not conveyed well enough. But that is just my opinion, and live footage will never please every performer in something of this magnitude. I can't imagine what it must have been like being in the editing room on such a momentous occasion.

As the footage jumped from close ups to wide shots, cameras panning to quick cuts, I could see just how incredible it all appeared. The images on screen looked stunning. Every volunteer was in the moment. Yet the sense of stupefaction that the viewers and audience must have felt was missing. I knew exactly why this was. I once saw an interview with Peter Jackson, the director of the incredible Lord of the Rings films, which left so many people astonished and entertained beyond measure upon first viewing them. He mentioned how much he would have loved to watch those films as a normal filmgoer who was seeing them for the very first time, so he could also experience the sheer wonder and breathtaking fantasy unfolding before him. That would always be impossible, since he had spent years at the helm. He knew every single shot and there were no surprises whatsoever. In a similar vein, I would never be able to experience seeing seven chimneys magically appear from nowhere without having known about them before, or being knocked for six at the rings converging, and then gasping at the completely unexpected pyro shower. The full intensity of that emotion was forever lost as soon as we signed up to be volunteers and a part of the show. All I had were the sentiments I felt when all of these things were revealed during rehearsals, which wouldn't quite match seeing the final version of the show for the very first time, with no prior knowledge. Of course I would never have traded places with a spectator, not for a second.

I watched the rest of the Ceremony, and for the most part, I did have that luxury. I watched volunteers and seasoned performers, musicians, dancers and actors, all sharing the same stage and making it all look so professional, so effortless. It was indeed every bit as incredible as the reviews claimed, and I was a small part of it. I felt immensely proud, and as ever, privileged. Part of the cultural record of London, forever. Steve had said it how it was. The enormity of his claim was not to be underestimated.

52

A Spectator's View

Monday 30 July 2012

Today I was finally able to talk openly with my team at work about the Opening Ceremony. The comments on the whole were very positive. Most people had missed me on TV so I showed them a screen shot that Josh had kindly emailed to me. I'm really not one for drawing attention to myself but this had to be an exception, and I must confess that I did rather enjoy it. I think my high was renewed with the accolades received about our segment, which was most people's favourite part.

I briefly spoke to Jack in the afternoon. He was still excited about having seen the dress rehearsal live, five days after the event. He told me he had applied for tickets to the Opening Ceremony but was not a bit surprised to have received nothing in the ballot. When he'd seen my poster for the raffle in the office he was thrilled at the chance to see the rehearsal, and then when he won he couldn't quite believe his luck. I was glad that the ticket had gone to somebody who had really wanted it. I asked him if he could send me some written feedback about his experience. He was kind enough to offer me the following summation of his night:

As I made my way to Stratford after work, I did something very unlike the English and began to get excited. It was a kind of child-like excitement you rarely feel as an adult. I had followed every twist of the Olympic story, ever since I had sat in my room at university in 2005 and read the news that we had won the bid. Now I was to be amongst the first people in the world to see the Opening Ceremony.

Walking from the station there was such a great atmosphere of enthused excitement. There were huge crowds. Everyone was friendly and the staff did a great job to help people. I started to believe that it actually would be amazing and bragged to my friends on Facebook about where I was.

My post provided me with a chance encounter with an old friend before we went in.

By now I was so excited. It was like the first time you walk into a football stadium, but this was the biggest I'd ever seen. It was hard to take it all in! Then I noticed the set – an amazing and surreal vignette of green fields and farm animals.

Once seated we were immediately involved in the performance. There was a small LED panel in front of every seat which created a great effect in the Stadium. We were told to wave it around which made everyone feel part of the show. We were also told a huge sheet would come down over us which we had to help with. Danny Boyle personally introduced the event, which made it feel very special as he was clearly passionate about his work.

Once the performance started the energy was incredible. The powerful words of Shakespeare and the emotive music helped build a breathtaking atmosphere as the number of people in the scene grew with the intensity of the spectacle. It was amazing to see so many people as part of one performance. I didn't know where to look, trying not to miss anything.

When the chimneys were raised there were genuine gasps. The purpose of the ring that was forged was not immediately obvious until the middle one began to rise. As the work of all the people culminated and the performance grew to a crescendo, it became clear that this was one of the Olympic rings.

The whole segment was an incredible sight, and so inspiring. Aside from the work of all the volunteers, for me it also represented mankind itself – giving us the message that from working together, freedom is born. For me this really encapsulated the spirit of the Olympics.

Afterwards I really wanted to tell everyone how great it was, but I wanted to 'save the surprise', as the message on the big screens asked.

Now that the Ceremony has taken place, all of my friends who were actually there agree that it was an amazing experience, one that we'll remember our whole lives. I feel privileged to have been there. Thank you to everyone involved.

Jack's last few lines very much echoed my own thoughts and feelings towards the experience. I was really beginning to register just what we had been involved in and how it had affected so many people in different ways. I couldn't express in any coherent terms just how lucky I felt to have been an integral part of such an enormous spectacle. Unlike Jack and everybody else at work, I had a performer's view. It felt immense and overwhelming.

WAVE SEVEN

GAMES TIME

53

Games Maker Shifts 2 – 9

Tuesday 31 July – Saturday 11 August 2012
Olympic Park

Within a few days of the Ceremony, it was clear that we hadn't seen the end of the experience. The Facebook page was as active as ever with people posting and writing messages on anything related to the Ceremony and Games. I wasn't the only one who would have loved to do another strike. People needed their weekend fix of rehearsing and rolling turf, but sadly we all knew the reality.

We could now upload and share photos, and hundreds appeared. A few performers were quick to put their costumes on eBay. Others scoured the internet for photos in which they unsuspectingly appeared, often with some success. The world's press had been present and snapping away, after all. Some people managed to arrange for articles to be written about them in their local press. My favourite story was about a member of Fife, Adam, who was invited to the press conference at the International Broadcast Centre the morning after the Ceremony. He was then interviewed by HELLO! magazine. Finally he managed to be taken out for a VIP trip on the London Eye by a Turkish TV station for a filmed interview. It must have been a very surreal experience for him. A lot of us were able to let go immediately, but I think some of us were trying to keep the experience alive in some shape or form for as long as possible.

I now had my shifts as a Games Maker, interspersed with my usual work and all of the online activity that I couldn't help but follow, and sometimes contribute to. My first shift after the one before the Ceremony was in the afternoon, from 1pm until 8pm. With travel included it took up most of the day. Upon arrival at the Cherry Park registration area, I checked in and received my gift for the day, a silver Games Maker pin badge, before joining a queue of Games Makers waiting to be allocated a team leader. Somebody asked for volunteers for the Greenway Gate. Only a couple of people put themselves forward. She needed eight so I also volunteered, wondering at the reluctance of the others. She did eventually get a full team together and we made our way to the gate, going through security first which got us into the Park.

Greenway Gate was a bit of a walk, but after going back and forth between Eton Manor so many times, it wasn't as bad as some people thought. It was good to see a part of the Park that I didn't even know existed as I had never walked this far beyond the Orbit before. On the way there it was hard not to notice the landscaping. Entire banks beside the river were covered in all sorts of flowers which added splashes of colour to the verdant patches that lined the pathways. Now that the Park had been opened, and all of it was fully accessible, there was going to be a lot to discover. I was thankful that all nine of my remaining shifts were going to be based here. Everywhere I looked there was a photo opportunity. I was going to have a lot of fun with my camera.

When we reached Greenway Gate it was very quiet and they were not quite ready for us, although I wasn't sure why. Whilst we waited our team leader helped us break the ice by asking us all about our highlight of the Games so far. Naturally I mentioned that I had been in the Opening Ceremony on Friday, which was met with the kinds of exclamations that were to be expected, one person even confirming that he had heard me correctly. For about two minutes I felt like the most important person in the group as people asked me what my role was and what it had been like.

After more waiting we were assigned roles. Almost two hours of my shift had by now passed and I had barely done anything, which had an air of familiarity. I was on soft ticket checking, so just making sure that people's tickets were for today, and that their event was indeed in the Olympic Park. We were positioned outside the PSA. In answer to the obvious query, we were told that some people did arrive on the wrong day and at the wrong venue, despite the full details being printed very clearly on every ticket.

So for the next couple of hours, my partner and I checked tickets. There was never a constant flow of spectators. Most people entered the Park through Stratford Gate; all of the other gates were quiet. I was now beginning to understand why people were not keen to work here. It was too lacking in activity and led to boredom, which both of us were feeling a little of already. It just made the shift pass slowly. We filled the many quiet spells with small talk. My partner asked me about the Ceremony and how we managed to coordinate ourselves, so I told him about our IEMs and that we were getting cues. To this he speculated that it must have been chaotic, being told to move a fence here and then go to another one, and then get some of the turf off. I explained that in actual fact we were so well rehearsed that we only received a few vital cues, and that most of what people saw was down to us knowing exactly what to do.

After a short break we had a change around so we were now a little further from the PSA, greeting spectators and asking them to have their tickets ready for inspection. Even with just two of us doing this there was rarely a time when we were both occupied, the flow of traffic was that slow. Further down from where we were another set of volunteers were asking spectators to dispose of any liquids if they were carrying any, but to keep the bottles as there would be places to fill them up once inside. I was moved to this role too after some time. We had been told that things would pick up because Transport for London had started to tell spectators to alight at West Ham if they wanted easier entry into the Park, but it was still very quiet and the number of volunteers present seemed excessive. What also seemed unnecessary was that there was a separate entrance for accredited people and spectators, both of which needed to be manned. There had been no real queues throughout my shift, just small clusters of people entering the Park. Eventually they closed our entrance down and moved us all inside the PSA to help there.

I was now queue pacing, which seemed ludicrous to me as there was no queue at all, just the occasional person or, if lucky, family or group to direct to one of the lanes where bags were checked. One of the team leaders from G4S, who were in charge of security at this gate, made sure I knew which lane was for which type of person, meaning that I sometimes had to send people to a lane where there was already somebody being checked, when the lane directly in front, reserved for accredited people, was empty. Some spectators complained about this but I had to follow instructions. I would have preferred to use my discretion and directed people in a more logical fashion, but it wasn't my decision to make. The only time I had to really do anything, and that only relatively speaking, was when a mixture of accredited people and the general public arrived at the same time.

So went the rest of my shift until it was time to go home. I left with my team leader and one other by the Greenway Gate as there was little point in walking back through the Park to Stratford, which would in effect have meant going the wrong way on the Jubilee Line only to come back in the same direction.

Along the way there were Games Makers posted at various intervals, chiefly to inform spectators that they were now on the 'last mile' to the Park. There was a nice view of the Stadium from here as we were on a raised walkway. Just outside the tube station about ten minutes later there were more Games Makers lined along the road, once again posted there essentially to greet visitors and give directions. These volunteers did not have the required accreditation to give them access to the Park, even though they were but a stone's throw away, doing a job so dull that they surely deserved a look at least inside the place they were giving directions to. Yet the very strict rules were in place and they would not be given any special treatment. They had been here all day, but despite this they all had a welcoming smile for everybody who walked past, whether arriving or leaving. I remember thinking that despite my own boredom I had to feel thankful that I was in the Park, a place that I had grown to be very fond of. These volunteers spent their entire day on a very quiet road in West Ham. It was all about perspective.

On the journey home, at the start of sunset, I broke my fast using the meal I'd saved from the dinner break on my shift. The workforce canteen was situated just behind the world's largest McDonald's, for which there had been an incredibly long queue, although I'd been told that it was very fast moving.

Our own canteen was only open to accredited staff, and wasn't even visible to the general public. It served a selection of sandwiches and salads (the same type that we had during rehearsals), snacks, drinks and a choice of hot food. We were given one meal voucher per shift and this entitled us to either a hot meal or the cold option, plus a drink, a snack and a piece of fruit, usually an apple. Tea and coffee were available, often with a basket of the same granola bars that I had eaten so many of over the last few months. In masochistic fashion I sometimes took more than one when it was clear that there was an infinite supply of them. On each side of the very large room there were TV screens set up showing footage of the various events taking place that day.

For two weeks I attended my shifts as required. After the third one it became clear to me that being a Games Maker was never going to surpass being a Ceremony performer. The latter had simply been too big an experience and was always going to dwarf what it meant to be a Games Maker. The work was also too monotonous for me, and I simply didn't have the opportunity to serve and interact with the public as I would have liked.

For the most part people wanted their passage through security to be as quick as possible. They had no desire to chat, and the majority of people were not looking for help of any kind, at least not at that stage of their visit. They were in and out. Yet we always greeted guests with warmth and enthusiasm, and that was one of the things that visitors often appreciated, even if at the same time we were asking them to empty or discard their perfectly good drinks, or making them remove their belts and empty their pockets.

The queues through security were rarely long, even at Stratford Gate, which was by far the busiest entrance. We all contributed to a very efficient security operation on the whole, and it was rewarding to be a piece of that. I often played my part in keeping the queue moving whenever there was one. Spectators had been advised, when purchasing tickets, to allow up to two hours to get through security, but in most cases they got through in a matter of minutes.

Most people I spoke to agreed with me that the work wasn't the most stimulating, but we were all glad to be a part of the wider team. Lots of people did love working as volunteers and their enthusiasm was almost enviable. I often wondered how much I would have enjoyed the experience if I hadn't been in the Ceremony.

Despite feeling a little underwhelmed at the Games Maker experience, with the work seriously lacking in variety and excitement, there were many aspects of my volunteering that I enjoyed. I never grew tired of arriving at Cherry Park for registration and being amongst a sea of people dressed in purple, red and beige. I loved wearing my uniform and being "part of the Olympic family", as one ticket inspector on the train said to me upon seeing my pre-paid Oyster card. It was probably the nicest way he could have described my involvement in the Olympic Games.

I spent hours and hours in the Olympic Park, seeing every corner of it, and taking hundreds of photos. I don't think I left a single stone unturned. During one break I walked along the river which was very picturesque and tranquil as it was down a deep embankment, accessible by flights of steps or a winding and descending path. You couldn't quite tell that there were tens of thousands of people on the upper level. There were benches for those who wanted to enjoy some quiet time away from the hustle and bustle. I happened across the perfect spot for a photo with both the Stadium and Orbit as the backdrop. I was asked by several people if I could take their picture and I was more than happy to oblige, thereby creating an iconic memory for them. It was some time before I could get somebody to return the favour for me.

Across the way and back down to the river the Gloriana was anchored. I had only seen it from afar on show day but now I could stand and take in the full splendour of it. This was another very popular spot for visitors, as was the incredible word fountain a little further along, one of my favourite features in the Park. It was so easy to be completely transfixed by it. When I had seen it that night after rehearsals, I hadn't realised that there were two of them operating at the same time, side by side. It is an incredible thing then, that I never saw the same word twice. Armed with my proper camera this time, I was able to capture lots of different words, made up of thousands of droplets floating in the air for just a single second. It was a truly beautiful thing and I spent several minutes just watching random words fall.

I was often able to explore like this when I was on shifts at quieter gates that were so free of spectators that we took turns to have extended breaks, allowed to do whatever we pleased. Although most of my common domain shifts were at Stratford Gate, I did make a point to work at the quieter and less popular gates too, just for the experience, even if the day seemed to pass much more slowly as a result.

Victoria Gate was a long walk from Stratford, which required us to go past the back of the Stadium where all the vehicles entered, a view I hadn't had before and would not even have known about had I not volunteered to work there. The view from the approach to this gate made the Olympic Park look like a large compound owing to the high fences all around.

It was during this shift that I was asked more than ever if it was possible to enter the Olympic Park just to explore and take photos. Sadly we had to decline every time. It was the same for ticket holders to venues outside the Park. They weren't allowed to enter here, although many did try. There had been an allocation of non-event tickets for visitors who only wanted to see the complex, but clearly not enough to satisfy the demand. They sold out very quickly. John Lewis, who had a store in Westfield that overlooked the Park, had arranged a viewing area for use during the Games. For a fee people could go and take photos of the Stadium and see some of the Park from afar. I recommended this facility as the best option to those people who we had to turn away. There were often lots of tourists standing outside Stratford Gate just to take photos of the Stadium.

On one shift I volunteered to work at Eton Manor Gate. I wanted to do this at least once just to see it again. That was one of my early shifts, starting at 6am. Unlike my very first morning shift, when there had been transport delays resulting in half a train load of Games Makers arriving late, I managed to get to the Park on time. When registering I received my gift for the day, an exclusive Games Maker diary, which I could now add to the three pin badges I'd received.

One of the perks of being a Games Maker was a ballot that we could all enter to win tickets to events on the same day. They were limited in number, and winners couldn't choose which event to attend, but it was something for nothing. We just had to enter our name and number in a box and be ready to answer our phone in case it rang. Some volunteers had won tickets to the Athletics in the Stadium; others had been to non-Park events. This was the first time I had entered so far and I was hoping that I would get tickets to the Aquatics Centre or the Athletics, if I was lucky enough to be chosen of course.

As soon as the team for Eton Manor Gate was assembled we started the long walk there. Most days by now were hot and sunny and this was no exception. We took the scenic route by walking along a section of the river I'd not covered thus far. This was the same section of river that I was looking over when viewing the Stadium for the last time, after we had finished our segment on show night, and before walking back to where I was headed now. At that time this part of the Park hadn't been opened.

Along one path there were some red phone boxes, or at least that's what they looked like when approaching. Upon closer inspection, however, I could see that they were simply sculptures, just the shells of phone boxes, and not all sides of them either. This was one of the things that I loved about the Park. There were things to discover at every turn, whether it was the word fountain, a reflective wall, a hidden path, a rock feature, a message board, or just a different group of flowers or plants. There were so many nooks and crannies to discover which could only be done by walking indiscriminately.

Being at Eton Manor again wasn't quite what I was expecting. For some reason I thought I could gain access to the cast area, just to take a look around and see if it was the same as we had left it, but of course I was there solely to help in the PSA.

For the duration of my shift that morning I switched between welcoming guests and soft ticket checking, queue pacing and tray loading. It was as quiet as expected so most of my time was spent chatting to whomever I was working with. One girl I spoke to was looking forward to taking lots of photos of the Park, but wished she could have been there when hardly anybody was present. I was glad to have had that opportunity, and felt relieved that I had taken advantage by not only documenting my walk to Eton Manor, but also taking photos during rehearsals and venue training.

Whilst posted here I received a phone call from an unknown number. I didn't even consider that it could be about the ballot I'd entered, but that is what the lady on the other end had called to tell me, that my name had been chosen. I couldn't quite believe my luck – I'd been very fortunate in Olympic-related ballots and my luck was continuing. I was told that I had a ticket for the Basketball Arena, although the event was handball. I was given some instructions and I thanked the lady profusely.

After my shift ended at 2pm, I had a couple of hours before I had to report to the designated area. From here everybody who had been chosen that day would be taken to their venues. Even though I'd been up since around 4am I couldn't miss this opportunity so I decided to stay after my shift and wait for the event. There was more than enough for me to do beforehand.

There were lots of concessions in the Olympic Park, run by corporate sponsors. Earlier that day, during my break, I'd visited the Samsung area where you could have your photo taken using their latest phone, and then have the result made into a badge. The backdrop was the Velodrome, which was opposite the concession, and you could have a flag of your choice as the surround to the image. It was another souvenir at no cost so I got one with the Union Jack and one with the Pakistan flag.

I'd heard that the Coca-Cola Beatbox, as it was called, was worth a visit, and you could have your photo taken with the Olympic torch, so I headed there after my shift ended. There were a few tents set up throughout the Park for photos with the torch, but these were charged for. This was free so a better option.

The queue was long, which translated into almost an hour of waiting. The sun was beating down that day, not a single cloud to be seen in the perfect blue sky. Usually I would have welcomed this, but today, as I was fasting and therefore couldn't keep myself hydrated, I found it a very difficult and long wait. There was no shade to ease my passage to the entrance. Indeed I was almost gasping for a drop of water, but as always my resolve proved to be far stronger than temptation. Using the bottle I had I rubbed cold water over my arms and into my neck and face. Throughout my shifts I would do this to keep my body feeling cool as I would often have to stand in the sun as I worked.

Eventually I was at the front and I made my way through the pavilion. I wasn't sure if it had been worth the wait but I knew what was at the top so I didn't mind. Besides I got lots of nice shots overlooking the Park through the red and white panels as I went round and climbed upwards.

Holding the torch at the top was indeed the highlight of this little visit. It was one of the official torches that had been used prior to the Opening Ceremony. There were eight thousand little holes covering the surface of the torch, representing each of the official torch bearers. One of those was for David in Fife, giving him another small place in Olympic history. Somebody took my photo and I was given a link to where I could download it in my own time. People were told to stand in a specific position, so that the Stadium was in the background, which made for a nice photo.

Having finished here I made my way down. At the bottom they were handing out free bottles of ice cold Coke in a special edition London 2012 bottle. I kept the bottle but poured out the contents as there was no cap so I couldn't save it for later.

I still had some time before I had to go to the staff area so I did some more exploring and just soaked up the atmosphere. There were thousands of people everywhere you looked, the vast majority of whom were clearly enjoying themselves. The Park Live facility was very popular, so much so that they had an entry system. I could remember when it was still being built during my venue training, which had happened around a month earlier. Back then the Park was largely unfamiliar and only parts of it were open. I could recall standing and looking at the Basketball Arena from a distance, the Coca-Cola Beatbox behind me, with the Velodrome and Athletes' Village on either side of this white building that looked almost like a massive meringue. Just like the Stadium and Aquatics Centre, it had something that appealed to me and I immediately added it to my list of favourite venues.

Around an hour later I found myself outside the very same meringue-like structure, waiting with a crowd of Games Makers in the scorching heat, trying to find some shade and attempting to deal with my dehydration and hunger. I was having a bad time of it today.

My mind kept going back to the free Coke I had poured out and wasted. I had a bottle of water in my bag that I just wanted to open and drink in one gulp; at the same time it was the last thing I wanted. This was simply temptation taunting me and playing with me. I knew that this was as far as it would ever get, but even this was a step too far. I had to control myself, but standing in the heat was not helping me. I was now glad that I hadn't won a ticket to an event in the Aquatics Centre. Seeing all of that water would indeed have been mental torture. I reminded myself that fasting without suffering a little was almost missing the point of doing it. These moments would come and go on some days, and right now I was in the deep end, but from experience I knew that it would soon pass.

I had no idea why we were being kept here for so long, but we had to just wait until we were allowed through the ticket barriers. When that time came I think most of us breathed a sigh of relief. We just wanted to sit down, relax and watch some sport.

The Basketball Arena was not what it first appeared to be from a distance. The white walls were actually just an outer casing, a shell that surrounded the actual building, as if it had been placed on top of and around the venue, with space in between. We now had to wait in this space, but at least it was out of the sun and a lot cooler. My dehydration and hunger slowly abated and I felt more comfortable.

I now discovered that seats for Games Makers were never guaranteed. It all depended on what was available at the time. There may have been unsold seats, or ones that had been reserved for the press, but were not being used. Around 20 people were allowed in initially, but the rest of us had to continue waiting.

The wait lasted around 30 minutes. We were all led into the arena up a flight of steps, along the back of one of the blocks, and then all the way down to the front rows. We had some of the best seats in the arena, positioned behind the judges and officials. It had been worth the wait. The game was between the Norway and South Korea women's teams. I knew nothing about handball, but I found it very entertaining and energetic, with lots of goals scored. The atmosphere was great and I felt very lucky to be experiencing an Olympic event for nothing, so unexpectedly and from such a prime position too.

We had joined the match during the first half. Throughout I was willing South Korea to close the gap, being a neutral and wanting to see a closer contest, but it wasn't to be and Norway prevailed quite comfortably. Seeing the Norwegian team celebrate together made me think about our own triumph a couple of weeks earlier, although we hadn't been competing for medals. It would have been very special if we had all been in one place at one time afterwards, and we could have all congratulated each other and revelled in our collective triumph, as one. Sadly it didn't work out that way. Everything had been on a much larger scale and it wouldn't have been possible.

My penultimate shift was another early one at the Main Press Centre. It went as any other shift, except it was a different setting. Some Games Makers often mentioned that they had seen celebrities, Amir Khan, John McEnroe, and Gary Lineker amongst them, but I never once saw a famous face, except for Gabby Logan during my very first shift.

When it was time for my break, instead of heading for the canteen, I took out my camera and began to take photos of the Media Village, as this would realistically be my last chance to do so. I entered the Press Centre and walked around freely, taking photos of anything that would help create a visual record of the place. I didn't think that this would be one of the buildings to survive beyond the Games, so now was the time to capture everything, making up for what I'd missed out on during my venue training. There were a few journalists working, so I was careful not to cause a disturbance, but on the whole it was very quiet at that time of the morning.

Crossing over to the International Broadcast Centre, I attempted to get inside to see if I could have a look around, but I was stopped immediately. I didn't have the required accreditation so was not even permitted into the lobby area. It was worth a try.

When returning for the remainder of my shift I was reminded that there was going to be a get together and celebration for all of the security workforce in the staff canteen the same afternoon. I considered whether or not to attend, but thought against it. I am never good in those situations. I can very easily walk into a room full of strangers, have a good walk around, and then leave without anybody knowing I was actually there. It is an undesired skill I have developed over the years. And strangers these largely were. I hadn't worked with the same person twice. On every shift I had a different team leader and team, which did mean that I met lots of people, many of whom were very friendly, but after the shift ended I never saw them again. Some Games Makers had seemingly known each other for years, either because they in fact had done, or they were simply better at bonding than I was, something that I sometimes envy in other people.

After my shift ended I headed straight home. If there had been a gathering of my fellow Ceremony performers, I would definitely have attended. We had seen and worked with each other week in week out; it was hard not to form some kind of bond, even for me. I was a part of that group as much as everybody else and it would always be good to see them, at any stage. We were on the whole such different people leading completely different lives. Had it not been for the Opening Ceremony, it is fair to say most of us would never have met, and would certainly not have had anything in common.

I had just one more shift remaining and then it would be over. This time for good. The difference in emotion between this and the day before the Opening Ceremony, when that was going to be over for good, was vast. Two very different experiences, one unbelievable, the other somewhat disappointing, but mainly because the one had dwarfed the other, making the latter impossible to live up to expectation.

I wished that I could perform our Ceremony just once more, but then where would the cycle end? After my final Games Maker shift, I had no desire to opt for one more. I just wanted it to end. Nevertheless I really was thankful that I'd had the opportunity to experience both. Tomorrow was going to be the end of the Olympic Games for everybody. And I was definitely pleased that I would also be here in the Olympic Park, one final time.

54

Games Maker Shift 10

Sunday 12 August 2012
1.00pm – 8.00pm
Olympic Park

Today is somehow different as I leave the flat. It's probably the knowledge that this is the very last day of the Olympic Games. Just as soon as they came, they are over. It's been an incredible couple of weeks. Amongst all of the medals for Team GB, the highs and the lows, the laughter and the tears, the joy and the despair, I have been one part of an army of volunteers who have been given such accolades as the people who have made the Games. I still don't feel like I have contributed a great deal, but that isn't from a lack of wanting to do so, and I could of course be completely wrong here. Who knows what the security operation would have been like if there were no volunteers.

I reach Stratford with no incident. So many people, myself included, believed that the transport system would crumble completely, or at best, would cause chaos in every direction. On the contrary, I have to congratulate Boris Johnson for proving the doubters wrong. I have had very few problems on the way to my shifts, and any disruption, in my personal experience, was kept to a minimum, and certainly not beyond what could reasonably be expected at such a time.

Upon leaving Stratford station I walk to the path that leads straight to the Park, avoiding Westfield, and show my accreditation to enter the lane reserved for those with the necessary credentials, thereby easing past the thick crowds, except today things are far more subdued as there are only a few final events taking place here: two disciplines of the Modern Pentathlon and water polo. The Stadium is reserved exclusively for the Closing Ceremony.

When we register we receive our final gift. We have had a selection of pin badges and a journal. It hasn't quite been one gift per shift, but we have a nice set of souvenirs to keep. Every Games Maker on their final shift has received a commemorative baton with a note from Seb Coe inside, a certificate signed by Jacques Rogge, and a pin badge simply stating 'Thank you' and 'Merci'. The silver baton is by far the best present I have received from both Ceremonies and LOCOG. It has been made to the approved Olympic relay baton specification and has been etched with the words "London 2012 ...I made it happen!" It's a fantastic souvenir and one that I am very proud to receive.

As usual I am allocated a team leader and meet a new group of people, except for one girl who I have in fact worked with on a previous shift. We are going to be on Stratford Gate, not actually in the PSA, but outside on soft ticket checking. This suits me fine as it is slightly different to what I've done before, and it means I will have a view of Westfield where crowds will no doubt gather. It's a bit like the Opening Ceremony, when the entire vicinity was brewing with activity and excitement.

We are briefed that ticket holders are going to be held behind a barrier until around 4pm. Before that all spectators from the remaining morning sessions will be asked to vacate the Park, in preparation for the Closing Ceremony. There is relatively little for us to do before then so we are allowed to have a break and go for a walk. For the last couple of weeks I have spent many hours in the Park, not including all the time I spent here during Ceremony rehearsals. I have seen everything I wanted to see, more than once in a lot of cases. I actually need a break from being here as I have had more than my fill of exploring. From that point of view at least, I am glad this is my last day here.

Nonetheless I re-enter the Park and take a walk with a few Games Makers from my team. The crowd of spectators is sparse and you can tell that things are being wrapped up. The concessions are beginning to wind down and announcements about the pending exodus are being made at regular intervals. Soon everything will be about the one remaining event.

I decide to take some final photos as I walk around, keeping in mind that I won't get another chance to do so, at least not during Games time. I look for small things that I may have missed, and the more quirky aspects. Whilst doing this, from one of the McDonald's I have a view of the Stadium, and to the side I can see the same set of stairs that we used to go down after registering and collecting our meal packs before rehearsals. There are lots of people doing the same now, presumably the performers in tonight's Ceremony. I smile as I reminisce and feel nostalgic. I wonder how long it will take to put the experience behind me completely. I suspect it will always be there.

When we return another group of people go on their break, and we man the entrances, still waiting for the crowds to be released, which will happen soon. We fill the time with conversations about our experiences over the last couple of weeks. Most of us agree that the security role hasn't been the best thing about our experience of the Games, but we are all unanimous in our assertion that we have enjoyed being Games Makers, especially here at the Olympic Park. My thoughts are once again with those poor souls whose entire Olympic experience has revolved around being in the PSA at Earl's Court, for example, or any other non-Park venue.

When somebody asks what we have liked most about the Olympics I can't help but mention the Opening Ceremony once again. Everybody is very impressed that I was a part of it. I receive more positive feedback about the Industrial Revolution segment, and I can only feel proud that I was there with everybody else. My own favourite moment of the competitive side of the Games was Andy Murray's gold medal, beating Novak Djokovic in the semi-final and then Roger Federer to deny him a Career Golden Slam. He didn't even drop a set during those last two matches. Lots of people would maybe choose Jess Ennis's or Mo Farah's triumphs, but for me Andy Murray's victory was very sweet revenge for his tearful Wimbledon loss, and one that he really did deserve after so many disappointing results in the majors. It made me very happy.

All of that has now passed and the evening of the Closing Ceremony begins when the first wave of ticket holders are allowed through. Although we are only doing soft ticket checking, ensuring that the tickets are indeed for tonight's Ceremony, we are kept very busy by the sheer numbers of people coming through. They are entering in droves and after some time more Games Makers are brought in to direct people to different entrances.

Some people can't wait to get inside. Maybe this is their first and only visit here, so in wanting to waste as little time as possible in security, they try to rush past, barely giving us a chance to see their tickets. We have to ensure that we see every single one and account for everybody who walks past us, so we need to be vocal when asking to see tickets properly. At the same time we are greeting people, welcoming them, wishing them a good afternoon, saying the same things, always with a smile, over and over and over again. It is relentless, but they all deserve the same care and attention.

This continues for the next couple of hours. Some of the guests who come through have tickets for the corporate hospitality venue, the Prestige Pavilion, which has a separate queue. When I worked at the Victoria Gate I had to walk past this building, which is situated a stone's throw from the Stadium. Even from the outside it looked very swanky, not the type of venue I would ever frequent. I wouldn't like to guess at the cost per ticket on a night as exclusive as this. Looking at some of the prices on the normal tickets, I see that some people have spent a small fortune for the privilege of seeing live the final night of the third Olympic Games in London. Tickets are as dear as £1,500 each and there are families coming in, having spent this much on each member. Conversely people have paid as little as £20.12 for the highest views of the show.

When it is time for our breaks, we are relieved and allowed to go. Tonight the Games Makers are eating in an alternative canteen, near the Aquatics Centre as the main one has closed. For a time I thought I was finally going to see inside that magnificent building, but it isn't meant to be, although it does mean I get to see the other side of it where the main entrance is situated. I thought I had seen every corner of the Park, but I was wrong in my estimation. This really is a wonderful place and I am going to miss being here, even though I do need that break from it for the time being.

Later on in the evening, when our shift is over, some of us go back inside the Park, before the Ceremony has begun, and see if we can somehow get into the Stadium. It is a very long shot, but maybe somebody will suffer a lapse in concentration and unwittingly allow us to walk in without the correct accreditation. As we all discover there is no chance of this happening. We try this more than once at different entrances, but the result is the same. And rightly so of course.

We realise that they are running the same system as the Opening Ceremony, where you need to have a sticker of a specific colour on your accreditation card. We also find out from one of our own supervisors that if we are to have any chance of getting in tonight, we need to find a certain individual who should have the necessary stickers, and may even go as far as taking pity on us and giving us one. We all know that we are not quite acting in the spirit of the Games Makers by expecting something that we agreed at the very beginning to not expect, but this is the final night and we are finding it difficult to turn our backs on it without at least trying. Personally, I just want to be inside the Stadium one last time, to stand on the podium level, look over towards Vom 5 and just let my imagination do the rest. I want to feel the crowd's energy, even though I will never be at the centre of it. Aside from that, there is simply something about the Stadium that draws me in. I have always felt that and I want to go inside once more.

In vain we attempt to locate our mystery man. This is a lost cause and there is no sense in continuing. We all disperse, going our separate ways. By now the sun has almost set so rather than break my fast on the train home, I stay just a little bit longer and enjoy my evening meal, which I kept from my break. In truth I think I am simply finding it difficult to let it go for good.

The Stadium is now doused in light, the colour changing periodically, going from yellow, to blue, to green, red and purple. From inside the roar of the crowd is the prevailing sound as the show is about to commence. I have no idea what is happening in there but the audience is clearly excited and more than willing to contribute to the proceedings with their applause, cheers, and outright appreciation of the occasion that is unfolding before them.

I am now standing in front of the same bridge that runs between the Aquatics Centre and the Water Polo Arena. Looking up at the Stadium all I can hear is the crowd and the sound of the Pet Shop Boys' West End Girls. Listening to Neil Tennant sing, I am taken back to 1985 momentarily, before I decide that it is time for me to leave. I am not going to stand here and listen to the whole of the Closing Ceremony. As I turn I notice large crowds of what can only be performers standing on the bridge that runs parallel to this one. I inwardly wish them the very best of luck and complete my about turn, the Stadium now behind me. Some people are still trying to get into the show. I have tried and failed. No more. I am going home to my wife and kids.

On the way I get talking to somebody who has also decided that there is no sense in staying. He spent his shifts in the Transport functional area and had a good time of it. He has loved meeting lots of new people, just like he is doing now, brief though it will be. Some members of Fife are in the Railway bar right now, watching the Ceremony that is taking place behind me. I said that I would try to make an appearance after my shift, but it is later than I was expecting. I turn around and take one final look at the Stadium, coloured in blue. To my left is the side of the Aquatics Centre, illuminated in yellow, with the Olympic rings in the centre. That is the last image I see before I turn and walk with a purpose to Stratford station, not looking back again. My wife is at home waiting, and she deserves to have me back completely.

55

This Is The End

On the train to London Bridge I reflect on the past few months. It really is all over now. I cannot begin to describe just how incredible it has been. I think any adjective would fall short, but one that may come remotely close is profound. There is without doubt an immeasurable depth to what I have experienced ever since I applied to be a Games Maker, and then a Ceremony Performer. It all began around two years ago, and as with all things there is an end.

It has indeed been a journey, a very long one. I began with a desire to be a Games Maker and that is how my Olympic experience has ended, yet it is my role as a Ceremony performer that I keep coming back to as my train continues its course on the Jubilee line. Without doubt that is the aspect of the Olympics that has moved and affected me the most. Therein lies the most profound of all of my experiences.

I tried to get into the Stadium tonight because I wanted to see just once more the place that was a big part of my life for over a month, and where all of us performers cemented our very small places in Olympic Ceremony history. Now I have no idea if I will ever see it again. And even if I do it won't be the Stadium as we left it. It won't feel the same.

I still count myself as very lucky. For over a month I was part of a very exclusive group of individuals who were allowed in there regularly, before anybody else. We walked beyond the public areas. We saw the Stadium when it was still deemed a construction site, a testing area for show night, still incomplete and a work-in-progress. We spent over 70 hours in there – more than most people, even a lot of the athletes who competed there. We owned that Stadium. It was ours.

For over a month we collectively kept its secrets and then revealed them to the world. When the time came we passed the baton to the athletes, the spectators, the journalists, broadcasters and photographers, Olympic personnel, dancers, musicians, and singers, celebrities and VIPs, even The Queen and James Bond. It was hard to let go, but in the end we had to. We had no choice.

When we walked up those aisles after our performance, we had our backs to our field of play. And play we did. But it wasn't all play. Ever since we had applied and been chosen, auditioned and succeeded, we worked so hard. All the work we put in, as part of our play. Along the way we smiled and laughed, were enthused and inspired.

When we began we watched, in disbelief and wonder, then began to believe, and wondered no longer. We started with moves, repeated and practised, pulled and prepared, repeated and practised, chiselled, hammered, dialled and shovelled, perfected en masse, in two mills and then one.

One to one, we travelled further, along the green and into the east. Our base was blue, yellow and pointed, between two fields of concrete for play. Day one we rotated, and learned all the stages, of taking the green and creating the grey. Day two we divided and counties were formed. Such a large team couldn't always be one, but divisions were tenuous for when we performed.

For weeks we waited, in lines of twos, whilst our leaders decided on how to resume. We waited longer, in the wind and the rain, as it blew and fell, not a thing could restrain it. When we struck we lifted, dragged and pulled, we repeated the same, again and again. So many times, we failed and failed, but also succeeded, our attempts rewarded. Sometimes we basked and lay on the turf, but so often we stood, with no aim and no clue.

A trial in rolling meant an end to dragging, an experiment it was, but we altered and adapted. Adopted by all, we rolled and rolled, until all of the rolls were piled up high. Reset and repeat, the chaos continued. We changed and we guessed, we realised, we applied. The only constant were the changes we made.

The music developed and we practised our moves, when time allowed, and it rained as a rule. We sheltered and doubled, our timing and quickness, to make it much easier when the speed was normal. Moves perfected, fine-tuned and corrected, we moved back to turf, to perfect our striking. Through talking and listening, we opined and we offered, ideas to consider, then agreed and accepted.

We stretched and avoided injuries and pain, whilst stopping the bus, oh yes, we were ready. Yet we tarried and waited, but soon rushed and then hustled, when cues were given we slowed down and then stopped. With whistling we reflected, respected and remained, silent and still for seconds, up to sixty.

We moved to the Stadium, where ramps were so real, so we

skidded and slid, slipped and fell down. We ate and crunched, popped and stopped, sipped and drank, caused stains so refrained, only tea and coffee were allowed to remain.

When turf removal had become second nature, we moved past Hail Mary, and on to the last waves. We listened to drums, they pounded our ears, they empowered and emboldened, the drama was born. Chimneys rose, seven in all, beam engines came, bellows blew. Weavers weaved, and workers shovelled, whilst metal was molten, and then it was smelted. Forgers swung, hammered and hit, a single ring, before four more converged.

We rehearsed and rehearsed, practised and practised, until we were ready for an audience of faces. We dressed in our costumes, sartorially shabby, we dirtied our faces, no longer angelic. From afar we walked to the field where we played, we waited in voms, at the ready to bulge. Presents were given, hugs exchanged, words of encouragement, a lifetime as friends.

We stood by to strike, and then we performed, just like we had done, on countless occasions. We performed to perfection, so proud they all were, a shower of pyros, wonder and awe. We turned and applauded, then turned back and signalled, we showed our work, then took one small bow. Our curtain call complete, we had performed so well. Over it was and time to vacate. We moved up the aisles and had to let go.

There is no way to really describe this entire experience in a few words. All I know is that I have been on an immeasurably exciting journey and it has now ended. On the walk home I recall doing this a couple of weeks ago, but this really is the last time as I now return to normal life.

I think of one of my favourite books, a very long and deeply entertaining work. I can see the parallels between that and the last couple of years. Both involve rings, a very long journey, overcoming challenges, and making friends. Each of the principle characters embarks on their own personal journey. All of the volunteer performers in the entire Ceremony have also been on thousands of separate and very different journeys, all containing common threads, and culminating in one place and one shared moment. The book ended very abruptly but I remember how it continued to stay with me for a long time after I had finished it, and still does. My own personal journey has ended but it too will always stay with me. I am so glad I had the opportunity when so many others didn't. I am proud to have been both a Games Maker and a Ceremony performer. I will always be able to claim that I was there.

I am equally proud to have been a part of the Kingdom of Fife for a few months, part of a beautiful group of people. Whenever I see that place name in any context, I am sure I will smile or at least feel an affinity with it, even if I have never even been there. That will also always be a part of me. Games Maker. Member of Fife. Forever.

I walk through the door and although it is late, Misbah is still up. She walks over and greets me, this time with a smile that betrays her relief at seeing me home. I am well and truly back.